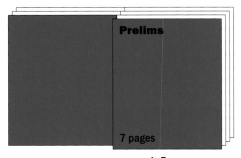

Prelims

7 pages

pages 1–7

Foreword

2 pages

pages 8–9

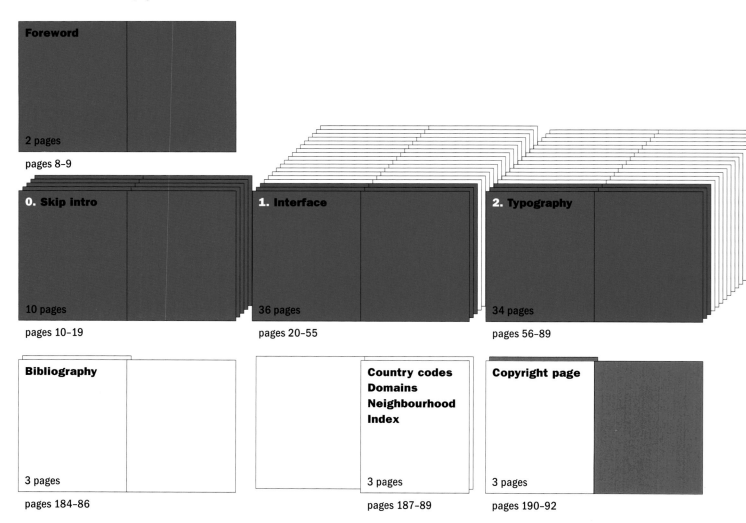

0. Skip intro

10 pages

pages 10–19

1. Interface

36 pages

pages 20–55

2. Typography

34 pages

pages 56–89

Bibliography

3 pages

pages 184–86

**Country codes
Domains
Neighbourhood
Index**

3 pages

pages 187–89

Copyright page

3 pages

pages 190–92

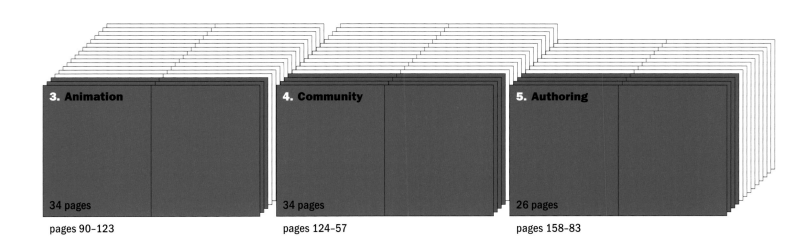

3. **Animation**

34 pages

pages 90–123

4. **Community**

34 pages

pages 124–57

5. **Authoring**

26 pages

pages 158–83

Despite still unstable technology and a general lack of standards, the web is coming into its own as an information, entertainment and communication medium with much to discover and enjoy – once the technology is in place. One of the primary aims of this book is to show that the overall quality of design for the web is improving all the time. Another objective, instead of desperately browsing the web for coolness, is to scrutinize some of the areas in which innovative approaches to web design are most essential, or should be, from a visitor's or user's[1] perspective.

Each chapter begins with a critical essay that further investigates one of the themes outlined in the introduction, discussing the criteria that have guided the selection of work. The essays are followed by short reviews of individual sites, which help the reader to arrive at a deeper understanding of the processes and ideas that drive state-of-the-art web design and e-culture.

In many cases, the site assessment is indicative of what the web might look like in a couple of years when problems of bandwidth, computer power, application instability and interaction on the web have been overcome. The sites that most inspire me may not always be polished achievements and some may be limited in scope, but they do represent a keen awareness of the complexity of the web as a communication medium, finding viable ways of structuring, visualizing and interfacing that awareness. Essentially, these are the environments where design on the web takes place: the sites of design.

1_I use a variety of words for what are mostly called 'users' in web environments. Since one of the main characteristics of the medium is its multifaceted nature comprising and converging different roles for those who make use of it, I will refer to 'users' as 'visitors', 'readers', 'players', 'listeners' or 'viewers' whenever these roles are implied in the content and behaviour of a site.

Max Bruinsma, 2003

0.

0. Skip intro

0. Skip intro

0. Skip intro

0. Skip intro

0. Skip intro

0. Skip intro

0. Skip intro

0. Skip intro

Instead of desperately browsing the web for coolness, we will scrutinize the areas in which innovative approaches to web design are most essential, or should be, from a visitor's – or user's – perspective.

It seems like pre-history now, but in fact it was only a few years ago that critics and the public alike complained about the lack of design quality in all but a few websites. The graphic-design profession appeared to have left the web, with its low-resolution computer screens and its severe limitations of bandwidth and display technology, to the 'desktoppers' and, above all, the software developers. Unencumbered by any deep understanding of editorial structure or aesthetic matters, they took the standard paper-based office routines for visually structuring document content and from these devised the defaults that became the modi operandi for web-related software and design. For some designers, however, the crude state of the new medium was a welcome diversion from standard practice; instead of trying to adapt the time-tested conventions of paper publication for the web, they sought to introduce new ways of interfacing content. The visual metaphors that resulted from these experiments were at first read as a new cultural code for an artistic underground. Bitmapped letters, intricately linked hypertexts in primary colours and plain HTML became the starting points for a design approach that turned the formal constraints of the medium into an expression of its great potential for structuring and expressing content in new ways.

Just a few years on, and the picture has changed radically; any complaints today are more likely to be about design overkill than lack of design. Instead of helping, endless animated introductions, showcases of visual ingenuity and design bravado often block easy access to information on a site, which becomes buried in layers of moving graphics, thumping beats and a plethora of decorative paraphernalia. Form over content seems to be the new condition on the web. A new generation of (graphic) designers have embraced the medium, aided by faster computers, broader bandwidth and a new breed of web applications that grant a much greater control over the visual – and aural – end result. In short, the web has become flashy.

Complete websites are now being made in Macromedia's Flash software, but the least one can expect is an 'intro', an opening page with moving type, animated figures, sounds and shifting colours. **<u>3. Animation</u>** The small interface element on such 'splash' screens, called 'skip intro', has become the ultimate user-friendly icon. Superficial displays of design cleverness aside, the growing importance of design for the web is remarkable for a variety of reasons. First, technology seems to have caught up with the demands designers make on the degree of manipulation and the quality of detail in their tools and presentation media. For designers, few things are as annoying as seeing a carefully orchestrated arrangement of texts and images fall apart on every other computer screen than their own. Conversely, there is a greater awareness among designers that they are unable – and should not want – to control every aspect of design for this medium with its ever-increasing array of output devices and technologies. Rather than meticulously laying out a wealth of details, as they are used to doing, web designers increasingly concentrate on making the basic structure of a site work on any conceivable platform and compensate proactively for differences in display and bandwidth. In short, a new design strategy is developing that focuses less on formal aesthetics and more on designing the behaviour of information and users.

Greater control over what users see on their monitors or other display devices and a deeper understanding of the web's idiosyncrasies have certainly made the medium more attractive for designers. It is, moreover, important to remember that the web allows designers to combine aspects and characteristics of other media in ways that were hardly thinkable before its invention. Applications like Flash and Shockwave and the development of code in such

Designers are taking up the challenge to truly 'remediate' – instead of just copying

14

1_Jay David Bolter and Richard Grusin.
Remediation: Understanding New Media
(Cambridge, MA: The MIT Press, 1998).

languages as Java, Javascript, Dynamic HTML and XML have given the web the tools to fulfil its promise: to be the medium to embrace all other media. Designers are taking up the challenge to truly 'remediate' – instead of just copying – the communicative know-how developed in older media. Remediation, according to <u>Jay Bolter and Richard Grusin</u>[1] at the Georgia Institute of Technology, is a natural and necessary operation that occurs whenever a new medium is invented. Since the usage of a new medium is embedded in the experience of older media, the question that concerns Bolter and Grusin is: how to translate or transcend this experience into the practice of the newer one while, at the same time, realizing the latter's extended potential. Communication is not reinvented from scratch each time a new medium arises, but if the new medium is to be used to its best advantage, the rules and routines of communication do have to change. Therein lies the challenge for designers: to research how existing methods of communication and tried and tested visual languages and techniques can be transferred, translated, transmuted or overcome for the new übermedium.

On the surface, it looked like a dream come true. Television, radio, magazines, books, records, all media known to humankind were being incorporated within a single encompassing communication space, the World Wide Web. **1. Interface** The same space could be used for communicating visually and verbally, for archiving notes or libraries, for playing online games or for accessing online applications. More recently, however, practical experience has dispelled this rosy view of the web. For many, the unbridled commercialization of the web has vandalized what was once a free information space and turned it into a quagmire of themed shopping malls that look the same and, from a design perspective, impose a very limited set of formats, just as commercialism did to mass media like television and cinema. Quite apart from informational ver-

Too often, the fancy of 'total infotainment-space' is cruelly shattered as soon as you try to make something work

sus commercial policies on the web, the medium is still very young and unstable. Too often, the fancy of 'total info-tainment-space' is cruelly shattered as soon as you try to make something work, or the moment you discover that the medium's promise can only be fulfilled after installing a zillion plug-ins. And then it might function on a PC in Explorer, although perhaps not on a <u>Mac in Netscape</u>[2]. Lack of standardization and the piecemeal development of software have resulted in a kaleidoscopic technology, which will only gradually develop into something more streamlined. In this respect, developments in media technology follow a similar pattern to those of the steam engine or the automobile. In the foreseeable future, this multifarious technology will become more diverse, with the expansion of presentation media into the realm of small wireless devices like UMTS telephones and PDAs. In turn, these small-screen devices will pose alternative design challenges to the ones that are currently being addressed on the computer screen. As any typographer knows, size does matter.

2_For researching this book, Netscape 4.7 and 6 and Explorer 5.1 were used on 500 MHz / 128 MB PC and Apple PowerBook G3, with DSL connections. Installed plug-ins: Shockwave 8, Flash 5, QuickTime 5, Beatnik, Real Player G2, Windows Media player, Pulse Player, PDF Viewer. Plus a few plug-ins, which I have no idea where they came from or what they do. Screendumps were mostly made on a Mac.

Technology and the ways in which we are used to dealing with content are quite often still at odds, and designers are well advised to take this condition into account. Assessing the technological common denominator for potential audiences has become an essential aspect of serving them. Another reason for the frequent clash of technology and users is the tendency among designers, especially the more experimentally inclined, to use tools that are beyond most recipients means. The conflict of technology and content is further aggravated by the dismal typographic quality still prevalent on the web, which still channels vast amounts of pure reading material, texts. **2. Typography** The simple, but fundamental fact that the screen is a light-emitting medium, and not a light-reflecting one like paper, should have deep consequences on the treatment of type on screen. This is not just because of the physical aspects of reading, but more importantly because on the web the

3_'Wir sind nicht mehr Subjekte einer gegebe- nen objektiven Welt, sondern Projekte von alter- nativen Welten.' ('We are no more subjects of a given objective world, but projects of alternative worlds.') Vilém Flusser, *Digitaler Schein – Ästhetik der Elektronischen Medien*. Florian Rötzer, ed. (Frankfurt am Main, Germany: Suhrkamp Verlag, 1991): 184.

4_For further reading, see: Jonathan Crary, *Suspensions of Perception* (Cambridge, MA: The MIT Press, 1999); John Johnston, *The Medial Turn* (1998); George P. Landow, *Hypertext: The Convergence of Contemporary Critical Theory and Technology* (Baltimore, MD: John Hopkins University Press, 1997); Lev Manovich, *The Language of New Media* (Cambridge, MA: The MIT Press, 2001).

5_See: Richard Rogers, ed., *Preferred Placement – Knowledge Politics on the Web* (Maastricht, the Netherlands: Jan van Eyck Editions, 2000); Peter Weibel and Timothy Druckrey, eds., *Net.Condition – Electronic Culture: History, Theory, and Practice* (Cambridge, MA: The MIT Press, 2001).

6_Ted Nelson, *Computer Lib – Dream Machines* (Redmond, WA: Microsoft Press, 1974, reprinted 1987).

reader changes from a 'subject' to a 'project', to use <u>Vilém Flusser's analogy</u>[3]. Website visitors are much more active participants in establishing the content of the pages they access than in any other medium. Conversely, 'accessing' the visitor becomes a more complicated and interactive process. The relationship between sender and receiver, so unilaterally defined in paper communications, turns into a dialogue between two parties who project content and context <u>onto each other</u>[4]. Yet, print-based typographic routines and design approaches remain predominant on the web, as is clear from the multitude of only marginally linked corporate brochures that vainly try to mimic their glossy paper counterparts. On the web, true remediation is still in its infancy.

While the web may have lost some of its early utopian flavour, there remains enough to savour regardless of the problems to be solved and the promises to be kept. A key challenge for designers, for example, is to aid the develop- ment of new and more sophisticated approaches and metaphors for the dialogue between coauthors and co- recipients, which is inherent in the medium. **5. Authoring** It has been <u>remarked repeatedly</u>[5] that the new media promise (or threaten, depending on your viewpoint) to thoroughly mix up the established hierarchies between authors (or content providers) and recipients (or users); the two become, as hypertext pioneer Ted Nelson said, '<u>deeply intertwingled</u>'[6]. The web prompts a way of browsing that is quite different from old media, magazines included. 'Scanning' is probably the most accurate word for the average browser's behaviour. The web encourages a predator's glance, processing a vast amount of fleeting information fast, before focusing on a target. Designers – and editors – who fail to recognize this pattern will most likely make confusing choices in content structure, and ultimately leave their consumers hungry for guidance and substance. Designers, in short, must

Apart from solving problems for consumers and clients, design is a cultural force to be reckoned with

deepen their knowledge of and expertise in orchestrating human response.

Apart from solving problems for consumers and clients, design is a cultural force to be reckoned with. Designers have become 'cultural agents'; for better or worse, they essentially shape today's visual cultures. As such, they now stand alongside the content providers they once served as neutral craftsmen[7]. Considering the web from this perspective, designers cannot focus solely on visual virtuosity or superficial hipness, nor on mere functionality or 'usability'. Eye candy may certainly help to convey a message, but a critical taste will test its flavour against the contents and contexts for which it is served – if design amounts to 'authorship'[8] then it shall be reviewed as such, as an expression of today's cultural condition.

As in other realms of product or graphic design, web design is not simply about making things look good, or even making them work well. In essence, design is an editorial activity – it organizes disparate elements into a structured whole on the basis of content-driven choices. It projects a given content onto its cultural context. On the web, where content and the technologies used to communicate it are so intricately ensnared, the editorial core of design acquires even more significance. The structure design brings to a site's content largely determines the visitors' experience. Beyond the crude functionalism of 'usability' advocates like Jakob Nielsen[9], then, the formal expression of a site's structure is an integral part of its content – the interface and its visual representation do not hover generically over a site's subject matter, rather they are part and parcel of it, expressing, among other things, its targets, its cultural context and its audience's aesthetics.

The web may appear to treat all data equally, but there remains a huge difference in accessibility between, for instance, online artworks and search engines. In both, however, the relationship between the content, the interface,

7_See also, Max Bruinsma, 'An Ideal Design Is Not Yet' in *The World Must Change – Graphic Design and Idealism*, Leonie ten Duis and Annelies Haase (Amsterdam, the Netherlands: Sandberg Institute, 1999). www.xs4all.nl/~maxb/ideal-e.html

8_See also, Max Bruinsma, 'Designers Are Authors' (lecture, 2001). www.xs4all.nl/~maxb/authors.html

9_Jakob Nielsen, *Designing Web Usability* (Indianapolis, IN: New Riders Publishing, 2000). See also the review of his site, p. 36.

18

the context and the visual expression is crucial. It is the balance between these and related factors – the editorial structure, the brief, the projected audience – that determines whether the visitor's experience of the site is positive or not. Correspondingly, in not just 'serving' the message but co-constituting it, the design of a website is a crucial factor in establishing the kind of intertextuality that is such a key element of the medium. The cross-referencing potential of hypertext was one of the fundamental ideas behind the technology to begin with, and it has since proven to be the single most discerning aspect of the new medium. The activity of creating and navigating links between such disparate formats as texts, streaming video, live sound, archived images and constantly updated information and the exchange of these with other users makes the technology a constituent part of the content. Therefore, instead of merely following function, as the modernists would have it, standard hierarchies dissolve. In complex communication environments, such as the web, form equals function equals content. And, vice versa.

Another, and deeply cultural, consequence of the web's ability to link is that websites hardly ever stand alone – they cluster. Visitors gather through portals, link lists, webrings, blogs, online clubs: they form communities.

4. Community From topical online support groups to forums and gaming communities, the web is used as an information and entertainment medium *and* a communication tool. A case in point is the networked activism that is gaining momentum in international protests against globalization. Again, linking is a fundamental component: linking information, linking communities of activists and linking critical dissent directly to its sources. The web facilitates simultaneous traffic of one-to-one, one-to-many, many-to-one and many-to-many exchanges, a concurrency that accelerates and intensifies its potential for spontaneous social action and interchange. A case in point are the

It may be strange for a book on web design to also look at the dilettantish side of the medium

myriad pages and sites that immediately sprung up after the terrorist attacks on 11 September 2001.

It may be strange for a book on web design to also look at the dilettantish side of the medium or at sites that are virtually undesigned, but there is no denying that these two elements make up the vast majority of what is available on line. Furthermore, a number of them are exemplary of the web's potential as a tool for social and cultural interaction. Amateurism aside, good design can have a tremendous impact on these types of communication not just in terms of the visual quality of individual sites, but also on the quality of the interface, interaction, editorial clarity and cultural integrity. This means a shift in focus for design criticism; ultimately, the test of design on the web lies not in fancy splash screens, but in the consistency, structure and articulation of the networked data behind them.

1. Interface

1. Interface

1. Interface

1. Interface

1. Interface

1. Interface

On the surface, it looked like
a dream come true. Television,
radio, magazines, books,
records, all media known
to humankind were being
incorporated within a single
encompassing communication
space, the World Wide Web.

In the age of converging media, one of the main challenges faced by (graphic) designers for the web is the organization and fine-tuning of the visual relationship between interface and screen design. To prevent an aggregate of buttons, arrows, scrollbars, pop-up menus and windows from clogging the screen and dictating its look and feel, new ways of navigating a site and accessing its contents are being researched and developed, from apparently simple typographic solutions – sometimes combined with sophisticated scripting for screen size and font format and conduct – to integrated systems that react to visitors' behaviour instead of passively presenting them with list after list of options. Analogous to the design development of more traditional engines, such as cars, the mechanics of the machine are becoming incorporated into the bodywork. In some sites, clicking is no longer necessary, just moving the mouse over the screen will do the work.

Meanwhile, a heated debate has evolved over the best way of interfacing information on the web. Usability gurus, like Jakob Nielsen, hold that visual design should be limited to such bare essentials as text, colour, and placement on the screen. Any departure from the users' expectations will result in confusion and thus obstruct communication. Although there is much to be said for Nielsen's simple and intuitive rules, he accepts that the navigational standards developed so far are often not the best solutions from either a functional or an <u>aesthetic viewpoint</u>[1].

Taking the crudeness of standard interfaces and the ensuing users' expectations as a given is, for many designers, an overly defensive stance. Those who endeavour to develop new approaches to designing interfaces, such as Dutch designers Mieke Gerritzen (<u>see pp. 34–35, 37, 86, 107</u>) and Joes Koppers (<u>see pp. 26–27, 34–35, 107</u>), mean something quite different from Nielsen when they state that 'the visual aspect [of web design] is often underestimated – it has its own functionality'. Gerritzen adds, 'This

1_'The mother of bad web design conventions is the decision to make hypertext links blue. Other colors would have been a better choice and would have increased the reading speed of the anchor text by a few per cent. It is unfortunate to put the most important text on the page in a color that is known to reduce readability. If we were designing the Web from scratch, I would recommend using a different link color than blue. Since we are designing sites for the Web as it exists, I retain my recommendation to leave the standard link colors alone.' Jakob Nielsen, 'When Bad Design Elements Become the Standard', Jakob Nielsen's alertbox, 14 November 1999. <u>www.useit.com/alertbox/991114.html</u>

lack of understanding of the special character of a visual language often leads to shallow translations, mere renderings of flow-charts. _That_ is so boring!'[2] Here, she refers to sites like Nielsen's own, which are as functional as a screwdriver but also as visually bland. If graphic design in other media has taught us anything, it is that visually enhancing messages not only concerns bettering their usability, but also involves intensifying their cultural import and effectiveness. Design is as much about visually embedding a message in its cultural context as it is about strict functionality. In fact, in an increasingly visual culture such as ours, this aspect of design becomes all the more important – and functional.

Converging media not only pose technological problems; they are, as founder of one of the web's earliest magazines, _FEED_, Steven Johnson suggests[3], transforming our culture and, thereby, changing the way we perceive the world. Graphic User Interfaces (GUIs) are not just tools; culturally speaking, they simultaneously symbolize and influence the ways we understand and process information. Website visitors are becoming used to adding or linking information, even if they are not web mavericks. In fact, the tools they use, such as word processors, weblogs or web diaries, allow them to organize their own data in a hypertextual manner, which only a few years ago it would have taken a computer scientist to achieve[4]. Linking information to other information becomes as important as presenting the data. Faced with audiences that expect a high level of intertextuality, designers are increasingly challenged to facilitate interactive readings. They have to find new ways of organizing navigation within what George Landow termed 'borderless text'[5].

Browsers are a case in point, epitomizing what Internet pioneer Alan Kay said of computers in general, 'It's a whole new way to deal with relationships and ideas'[6]. In the borderless text, linear argumentation and the logic

2_Mieke Gerritzen, _Eye_ (no.26, vol.7, autumn 1997): 54.

3_'We will come to think about interface design as ... perhaps the artform of the next century.' Steven Johnson, _Interface Culture: How New Technology Transforms the Way We Create and Communicate_ (San Francisco, CA: HarperCollins Publishers, 1997). For a review of this title by Max Bruinsma, see www.xs4all.nl/~maxb/eye28-interface.htm

4_'Because hypertext systems link passages of verbal text and images as easily as they link two or more verbal passages, hypertext includes hypermedia. ... In practice, popular word-processing programs, like Microsoft Word, have increasingly featured the capacity to include graphic materials in text documents. Linking ... makes such integration of visual and verbal information even easier.' George P. Landow, _Hypertext 2.0 – The Convergence of Contemporary Critical Theory and Technology_ (Baltimore, MD: John Hopkins University Press, 1997): 59.

5_ Ibid.

6_Alan Kay's keynote address, 'The Computer Revolution Hasn't Happened Yet', at the ACM SIGPLAN Conference on Object-Oriented Programming Systems, Languages, and Applications in Atlanta, Georgia, October 5-9, 1997.

To experience these fragments as meaningful information, readers have to actively and consciously reassemble the parts

24

7_'Electronic writing is both a visual and verbal description. It is not the writing of a place, but rather a writing *with* places, with spatially realized topics.' Jay David Bolter, 'Topographic Writing: Hypertext and the Electronic Writing Space' in *Hypermedia and Literary Studies*, eds. Paul Delany, George P. Landow (Cambridge, MA: The MIT Press, 1991): 112.

8_'ToolToys are products that satisfy not only the requirements for functional tools, but also give the user the pleasures associated with toys.' Alexander Manu's lecture, 'Form Follows Spirit', 'Design and Cultural Diversity' conference, Florianópolis, Brazil, 1994.

(and logistics) of traditional discourse give way to a more 'rhizomatic' construction of relationships between fragments of data. To experience these fragments as meaningful information, readers have to actively and consciously reassemble the parts along the paths that are open for them to follow. Obviously, the design of the interface is crucial: it delimits the gamut of visitors' actions and it represents the editorial structure of the site. In other words, it maps its meaningful uses. Reading and writing have, as literary scientists argue, become 'topographical'[7], a term indicating that information resides as much in the way discrete collections of data are connected to each other as in the information contained within the data. When content is visually presented as a landscape of topoi or 'sites' of information, the way an interface facilitates or determines the routes through that information and between the sites touches on more than its accessibility, or usability – the interface becomes part of its contents. Thus, the design of the interface is essential in quite literally mapping out the information's topology.

Graphic designers and artists are becoming more and more drawn to the intricacies and potential of graphic interfaces on the web, delivering on Johnson's and other commentators' demands and predictions. Increasingly, designers and artists force the browser's own interface to the background, replacing it with their own – an appropriation that indicates a growing fusion of interface and content. In some cases, the interface becomes an expression of a site's attitude or even acquires gamelike characteristics. Just as the furniture in a living room is functional and expressive of the inhabitant's tastes and style, interfaces can furnish a screen. And, like the 'ToolToys'[8] that we buy to amuse ourselves and to perform chores, interfaces can provide an entertainment angle as well.

In this respect, online search engines are quite different from online artworks, portfolios or games, although each of

Searching the web can become a game, and games can be played by typing in search terms

25

these can incorporate the structural, editorial and interface elements of the others. Searching the web can become a game, and games can be played by typing in search terms, showing that choices made in the design of interfaces do not merely touch on a site's functionality, but are deeply editorial. With this, the designer of the interface effectively becomes coauthor, or at least co-editor, of a site's contents as much as authors and editors become co-designers.

Ever since winning the first International Browserday, Joes Koppers has perplexed even seasoned interface designers

www.usemedia.com

Usemedia
client_Usemedia, Amsterdam, NL and
New York, US
design_Joes Koppers
on line_2000

Ever since winning the first
International Browserday (see pp.
34–35) in Amsterdam in 1998
while still a graduate student at
Amsterdam's Sandberg Institute,
Joes Koppers (see pp. 34–35,
107) has perplexed even seasoned interface designers. His
interfaces at times equate pure
poetry – and they work too.

 Koppers's own site is a show-
case of highly aesthetic and functional solutions to such normally
intrusive interface elements as
scrollbars and pop-up windows.
Koppers makes the interface invisible, unobtrusive and playfully interactive. Sometimes his digital
objects seem to have a life of their
own; for example, windows choose
their own place on the screen, as
in 'new.usemedia.com', 'sub:way'
or his recent sites for Browserday.
By bringing the interface to life,
Koppers makes the visitor want to
search around for options. On his
screens, scrollbars and menus
appear only when the mouse point
touches a corner of the active window. Windows float over other
windows and can be used for
navigating and finding hot spots.

 The main interface for Koppers's
site ('say.usemedia.com') is a
page that starts with 'hello!', and
the question 'say?' It is a kind of
game; if the letter the visitor types
in the frame is the first letter of a
title in Koppers's database, that
title appears with a question mark
and, by pressing enter, a button
is displayed that will take the
visitor to the project. If it is not the
first letter of a title, the phrase 'I
don't understand' appears. You
browse the database by keying in
letters and choosing from what
the engine proposes.

www.usemedia.com

'NYC' is part of what Koppers describes as 'a collection of works that re-consider the window concept'

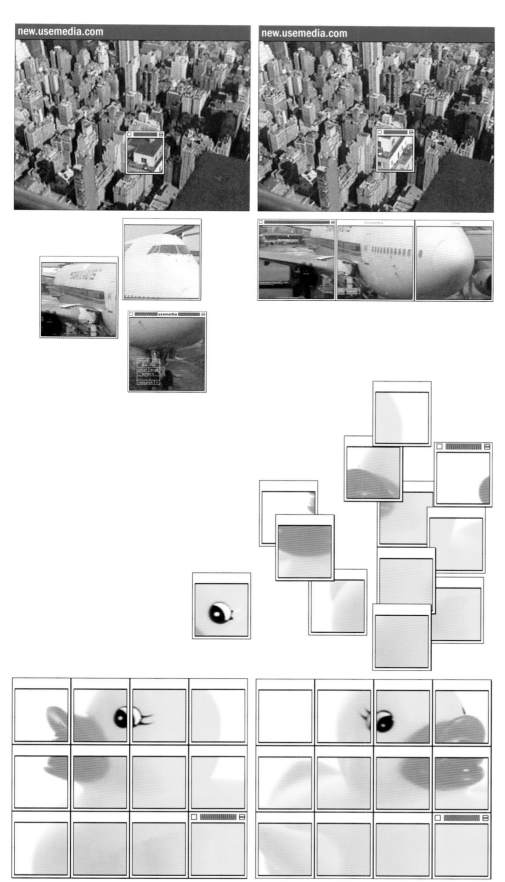

'NYC' is part of what Koppers describes as 'a collection of works that re-consider the window concept'. They all deal with using this Ur-frame of the graphic interface in a different way; windows become loopholes, allowing users to see information that is supposedly hidden behind the screen. The windows can be moved around to see more. Touching an area in the lower left-hand corner of a window brings out a small menu for exploring further experiments, like the view from the Empire State building in New York. Scanning this picture with the small transparent window, users may find hot spots, at which point the frame's function changes to a magnifying glass. A vague shadow on a rooftop, for example, turns out to be a small roof garden.

In other experiments, visitors can change the order of four frames showing a moving subway train without stopping the motion; or click to zoom in on a small video and open up alternative angles of view; or reassemble in the right order loose frames of a picture of a duck – on completion, the image locks in place and starts twirling round. Fun and technical bravado are certainly part of such exercises, but more important is their implication for the further development of GUIs. Imagine using Koppers's windows for examining details behind an overview of densely packed data, or his invisible menus for hiding a wealth of navigation options in a wide information landscape that can be scrolled through. A dream interface: breadth and depth on a single screen!

Erik Natzke uses his personal site to 'vent, explore, express, research, and share ideas' with visitors

www.natzke.com

Erik Natzke

content, design_Erik Natzke,
San Francisco, CA, US
on line_2000

Erik Natzke (see pp. 70, 101) is a graphic designer and Flash maverick originally from Wisconsin, who uses his personal site to 'vent, explore, express, research, and share ideas' with visitors. A very elegant interface slides into place and fills with entries as the site loads. Natzke experiments a great deal with Flash to make transitions from one page to another less awkward than the usual 'hard cuts' or empty screens that say 'please wait'. A number of his experiments are geared toward finding rhythmic ways of building a page or an illustration from separate elements, an almost cinematographic approach to the montage of a website. The status bars fill to a sound like cogs locking into each other, and the other sounds Natzke uses to indicate that something is loading maintain this association with machinery at work.

Obviously, Natzke revels in the nuts and bolts of his medium, which is further emphasized in his many exercises with mouse movement and the interaction between the user and the screen. In 'Portfolio Drag', for instance, merely moving the mouse controls the zoom in and out of a picture, while clicking and dragging changes its orientation. 'Pattern Reflections' is similar – the vertical position of the mouse point influences the zoom in and out, and the horizontal position dictates the speed at which the image slides to the left or right. Such exercises also constitute a training for visitors, who practise their navigation skills while exploring the screen.

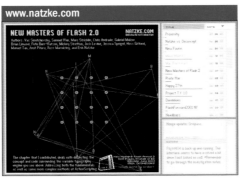
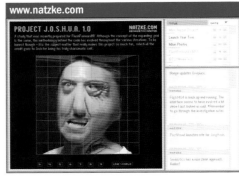

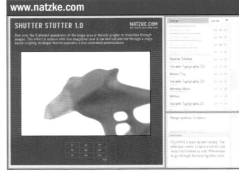

A box of 'errors, mistakes, bad judgement while working too late'

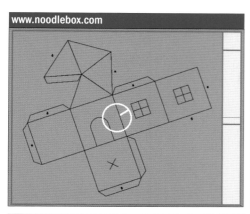

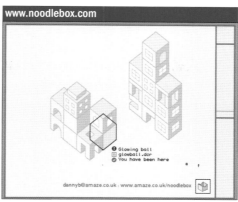

Noodlebox

content, design_Daniel Brown,
Liverpool, UK
on line_1997

A box of 'errors, mistakes, bad judgement while working too late' is how Daniel Brown describes his entertaining Shockwave toys collected in 'Mr Noodlebox'. It is a classic by now, a concise digest of how to make things alive and interactive on screen. The main interface is a set of building blocks that can be rearranged to the visitor's liking. Each block represents a small Shockwave adventure, which, on mouseover, is captioned in a way that betrays its origin in Director. The toys range from non-interactive waves of form and colour that gradually fill the window to interactive games. Considering these experiments were carried out in 1997, they were fairly advanced for their time, and some of them are still essential demonstrations of how digital objects may acquire 'physical' properties.

Perhaps the most poetic expression of how interaction between simple codings and human manipulation can result in lifelike behaviour on the screen is in Brown's 'More Butterflies' (www.noodlebox. com/danielbrown/screen08.htm). A swirling bunch of butterflies sits on the mouse point until the user moves it; if the user finds the right way of moving the cursor over the screen, the flock separates into five individual insects that gyrate around the cursor as real butterflies would around a flowerbed in summer.

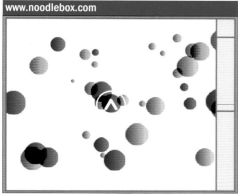

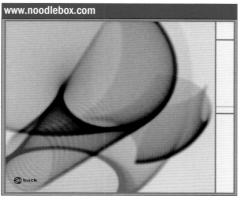

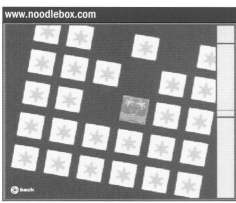

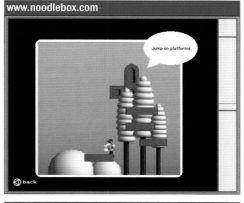

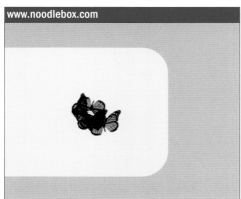

The main interface of this small portfolio site of Jayson Singe is a gem of structure and visualization

30

www.neonsky.com

Neonsky

design_Jayson Singe, Chapel Hill, NC, US
on line_2000

The main interface of this small portfolio site of multimedia designer and photographer Jayson Singe is a gem of structure and visualization. Elegantly crafted cabinets with sliding doors ripple and reveal their contents on mouseover. If one of the doors is clicked on it expands, pushing the other compartments aside to give more information and the option to launch the feature at hand. Singe is a documentary maker in Flash. His background in photography informs his work in the montage and pacing of images and texts. Online documentaries, like the one on an icon of African-American folk music, Joe Thompson, or the decline of America's tobacco farmers, mix good photography, spoken and written texts, atmospheric sounds and statistical material, resulting in a hybrid of television and magazine reports. Visitors might wish for more interaction than Singe's documentaries actually offer, but I am sure that will come at the next stage; for example, if visitors could zoom in on a map of Afghanistan in his 'National Geographic' feature, they would receive contextual information alongside the ongoing story. At this time, however, Singe is primarily transporting the documentary format into a new technology in a convincing way. The real remediation (see p.14) will be the next step.

www.neonsky.com/neonsky.html

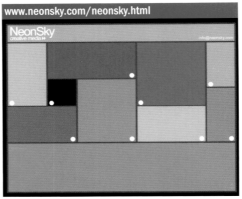

www.neonsky.com/neonsky.html

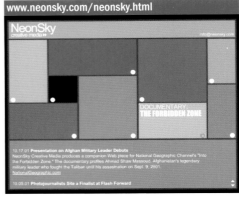

www.neonsky.com/neonsky.html

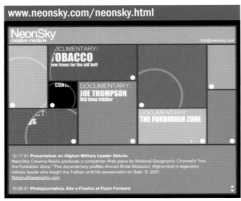

www.neonsky.com/neonsky.html

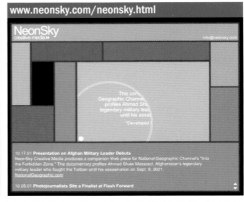

www.neonsky.com/neonsky.html

www.neonsky.com/neonsky.html

www.nationalgeographic.com/tv/channel/zone/frontline_flash2.html

Entering Snarg, visitors are tempted to remain staring at the slowly changing and rather vague but nonetheless intriguing images

www.snarg.net

www.snarg.net

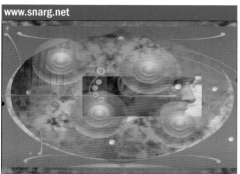

www.snarg.net

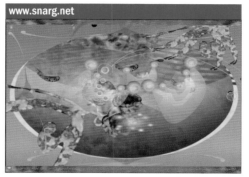

www.snarg.net

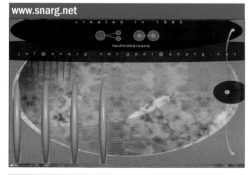

www.snarg.net

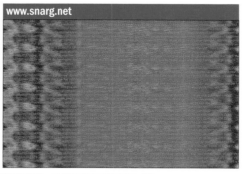

www.snarg.net/flash/physics.html

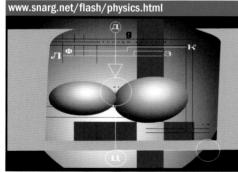

www.snarg.net/technobaroque/20_conta.html

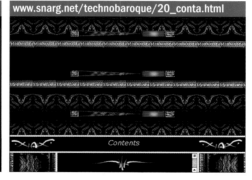

www.snarg.net

SNARG

design_Jef and Gael Morlan, Fidalgo Island, US and Antwerp, BE
on line_1997

31

Entering Snarg, visitors are tempted to remain staring at the slowly changing and rather vague but nonetheless intriguing images that continuously load in the otherwise empty screen. The only element that can be clicked on is a tiny '#', which offers the choice of entering either 'squeee' or 'framina'. From then on, the restrained aesthetics are rigorously discarded. What follows is called 'technobaroque' by its makers Jef and Gael Morlan, but the term does not correspond to the art-historic classification. 'Abstract Rococosurrealism' would be a more accurate description for these proliferations of serpentine tentacles, throbbing blobs and mauve colours. Snarg's screen designs are decidedly over the top, and interestingly critical of decorative excrescences in interfaces that at first sight may look extremely well organized in comparison. That they get away with it is because their site's interface and content are one and the same thing. Clicking on the blobs and other hot spots changes the overall image by adding new parts and deleting others. Meanwhile, the mysterious soundtrack slowly changes direction. Nothing else happens, but the surfer who commented in his web log 'Don't go there if you don't have a couple of hours to spend' was right; this is a visual variant of George Landow's 'borderless text' (see p. 23), and it seduces you to keep on exploring it.

The designers that formed Amsterdam–based group DEPT presented their homepage as a collection of huge buttons

www.dept.nl

DEPT

design_DEPT, Amsterdam, NL
on line_1998, 2002

The designers that formed Amsterdam–based group <u>DEPT</u>[1] (<u>see p. 97</u>) presented their home-page as a collection of huge buttons. To stress their solidity, the buttons depress with a loud 'thud' on mouseover, not doing anything else, however, until they are actually clicked on. It is one of many artful games DEPT plays with media conventions and codes, be it in the members' capacity as web designers or as graphic designers, V-jays or artists. DEPT's output ranges from printed books and fly-ers to art installations in galleries, characterizing the designers as representatives of the '<u>post-multi-media generation</u>'[2], which sees all media as pertaining to the same communication environment.

The 'More' section is DEPT's repository of past projects and small experiments, ironically laid out as an old-style archive in metallic filing-cabinet grey, com-plete with file cards and markers. The interface is in reality a parody on the records, ledgers and direc-tory metaphors so abundant in desktop environments. Pop-up after pop-up gives access to yet another seemingly nonsensical list of sub-directories – if you loose track, the whole card house collapses and you have to start over again.

www.dept.nl/dept.html

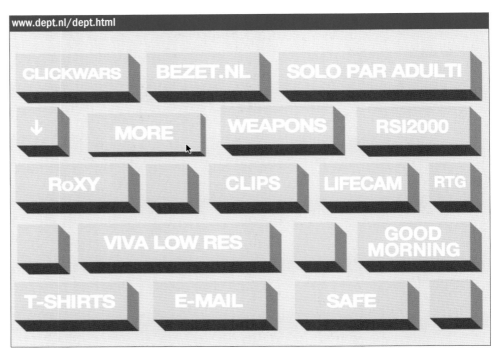

www.dept.nl/level01/level01.html

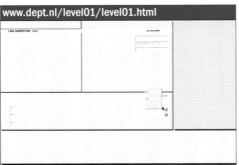

www.dept.nl/level01/level01.html

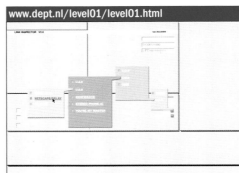

www.dept.nl/level01/level01.html

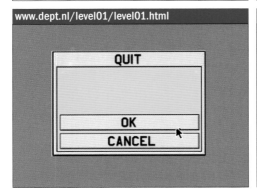

www.dept.nl/level01/level01.html

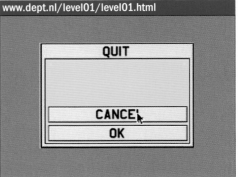

DEPT have made fun of standard procedures in on-screen navigation and the ease with which these protocols can be sabotaged

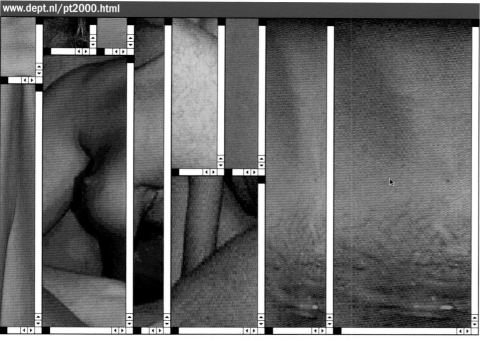

www.dept.nl/pt2000.html

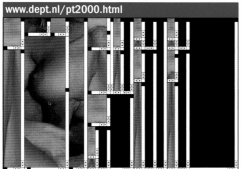

www.dept.nl/pt2000.html

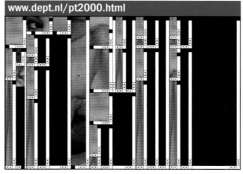

www.dept.nl/pt2000.html

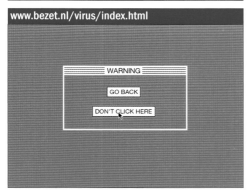

www.bezet.nl/virus/index.html

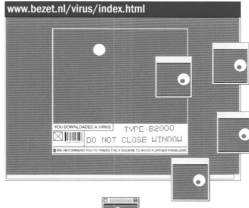

www.bezet.nl/virus/index.html

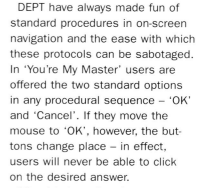

33

DEPT have always made fun of standard procedures in on-screen navigation and the ease with which these protocols can be sabotaged. In 'You're My Master' users are offered the two standard options in any procedural sequence – 'OK' and 'Cancel'. If they move the mouse to 'OK', however, the buttons change place – in effect, users will never be able to click on the desired answer.

'Virus' is based on Internet users' worst fears. A page warns visitors, 'don't click here'. For those who cannot resist the temptation, the next message informs them that they have downloaded a virus, which starts to clog the screen and the browser's memory with a hoard of small windows.

In a parody on the web's most popular content, 'Solo par Adulti' frustrates visitors in search of adult material by making each frame less visible the more they click on it until the screen shows only an array of fleshy tones with very little detail. Using one of the scrollbars results in the frames going altogether black. The soundtrack behind this page is a metallic female computer voice, frigidly reciting the most obscene proposals.

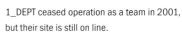

1_DEPT ceased operation as a team in 2001, but their site is still on line.
2_Max Bruinsma, 'Mode(s) d'emploi' (1999, www.xs4all.nl/~maxb/divers-mo-e.html).

The International Browserday competition has challenged students and young designers to find new ways of interfacing the web

www.browserday.com

International Browserday 5 & 6

client_International Browserday,
Amsterdam, NL
design_Joes Koppers, NL.Design,
Amsterdam, NL
on line_2001, 2002

34

Since 1998, the International Browserday competition, founded in Amsterdam by designer Mieke Gerritzen (see pp. 26–27, 37, 86, 107) and media theorist Geert Lovink, has challenged students and young designers to find new ways of interfacing the web. The first winner, Dutchman Joes Koppers (see pp. 26–27, 107), made the sites for the fifth and sixth events in Berlin (2001) and Amsterdam (2002).

On the Berlin site, four windows seem to land randomly on the screen. Depending on the order in which the user arranges the windows, they display different information. Placing the four windows in the 'correct' order makes them display the information the designers intended to be shown here. As a gesture toward impatient visitors, Koppers added a fifth window, the menu, where clicking on an entry automatically sorts the windows into their correct position in the centre of the screen. The words in the lower margin of the four windows are a fake interface – they cannot be clicked on, but help the user to find the right order of the windows.

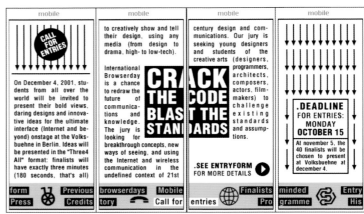

The site for the sixth Browserday works in a similar way, but without the interactive feature

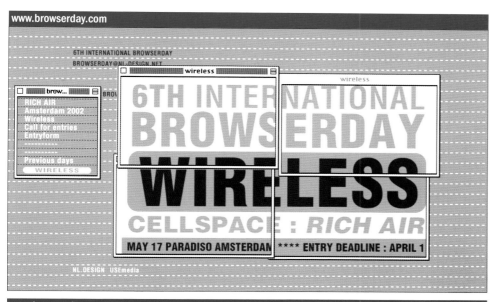

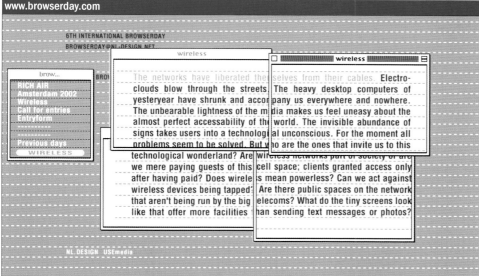

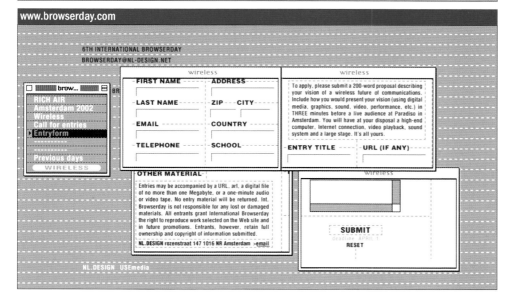

The site for the sixth Browserday, made in collaboration with Mieke Gerritzen, works in a similar way, but without the interactive feature of influencing the windows' content by moving them around. Instead, the windows keep moving slightly of their own accord, an apt metaphor for the instability of the web's content, certainly with respect to the sixth Browserday's theme, 'wireless'. However, in this case it makes focusing on the texts rather difficult.

Koppers incorporates smooth working interfaces with playful elements and gaming aspects in both sites. He experiments with the browser's behaviour, the visual metaphors of the Graphic User Interface and visitors' responses. Even if they are occasionally on the verge of form over function, the Browserday sites represent a strong and well-reasoned combination of content, design and medium, intended to refine our understanding of the particularities of the web. In this sense, Koppers's interfaces are educational as well as entertaining.

If usability guru Jakob Nielsen's philosophies were generally followed, this book could not have been written

36

Jakob Nielsen

design_Jakob Nielsen, Fremont, CA, US
on line_1996

If usability guru Jakob Nielsen's philosophies were generally followed, this book could not have been written (<u>see p. 17</u>). However sensible his views on interface design and his emphasis on functional details, his deep mistrust of visual designers and his rather low esteem of users lead to a kind of web design that, although functional, lacks all individuality. Nielsen's own site is a case in point. It is highly informative – the kind of content we just love to disagree with – and the austere visual design is completely consistent with Nielsen's belief that design on the web should follow established conventions of use. This may hold true for Nielsen – the site reflects *his* personality – but if, for instance, MTV (<u>see pp. 50–51</u>) or Dior (<u>see p. 114</u>) were to follow the same rules in their visual presentation, they would loose their constituency immediately. It seems ridiculous to pin down usability standards for a medium that is in its infancy. Nonetheless, Nielsen prefers to keep such common design mistakes as blue hyperlinks ('the mother of bad web design conventions', <u>see p. 22, note 1</u>) than to challenge users by finding better methods. As dangerous as ignoring the gist of his argument (respect the user) is to accept his disregard of the potential functional and expressive value of visual design.

---

www.useit.com/about/nographics.html

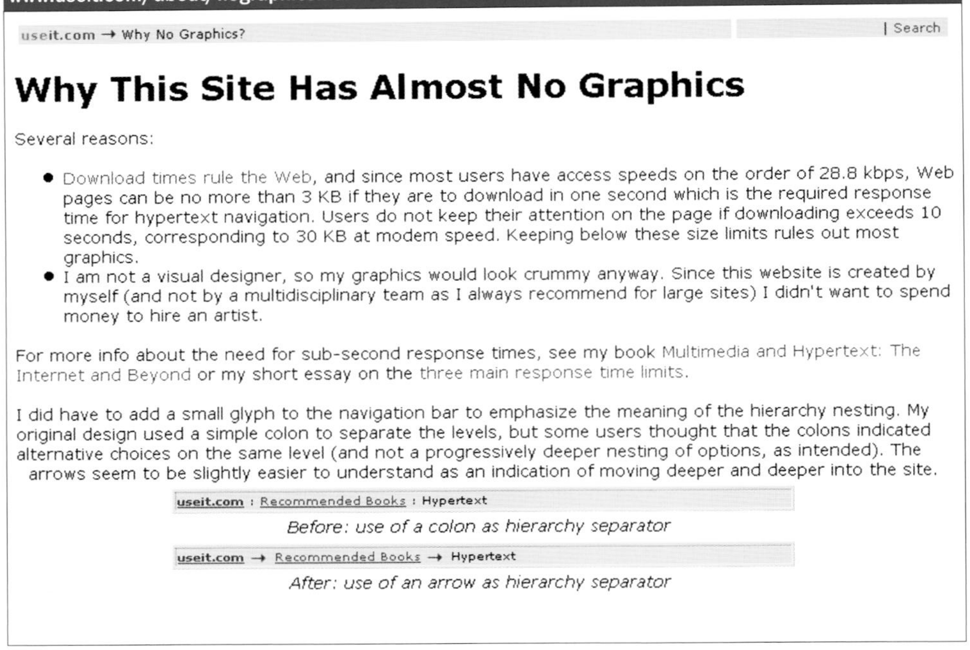

useit.com → Why No Graphics? | Search

Why This Site Has Almost No Graphics

Several reasons:

- **Download times rule the Web**, and since most users have access speeds on the order of 28.8 kbps, Web pages can be no more than 3 KB if they are to download in one second which is the required response time for hypertext navigation. Users do not keep their attention on the page if downloading exceeds 10 seconds, corresponding to 30 KB at modem speed. Keeping below these size limits rules out most graphics.
- I am not a visual designer, so my graphics would look crummy anyway. Since this website is created by myself (and not by a multidisciplinary team as I always recommend for large sites) I didn't want to spend money to hire an artist.

For more info about the need for sub-second response times, see my book Multimedia and Hypertext: The Internet and Beyond or my short essay on the three main response time limits.

I did have to add a small glyph to the navigation bar to emphasize the meaning of the hierarchy nesting. My original design used a simple colon to separate the levels, but some users thought that the colons indicated alternative choices on the same level (and not a progressively deeper nesting of options, as intended). The arrows seem to be slightly easier to understand as an indication of moving deeper and deeper into the site.

useit.com : Recommended Books : Hypertext
Before: use of a colon as hierarchy separator

useit.com → Recommended Books → Hypertext
After: use of an arrow as hierarchy separator

---

www.useit.com/alertbox

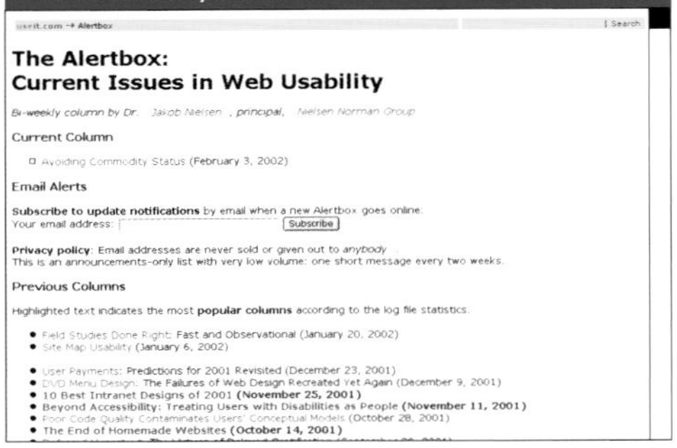

useit.com → Alertbox | Search

**useit.com:
The Alertbox:
Current Issues in Web Usability**

Bi-weekly column by Dr. Jakob Nielsen, principal, Nielsen Norman Group.

Current Column

☐ Avoiding Commodity Status (February 3, 2002)

Email Alerts

Subscribe to update notifications by email when a new Alertbox goes online.
Your email address: [ ] Subscribe

Privacy policy: Email addresses are never sold or given out to anybody
This is an announcements-only list with very low volume: one short message every two weeks.

Previous Columns

Highlighted text indicates the most **popular** columns according to the log file statistics.

- Field Studies Done Right: Fast and Observational (January 20, 2002)
- Site Map Usability (January 6, 2002)

- User Payments: Predictions for 2001 Revisited (December 23, 2001)
- DVD Menu Design: The Failures of Web Design Recreated Yet Again (December 9, 2001)
- 10 Best Intranet Designs of 2001 (November 25, 2001)
- Beyond Accessibility: Treating Users with Disabilities as People (November 11, 2001)
- Poor Code Quality Contaminates Users' Conceptual Models (October 28, 2001)
- The End of Homemade Websites (October 14, 2001)

---

www.useit.com

useit.com: Jakob Nielsen's Website

useit.com: Jakob Nielsen's Website

Permanent Content	News
Alertbox	The guidelines for improving usability for users with disabilities are now **available as an audiobook** (CD or tape, as you prefer). Great while commuting or exercising, or if you are looking for a human voice alternative to listening to a screen reader.
Jakob's bi-weekly column on Web usability	
Avoiding Commodity Status (February 3)	
PCs do not need to be commodities: a focus on quality can differentiate both products and services. Software has great potential for getting better, as shown by an under-appreciated feature in Windows XP that can save users $2,000 per year	Dave "DaveNet" Winer relates his experience with linkrot on various websites, prompted by a massive death of links into the San Jose Mercury News . Dave finds the New York Times to have the most robust archives. I have also noted that USA Today, The Guardian, News.com and WIRED keep their old URLs alive. **Linkrot impacts the way we write for the Web**: I am more
Field Studies Done Right: Fast and Observational (January 20)	motivated to link to a site if I have reasons to believe that the link will continue to work in a few years (let alone a few days or months, which is the lifetime of links
Site Map Usability (January 6)	on some sites — forget about linking to them). Since
User Payments: Predictions for 2001 Revisited (December 23)	incoming links are the main way to improve ranking in search engines, sites that don't preserve old URLs will
All Alertbox columns from 1995 to 2002	not only lose the traffic from the linking sites, they will also place poorly in search engines (one of the main tools of Internet marketing as far as attracting new
Reports	customers is concerned). In my opinion, see my articles from 1998: Fighting Linkrot and Web Pages Must
Intranet Design Annual: 10 best intranets	Live Forever (both articles have been live at the same URLs since 1998, so you can feel safe in linking to them
Site map usability	for background on this topic — these articles will be there
Users with disabilities (75 usability guidelines)	
PR sections of corporate sites – optimizing usability for journalists	
E-commerce usability (207 design guidelines)	
User testing: 230 tips	

---

www.useit.com/alertbox

- DVD Payments: Tradecard for 2001 Revisited (December 23, 2001)
- DVD Menu Design: The Failures of Web Design Recreated Yet Again (December 9, 2001)
- **10 Best Intranet Designs of 2001 (November 25, 2001)**
- Beyond Accessibility: Treating Users with Disabilities as People (November 11, 2001)
- Poor Code Quality Contaminates Users' Conceptual Models (October 28, 2001)
- **The End of Homemade Websites (October 14, 2001)**
- Deferred Hypertext: The Virtues of Delayed Gratification (September 30, 2001)
- Mobile Devices Will Soon Be Useful (September 16, 2001)
- Designing Web Ads Using Click-Through Data (September 2, 2001)
- Did Poor Usability Kill E-Commerce? (August 19, 2001)
- First Rule of Usability? Don't Listen to Users (**August 5, 2001**)
- Tagline Blues: What's the Site About? (July 22, 2001)
- Helping Users Find Physical Locations (July 8, 2001)
- Error Message Guidelines (June 24, 2001)
- Avoid PDF for On-Screen Reading (**June 10, 2001**)
- Salary Survey: User Experience Professionals Earn Good Money (May 27, 2001)
- Search: Visible and Simple (May 13, 2001)
- Japanese Products Map the Mobile Road Ahead (April 29, 2001)
- Collect, Compare, Choose: The 3Cs of Critical Web Use (April 15, 2001)
- Corporate Websites Get a 'D' in PR (**April 1, 2001**)
- Stationary Mobility (March 18, 2001)
- Retaining Key Staff: What High-Tech Employees Say versus What They Do (March 4, 2001)
- Success Rate: The Simplest Usability Metric (February 18, 2001)
- Are Users Stupid? (**February 4, 2001**)
- Usability Metrics (**January 21, 2001**)
- Mobile Phones: Europe's Next Minitel? (January 7, 2001)

- The Web in 2001: Paying Customers (December 24, 2000)
- WAP Field Study Findings (December 10, 2000)
- Security & Human Factors (November 26, 2000)

---

www.useit.com/alertbox/20000723.html

useit.com → Alertbox → July 2000 End of Web Design | Search

Jakob Nielsen's Alertbox, July 23, 2000:

End of Web Design

Websites must tone down their individual appearance and distinct design in all ways:

- visual design
- terminology and labeling
- interaction design and workflow
- information architecture

These changes are driven by four different trends that all lead to the same conclusion:

1. Jakob's Law of the Internet User Experience

Users spend most of their time on *other* sites. This means that users prefer your site to work the same way as all the other sites they already know.

This Law is not even a future trend since it has been ruling the Web for several years. It has long been true that websites do more business the more standardized their design is. Think Yahoo and Amazon. Think "shopping cart" and the silly little icon. Think blue text links.

2. Mobile Internet

Mobility drives small screens (because they are the only ones that can be easily carried) that will often be grayscale (to save battery). Mobile bandwidth will be much more restricted than wired bandwidth. Even

---

www.useit.com/alertbox

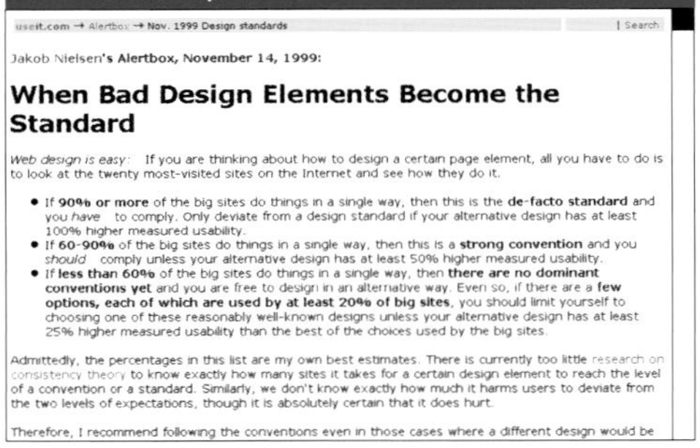

useit.com → Alertbox → Nov. 1999 Design standards | Search

Jakob Nielsen's Alertbox, November 14, 1999:

When Bad Design Elements Become the Standard

Web design is easy: If you are thinking about how to design a certain page element, all you have to do is look at the twenty most-visited sites on the Internet and see how they do it.

- If **90% or more** of the big sites do things in a single way, then this is the **de-facto standard** and you have to comply. Only deviate from a design standard if your alternative design has at least 100% higher measured usability.
- If **60-90%** of the big sites do things in a single way, then this is a **strong convention** and you *should* comply unless your alternative design has at least 50% higher measured usability.
- If **less than 60%** of the big sites do things in a single way, then **there are no dominant conventions yet** and you are free to design in an alternative way. Even so, if there are a **few options**, each of which are used by at least **20%** of big sites, you should limit yourself to choosing one of these reasonably well-known designs unless your alternative design has at least 25% higher measured usability than the best of the choices used by the big sites.

Admittedly, the percentages in this list are my own best estimates. There is currently too little research on consistency theory to know exactly how many sites it takes for a certain design element to reach the level of a convention or a standard. Similarly, we don't know exactly how much it hurts users to deviate from the two levels of expectations, though it is absolutely certain that it does hurt.

Therefore, I recommend following the conventions even in those cases where a different design would be

---

www.useit.com/alertbox/20000723.html

useit.com → Alertbox → Jakob Nielsen bio | Search

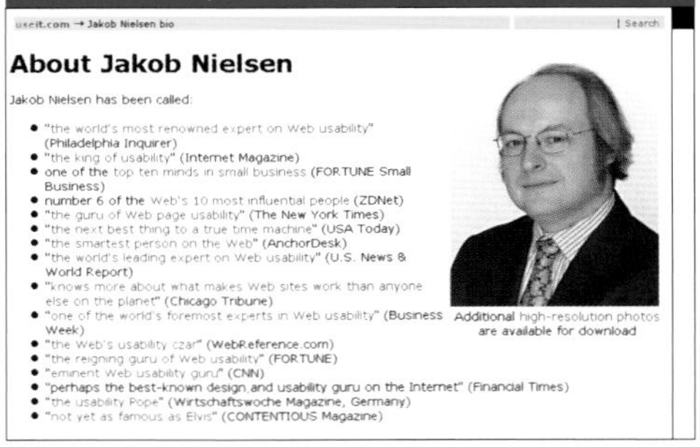

About Jakob Nielsen

Jakob Nielsen has been called:

- "the world's most renowned expert on Web usability" (Philadelphia Inquirer)
- "the king of usability" (Internet Magazine)
- one of the top ten minds in small business (FORTUNE Small Business)
- number 6 of the Web's 10 most influential people (ZDNet)
- "the guru of Web page usability" (The New York Times)
- "the next best thing to a true time machine" (USA Today)
- "the smartest person on the Web" (AnchorDesk)
- "the world's leading expert on Web usability" (U.S. News & World Report)
- "knows more about what makes web sites work than anyone else on the planet" (Chicago Tribune)
- "one of the world's foremost experts in Web usability" (Business Week)
- "the Web's usability czar" (WebReference.com)
- "the reigning guru of Web usability" (FORTUNE)
- "eminent Web usability guru" (CNN)
- "perhaps the best-known design and usability guru on the Internet" (Financial Times)
- "the usability Pope" (Wirtschaftswoche Magazine, Germany)
- "not yet as famous as Elvis" (CONTENTIOUS Magazine)

Additional high-resolution photos are available for download

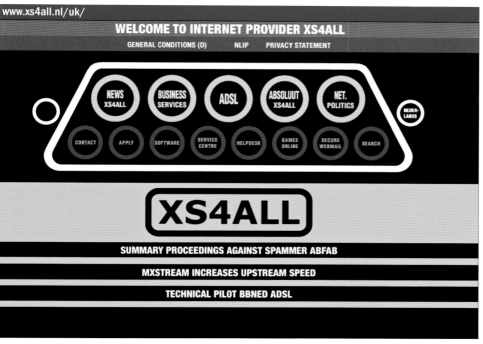

XS4ALL

client_XS4ALL, Amsterdam, NL
design_Mieke Gerritzen, NL.Design,
Amsterdam, NL
on line_2000

The Netherlands' first public Internet Service Provider (ISP) was the brainchild of a quartet of hackers who met through *HackTic*, a 'techno-anarchist' magazine from the late 1980s. As the name suggests, XS4ALL was intended to provide access for all instead of limiting access to the university and business accounts as had been the case in the Netherlands before XS4ALL was launched. Within hours of opening to the public in 1993, the new ISP exceeded the five-hundred-subscriber mark the founders had envisioned reaching after six months. Now, XS4ALL is one of the largest ISPs in the Netherlands and has been taken over by KPN, the leading Dutch telecom company. After a series of redesigns, XS4ALL homepages still reflect the no-nonsense, power-to-the-people attitude of the founders. The site has not given in to the temptation of becoming a portal for any other business than its own, which is assisting subscribers and customers and supporting the cause of free information exchange on the web. Mieke Gerritzen's signal style (see pp. 26–27, 34–35, 86, 107) of sturdy typography, strong colours and a clear and outspoken visual hierarchy fit the job perfectly, as does the main interface design on the homepage: a simple toolkit for users.

The site's opening page shows an outline drawing of a photography studio in which three faceless men pose in rabbit costumes

www.klimate.com

Klimate

design_Klimate, New York, US
on line_2001

The site's opening page shows an outline drawing of a photography studio in which three faceless men pose in rabbit costumes. Moving the mouse over the dotted outline of the question-marked bunny produces the caption, 'employer recruiting candidates; this could be you'. Who is 'you'? Is this the usual jobs vacant page? Or, is it addressing the visitor as a potential customer of the Klimate research and development group? Clicking on this bunny reveals a window listing 'past recruits', i.e. clients, with samples of work for Rolling Stone Radio, the David Bowie website and the webzine 'Word'. The other two bunnies represent Klimate's founders Jason Huang and Sam Frank and show their biographies. This is about the only conventional element of the site. You would expect to find the firm's portfolio behind the small screen captioned 'media, the end result'. Instead, you are transported to a scene with two bunnies in front of a television screen, absorbed in a dialogue about artistic practice and honest communication. They increasingly annoy each other as the visitor clicks through their endless conversation. This is 'irri-design', and the visitor is inclined to agree with the two bunnies in their mutual concluding remark 'asshole'. Of course, the content is meant to convey an image of self-critical media-awareness on a small site that looks cool to the target audience. Klimate plays with clichés of interactivity and mocks them. Bad bunnies!

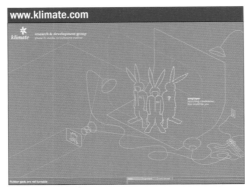 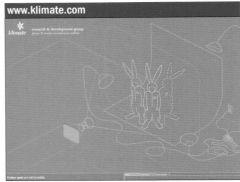

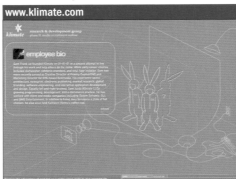 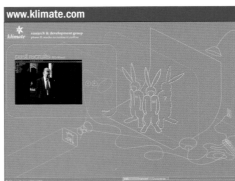

Portuguese photographer Rui Camilo, based in Germany, was smart enough to register two URLs

www.rui-camilo.de/main.html

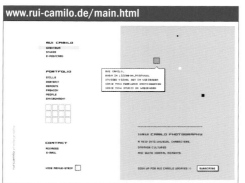

www.rui-camilo.de/main.html

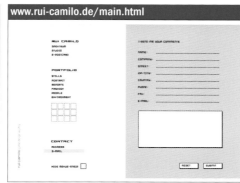

www.rui-camilo.de/main.html

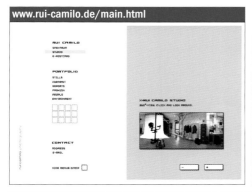

www.rui-camilo.de/main.html

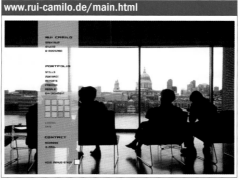

www.rui-camilo.de/main.html

www.rui-camilo.de
www.rui-camillo.de

Rui Camilo
client_Rui Camilo Photography, Nordenstadt, DE
design_Scholz & Volkmer, Wiesbaden, DE
on line_2000

39

Portuguese photographer Rui Camilo, based in Germany, was smart enough to register two URLs, certain that people would misspell his name. His site is similarly well considered apart from the ridiculous interface elements on the right side of the homepage, a few perpetually bouncing squares that, if one cares to catch them, display extra information. The rest of the interface, however, elegantly solves the tricky problem of how to prevent the interface from interfering with the work. Design studio Scholz & Volkmer devised a transparent strip that contains all the necessary elements for navigating the portfolio and a 'hide' button. The tiny, movable square that remains after collapsing the strip is unobtrusive, and stays functional in several ways – one shouldn't make copying too easy. The portfolio sections load as darkening green squares in the navigation strip, and, once loaded, the photographs appear immediately when clicked and a short caption comes up in the strip. The site is simple and straightforward, and, aside from a 360-degree overview of Camilo's studio (looks like a cosy place), the focus is entirely on the photographer's work.

If you are familiar with Posttool's award-winning 1997 website, the new version (2001) looks rather subdued in comparison

www.posttool.com
www.californiaclosets.com
www.palacepress.com
www.chroniclebooks.com
www.dwellmag.com

Posttool

client, design_David Karam, Gigi
Biederman, San Francisco, CA, US
on line_2001

If you are familiar with Posttool's award-winning 1997 website, the new version (2001) looks rather subdued in comparison. No doodles, no fluffy bunnies that challenge visitors to find out how they work. Still, playfulness prevails albeit in more subtle details, such as the ever-changing colours of the translucent blocks on the homepage, the hovering or twirling lines on sites for the San Francisco Museum of Modern Art and Palace Press and the turning book pages on the site for Chronicle Books. Much of Posttool's visible effort goes into coding the behaviour of the decorative aspects of sites, while a lot of invisible design labour is dedicated to making the database-driven sites work seamlessly. Even if the informational or text content of a page is a bit thin, such as the page for SFMOMA's exhibition 'Revelatory Landscapes', the decoration provides entertainment and associative imagery.

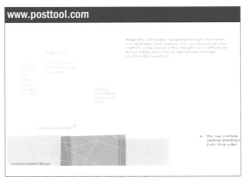

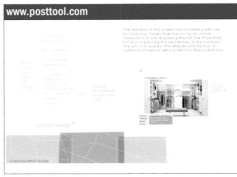

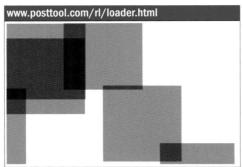

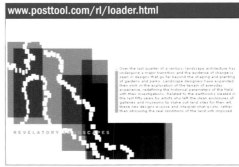

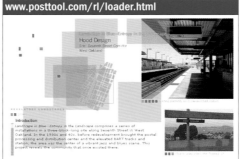

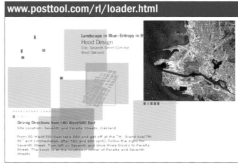

From an aesthetic viewpoint, the transition between sections and pages is the most interesting feature on the Chronicle site

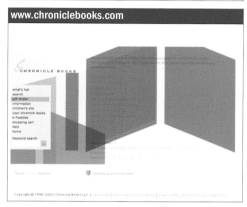

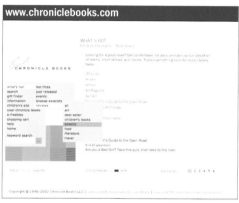

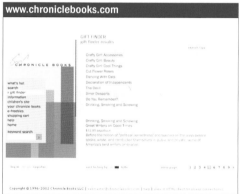

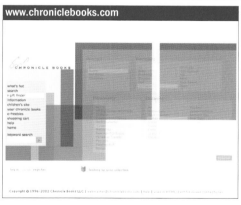

From an aesthetic viewpoint, the transition between sections and pages is the most interesting feature on the Chronicle site. Expanded menus collapse onto each other, while coloured boxes in the background slide into each other, open and close like books and melt and disappear behind new ones. Posttool uses such cinematic montage and transitional devices as blends, fades and pans in a graphic way for which the web seems to be the natural environment. That the designers rely heavily on visitors' bandwidth and CPU and that their work is sometimes quite sensitive about which platform or browser is used, is something you have to accept from people who write Flash faster than many computers can read it. We will catch up some time.

Joan and Dirk teamed up to form Jodi when the wonderland of technological innovation that is the web was still in its infancy

wwwwwwwww.jodi.org

jodi.org
design_jodi.org, Barcelona, ES
on line_2000

Belgian artists Joan Heemskerk and Dirk Paesmans teamed up to form Jodi when the wonderland of technological innovation that is the World Wide Web[1] was still in its infancy. They did not set out to become net.artists, being more interested in the processes that dictate the computer's inner workings; for example, what happens in the machine when you start up a CD-ROM, how does the operating system deal with unsolicited data sent via its Internet connection, what is the logic behind the dominant GUIs, and, most importantly, how can we hack all that? Jodi investigates – and thoroughly mixes up – the rules that govern the medium at an infrastructural level. Often considered to be net.anarchists because of their rather disruptive visuals and interactive models, Heemskerk and Paesmans are not necessarily out to do serious damage, but they do want to explore and make evident the cultural fabric that determines interfaces and operating systems. The visual panic of their output is a result of their modus operandi, which makes the computer do things that its very architecture forbids it to. Concurrently, Jodi hacks into our conventional expectations of how to operate this vast landscape of procedures and interfaces.

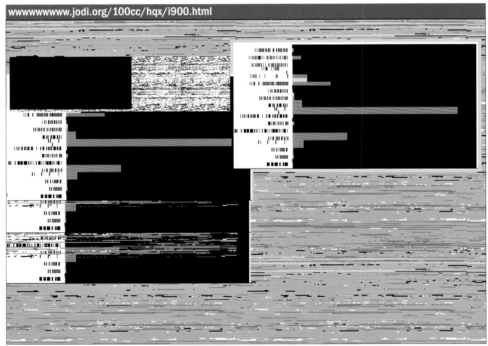

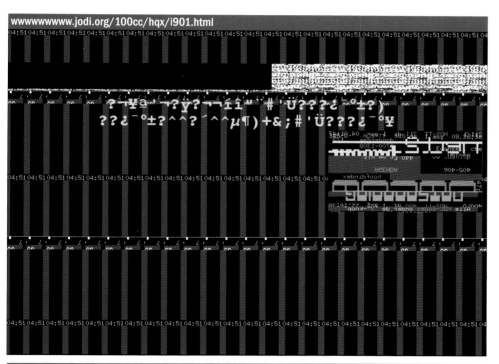

wwwwwwwww.jodi.org/100cc/hqx/i901.html

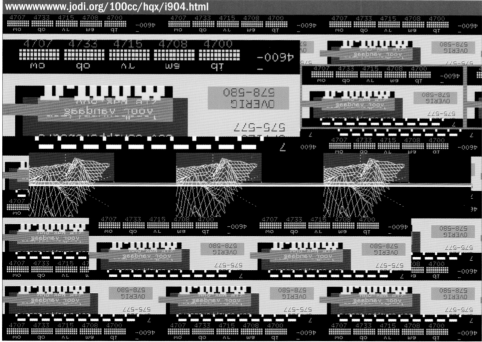

wwwwwwwww.jodi.org/100cc/hqx/i904.html

On the occasion of the Dutch Electronic Arts Festival (DEAF) in 1998, Jodi developed an alternative operating system (OSS) that manipulates and apparently all but shatters the system it is played on. Originally a CD-ROM work, Jodi later chose to make it available for downloading on the web (oss.jodi.org). It caused a major row resulting in their expulsion from their ISP after other customers complained. Time and again Jodi makes it clear that interfaces are decided by culturally dominant values and ideas, demonstrating at the same time that cultural and system codes can be altered without destroying all functionality. As Heemskerk and Paesmans explain, 'We learned from our first web mistakes that an error can be most interesting. If you forget a little HTML code tag, for example the bracket ">", then the text surface mixes with the code and becomes liquid, it flows all over the screen. This type of dynamic, tactile text is different from hard copy. We can't accept that print design rules define also the layout on a computer screen. Most websites still look like print. The possibilities of code and text exchange are not used, because it's confusing, it is not readable.' Jodi is opening our eyes to the endless possibilities of code expressing itself.

43

1_See also: www.jodi.org, oss.jodi.org, sod.jodi.org.

Peter Luining describes his work as 'little pieces of software that allow the user to make sound or audiovisual compositions'

ctrlaltdel.org

design_Peter Luining, Amsterdam, NL
on line_1998

A net.artist from Amsterdam, Peter Luining describes his work as 'little pieces of software that allow the user to make sound or audiovisual compositions within limits defined by the artist'. His sound engines are embedded in a distinguished tradition of experiments concerning the relationship between visuals, sound, motion and interaction in computer media, of which London-based Antirom is the best-known exponent.

Characteristic of Luining's work is its explorative spirit and abstract visual language: coloured or black-and-white blocks move in a relentless rhythm within the confines of the window until a player grabs them and alters their course, or clicks on them to change their sound or rhythm. When Luining states that 'you directly control components of the piece ... which are influencing the sound composition', he is not entirely accurate. You cannot control these engines as you would expect to control normal interfaces, and Luining is keen to subvert such expectations; in that respect, he is akin to Jodi (see pp. 42–43). 'Control', here, means that a player's action has an effect – what effect remains to be seen and heard. This uncertainty is inscribed in most of the objects on the site, for example, the derailing sequences of web debris, hardcore music and software booby traps behind 'Clickclub'. The last I saw of this particular piece before my computer went into a coma was a sign promising me an enriching experience. The site's name is its program.

www.ctrlaltdel.org/clickclub/macrec1.htm

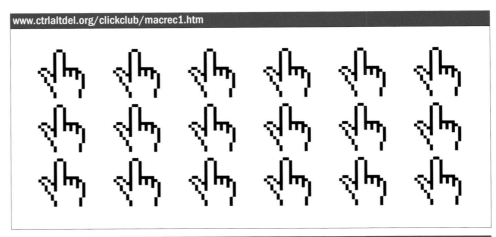

www.ctrlaltdel.org/clickclub/macrec1.htm

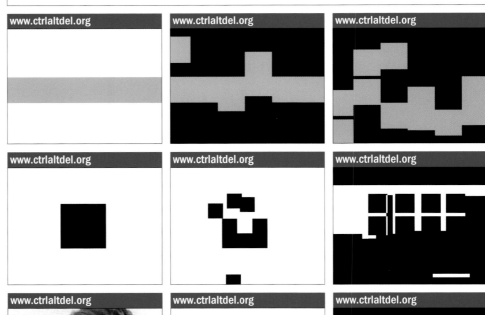

www.fu-fme.com/faq-use.html

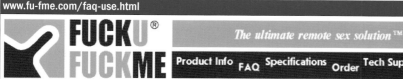

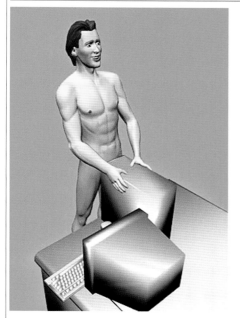 

FuckU-FuckMe in use.
Back to FAQ.

www.fu-fme.com/faq-use.html

Product Info FAQ Specifications Order Tech Support Warranty

Specifications

System Requirements	
Computer Requirements	Windows® 95/98 or Windows® NT 4.0 Pentium processor, 133 megahertz (MHz) minimum (166MHz recommended for H.323 connections) 32 megabytes (MB) of RAM 10 MB of hard disk space
Network Connections:	TCP/IP (Winsock compliant) IP address 33.6 Kbps (minimum) modem, LAN, Cable, or ISDN connection (56Kbps recommended for H.323 connections) PPP for dial-up connection
Technical Specifications	
Model	A013/F and A013/M
Type	Internal (bare drive)
Interface Connector	E-IDE
Installation direction	Horizontal, vertical
Power requirements	DC 5V
Power consumption	20 W (max)
Dimensions(W x L x H)	146.0 x 203.0 x 41.3mm
Weight	1,7 (model A013/F) and 1,8 (model A013/M)
Front Panel On	Software manual

www.fu-fme.com

FuckU-FuckMe
Changing the Feel of
Communication
design_Alexei Shulgin, Moscow, RU
on line_1999

As the product info page announces, 'FuckU-FuckMe for Windows 95, Windows 98, and Windows NT provides the most complete remote sex solution for the Internet and corporate intranet'. The site is no more and no less than an online advertorial, explaining what this ingenious and exciting interface is all about: 'changing the feel of communication'. This is done in the worst tradition of generic product pages in terms of design and text (read the FAQ, it's hilarious!). Inspired by the early online video conference tool CUSeMe (see you, see me), this 'point of view' invention offers a hands-on experience where other communication means remain merely eidetic. Who said computing could not be fun? This combination of derailing technology and design critique stems from the Moscow-based net.artist and curator Alexei Shulgin, who has done a great deal to make life on the web a more enthralling experience in his pieces collected on his site 'Easylife' (www.easylife.org). An early authority in the so-called net.art movement and a witty critic of the young medium, Shulgin is also a member of the low-tech cyberpunk rock band 386dx, which plays at any serious video-art festival near you. The 'FuckU-FuckMe' interface is a classic, a fine and outrageous example of interface innovation that points to the weak spot of the medium: its lack of corporeality.

'Neither art, nor those who make it, show it, and look at it can ever be the same again'

010101.sfmoma.org

010101: Art in Technological Times

client_San Francisco Museum of
Modern Art, CA, US
curators_Aaron Betsky, Benjamin Weil
design_Perimetre-Flux, San Francisco,
CA, US
on line_2001

'Neither art, nor those who make it, show it, and look at it can ever be the same again.' With this dec-laration, SFMOMA put together the '010101: Art in Technological Times' exhibition in 2001. The website was developed as an inte-gral part of the exhibition's media mix of gallery shows (sculpture, video, design projects, computer installations, online works), public events and the catalogue. The main interface tool is a small square made up of eight tiny cubes, which are increasingly surrounded by red and black dots that randomly appear with soft ploppy noises. When clicked, the black dots trigger quotes on computers, the media and associ-ated topics from a range of pundits from John Maeda to Albert Speer. The square provides access to the main sections of the site, such as the gallery overview, a range of specially commissioned artist projects, an archive of online presentations and backgrounds on the artists in the exhibition. Each section opens with an introduction that can be closed after reading but remains in the background for reference, along with other explanatory texts. A third interface element is an array of line pat-terns, which on most pages sits decoratively on the left side of the screen. On mouseover, the lines display key words that when clicked open a page showing quotes on the subject and visitors' reactions; a laudable attempt at using the medium for intellectual

010101.sfmoma.org/start.html

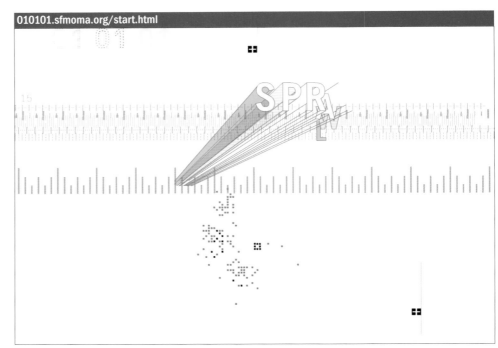

010101.sfmoma.org/start.html

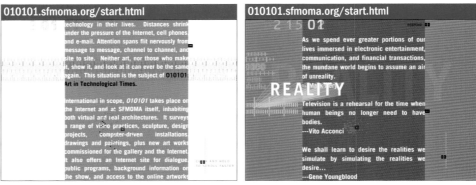

010101.sfmoma.org/start.html

010101.sfmoma.org/start.html

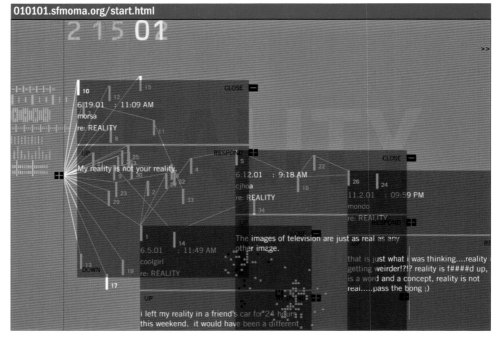

Leaving aside visitor participation, the site is a successful combination of content, interface and visual design

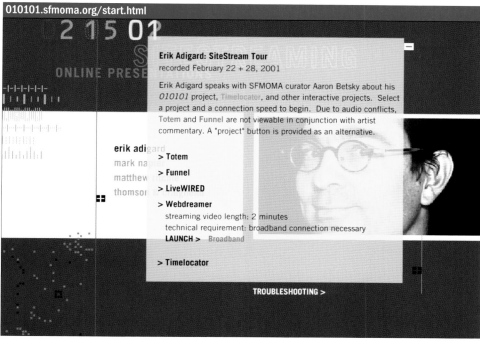

exchange, which, regrettably, too often results in comments to the effect of 'this site sucks'.

Leaving aside visitor participation, the site is a successful combination of content, interface and visual design. The frequent layering of information levels is well animated and always locks into a readable end state. Such dynamics, also seen in the texts that open or close in a lively fashion, suggest a fluidity of information that is, of course, purely virtual; the site's editorial structure is tight and quite linear. However, the movement and the smooth transition between topics do justice to the curators' cultural and theoretical points of departure: to see the web as a circuitous and tractable medium. On the site, this condition is more symbolized than realized, although in a few cases it is achieved; for example, hear Mark Napier (see pp. 176, 177) talk about 'Shredder' in the online presentation section and at the same time load the site's URL into this application – media at their best.

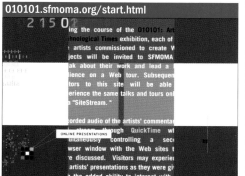

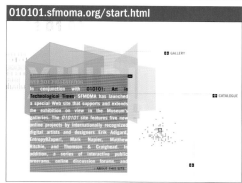

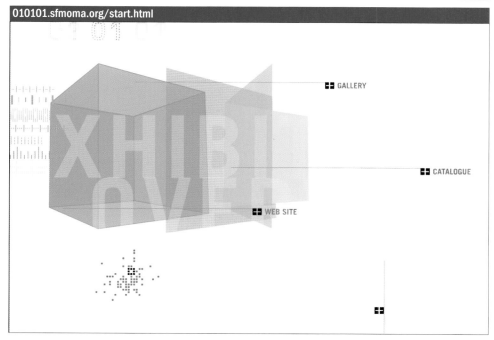

An Internet art exhibition, 'The Forest of Thoughts' grew over a period of six weeks in August and September 2000

www.zeit.de/forest

The Forest of Thoughts
design_Boris Müller and Sven Voelker
at Propellers, Berlin, DE
on line_2000

An Internet art exhibition, 'The Forest of Thoughts' grew over a period of six weeks in August and September 2000. Based on a design by Boris Müller and Sven Voelker from the young art-and-design network propellers.org and hosted by the German weekly *Die Zeit*, the exhibition was developed by fourteen contributors from different disciplines from around the world, including John Warwicker of Tomato in London, web artists Jodi.org in Barcelona (see pp. 42–43) and the Danish art group N55 in Copenhagen. These artists, designers, illustrators, architects and musicians exhibited and discussed ideas by sending images, texts and sounds into the 'forest' in response to four 'theme-seeds': body, pleasure, audience and reality.

Trawling through the interactive exhibition space, visitors can focus on these themes or on associative 'threads' that link one contributor's submission to the ones it has spawned, zoom in on the individual pieces or, using the timeline at the bottom of the screen, on the chronology of submissions. This kind of site is at once intriguing and irritating: if you are pre-coded for self-evident narrative structures, do not go there! You will get lost and bored within seconds. On the other hand, there is a great deal of serendipity to be experienced in such environments. And, for all its intangibility the interface looks cool and is well organized. Still, the complexity of the interface and the structures underlying the material, combined with an apparent lack of rigid editorial criteria, means that visitors may experience the forest, but have a hard time seeing the trees.

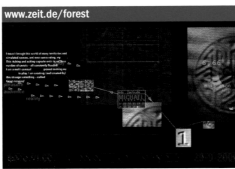 
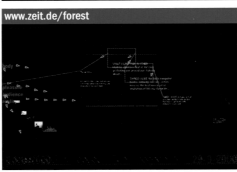 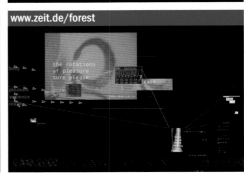
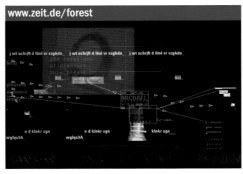 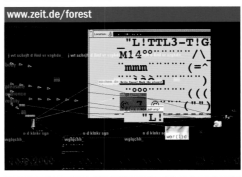

The splash screen betrays the fact that this site is not made in 1982 as the copyright sign on the following screen asserts

www.topscoreusa.com

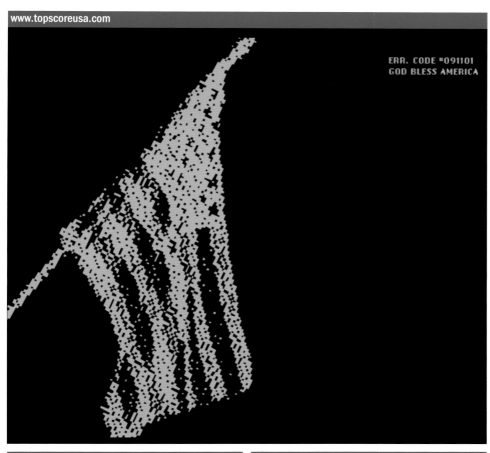

ERR. CODE #091101
GOD BLESS AMERICA

www.topscoreusa.com

Topscore USA
client_Topscore USA
design_James Schoenecker,
Milwaukee, WI, US
on line_2000

The splash screen, with its reference to 'error code #091101', betrays the fact that this site is not made in 1982 as the copyright sign on the following screen asserts. In other respects, however, visitors would indeed suspect that they had accessed an IBM work station from the 1980s: dark-yellow letters glow on a black background and the interface works exclusively from the keyboard (using arrow and enter keys, the space bar and keys 1–6). The site's visual presentation perfectly reflects young music fans' taste for the vernacular of the 1970s and 1980s. It is a pity that the pages don't contain more information – despite being a consistently sustained stylistic exercise, the site remains a gimmick. The real business is going on at the parallel site, Topscore USA store. That and the fact you can listen to online music samples on the pastiche site are further indications that this is no longer the 1980s.

49

www.topscoreusa.com

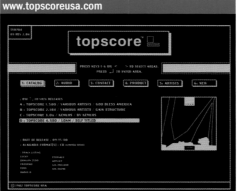

www.topscoreusa.com

www.topscoreusa.com

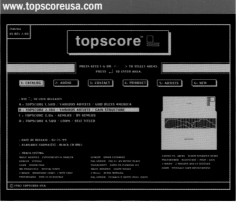

Connected to MTV's alternative music channel, the MTV2 website not only presented information about the channel

www.mtv2.com

MTV2

client_MTV Europe, London, UK
design_Digit, London, UK
on line_2000–02

Connected to MTV's alternative music channel, the MTV2 website[1] not only presented information about the channel (playlist, schedules, subscription information), but also allowed users to create an individual segment of programming and to communicate among themselves. The 3-D design (in Flash) with its nuts-and-bolts appearance may at first sight look quite over the top – who needs flying panels that zoom in and out of the screen just to say 'click here' – but the look and feel of the site is a serious component in appealing to MTV's target group of web-savvy youngsters with attitude. For all its overstatement, the design works well and is unquestionably aesthetic, a good example of the restrained typography and exuberant visuals so characteristic of today's hip visual culture.

The site's seamless merging of interface and design makes it less apparent that the screen layout is rather 2-D – nothing is really done with the suggested architectural space. On the other hand, MTV2's rendering of the time-tested metaphor of a digital city as a collection of sci-fi city blocks hovering in the media universe takes it to the cutting edge of 3-D environments. The sound design of the site deserves a special mention,

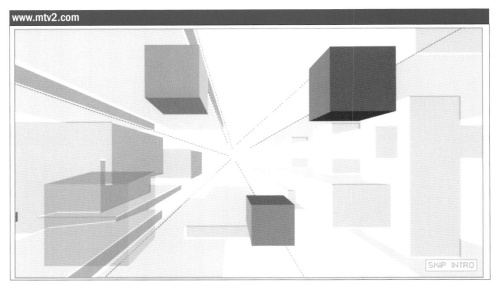

www.mtv2.com

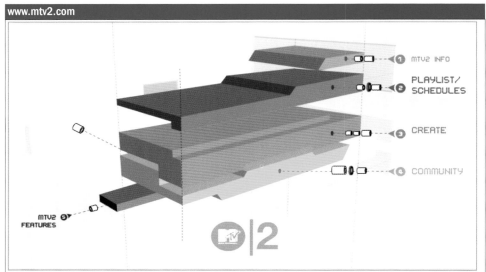

www.mtv2.com

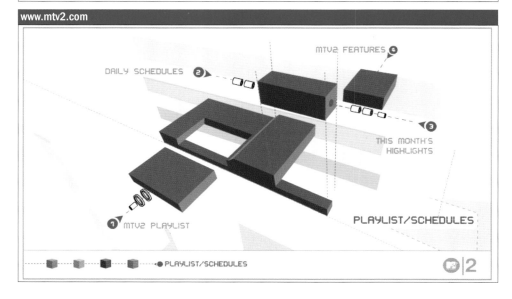

The overall site has an ethereal background noise

managing to steer clear of the hullabaloo of repetitive samples normally heard on sites that target a young audience. The overall site has an ethereal background noise, while on the homepage each floor of the MTV2 building comes with no less than three sounds that are individually triggered on mouseover. Attentive visitors will notice that just by sliding over the different floors they are able to make their own ambient music.

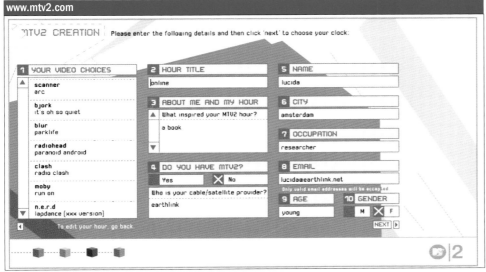

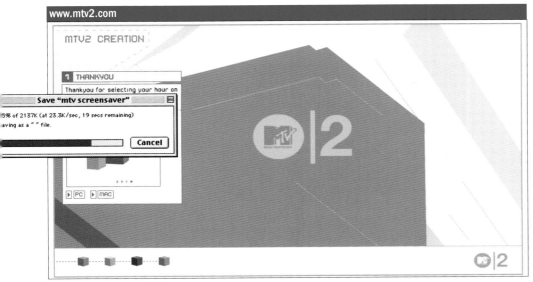

1_MTV has taken down the site. It can be visited at Digit's design archives, www.digitlondon.com/newDig/archive/mtv2

A non-profit organization founded in 1996, 'Rhizome.org' presents new media art through a website, a mailing list and events

| www.rhizome.org |
| rhizome.org/starrynight |
| rhizome.org/spiral |

Rhizome.org
design_Rhizome.org, New York, US
on line_1996

'StarryNight'
concept_Alex Galloway and Mark Tribe
production_Alex Galloway and Martin
Wattenberg

'Spiral'
concept, production_Martin Wattenberg
(with consultation from Steve Cannon)

A non-profit organization founded
in 1996, 'Rhizome.org' presents
new media art through a website,
a mailing list and events.
Geographically dispersed, this
important online community
includes artists, curators, writers,
designers, programmers, students,
educators and new-media professionals in more than eighty coun-
tries. The 'Rhizome alt.interface'
commissioning program
(rhizome.org/interface) is a combination of technological and artistic
innovation. Hybrids of net art and
functional design, the 'StarryNight'
and 'Spiral' interfaces list the
organization's library of over 1,700
indexed and edited texts – a huge
database of messages, discussions, reports and announcements
– in a radically different way from
usual indexing methods.

'Spiral' organizes the database
along chronological and categorical
lines, making the aggregate appear
like a galaxy through which one
can literally travel through time by
moving the scrollbar on the right.
The five fingers of the spiral

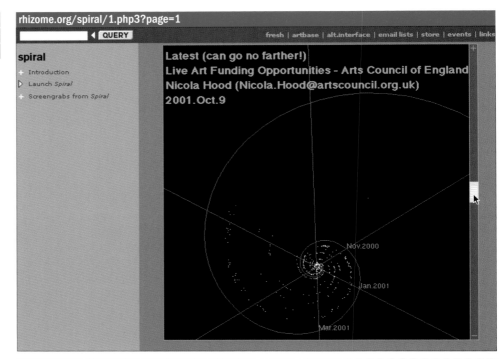

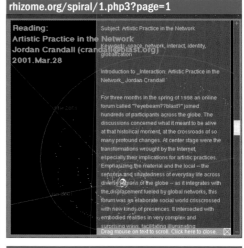

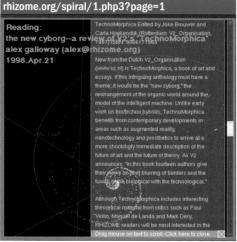

'StarryNight' shows all entries as stars against the night sky

52

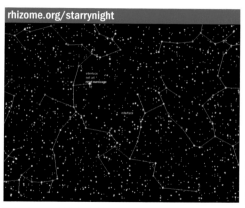

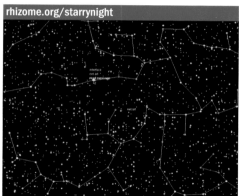

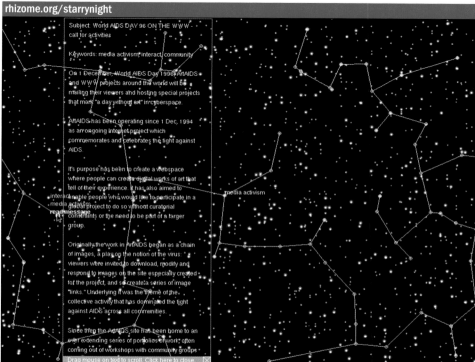

timeline represent the categories in which the texts are archived: listings and events, reviews, threads, statements and theory and commentary.

'StarryNight' shows all entries as stars against the night sky. Each time an entry is read, its star becomes brighter. Dragging the mouse over one of the stars brings up a pop-up list of key words that the corresponding text shares with other texts. On clicking a key word, the interface draws a constellation linking all the texts that share the word.

Such 'interface artworks', as their makers call them, may not provide the fastest ways of finding information, but they do conjure up an enticing image of linked data and offer viewers a new way of browsing and experiencing the site's contents associatively or contextually.

53

In 1999, Lisa Jevbratt started compiling a database that will, she hopes, eventually contain every website address in the world

cadre.sjsu.edu/jevbratt/c5/
onetoone/2/index_ng.html

1:1

concept and design_Lisa Jevbratt and C5,
San Jose, CA, US
on line_1999, 2001

In 1999, Lisa Jevbratt, a research theorist at the CADRE Laboratory for New Media at San Jose State University, California, started compiling a database that will, she hopes, eventually contain every website address in the world. She has also designed interfaces through which to view and use this database. Jevbratt began with the numerical addresses of websites (which all computers connected to the Internet have), called IP (Internet Protocol) addresses. A URL, a site's name that visitors are more familiar with (for example, 'cadre.sjsu.edu', the site 1:1 resides on), is actually a cover for the numerical IP address (in 1:1's case, '130.65.200.15') that is the 'real' address of a website. Crawlers (small programs that automatically collect data) were sent out on the web to search for sites with specific numerical addresses. If a site existed, whether accessible to the public or not, the address was stored in the database. In this way, about two per cent of existing websites in 1999 were charted, resulting in a database of 186,100 sites. In 2001, the same numerical spectrum was searched again to map the changes that had occurred in this very volatile field.

The five interfaces of 1:1 – 'Migration', 'Hierarchical', 'Every', 'Random', 'Excursion' – allow for addressing every site in the database, and, more importantly, they visually map the whole web.

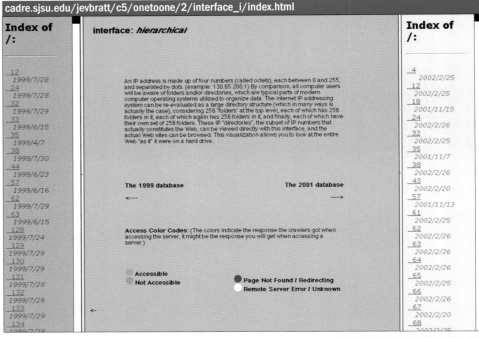

cadre.sjsu.edu/jevbratt/c5/onetoone/2/interface_i/index.html

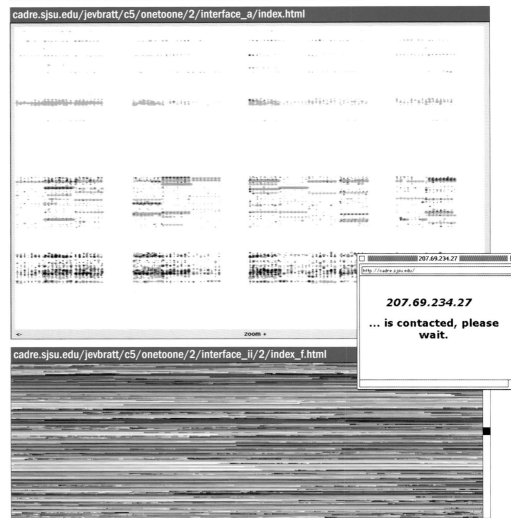

cadre.sjsu.edu/jevbratt/c5/onetoone/2/interface_a/index.html

cadre.sjsu.edu/jevbratt/c5/onetoone/2/interface_ii/2/index_f.html

The 'Every' interface shows the web as a range of differently coloured pixels

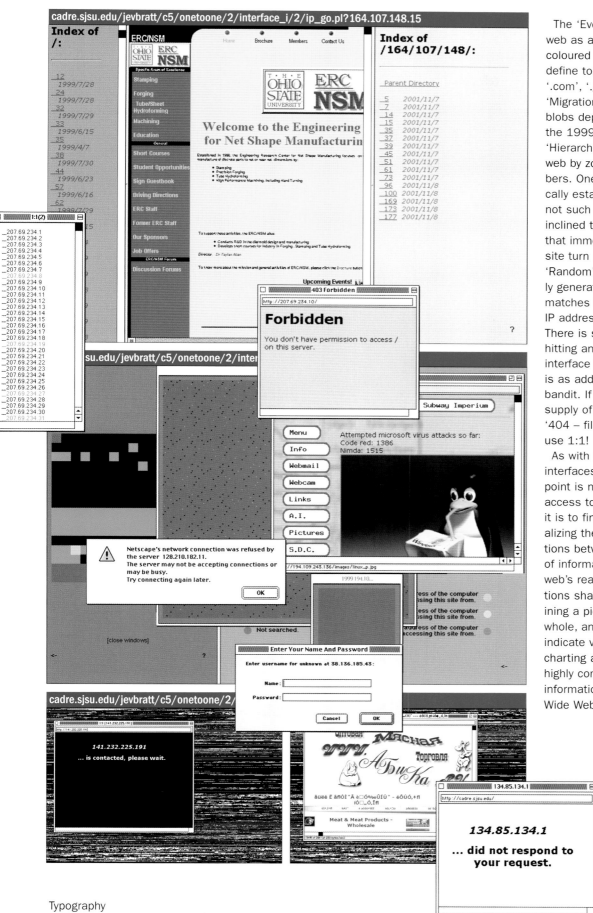

cadre.sjsu.edu/jevbratt/c5/onetoone/2/interface_i/2/ip_go.pl?164.107.148.15

Index of /:

_12
1999/7/28
_24
1999/7/28
_32
1999/7/29
_33
1999/6/15
_35
1999/4/7
_38
1999/7/30
_44
1999/6/23
_57
1999/6/16
_62
1999/2/29

ERC/NSM

OHIO STATE
ERC NSM

Specific Areas of Excellence

Stamping
Forging
Tube/Sheet Hydroforming
Machining
Education

General

Short Courses
Student Opportunities
Sign Guestbook
Driving Directions
ERC Staff
Former ERC Staff
Our Sponsors
Job Offers

ERC/NSM Forum

Discussion Forums

THE OHIO STATE UNIVERSITY
ERC NSM

Welcome to the Engineering for Net Shape Manufacturin

Established in 1986, the Engineering Research Center for Net Shape Manufacturing focuses on manufacture of discrete parts to net or near net dimensions by:

• Stamping
• Precision Forging
• Tube Hydroforming
• High Performance Machining, including Hard Turning

To support these activities, the ERC/NSM also:

• Conducts R&D in the die/mold design and manufacturing
• Develops short courses for Industry in Forging, Stamping and Tube Hydroforming

Director: Dr Taylan Altan

To know more about the mission and general activities of ERC/NSM, please click the Brochure button.

Upcoming Events!

Home   Brochure   Members   Contact Us

Index of /164/107/148/:

Parent Directory

_5   2001/11/7
_7   2001/11/7
_14   2001/11/7
_15   2001/11/7
_37   2001/11/7
_39   2001/11/7
_45   2001/11/7
_51   2001/11/7
_61   2001/11/7
_73   2001/11/7
_96   2001/11/8
_100   2001/11/8
_169   2001/11/8
_173   2001/11/8
_177   2001/11/8

1:1(2)

_207.69.234.1
_207.69.234.2
_207.69.234.3
_207.69.234.4
_207.69.234.5
_207.69.234.6
_207.69.234.7
_207.69.234.8
_207.69.234.9
_207.69.234.10
_207.69.234.11
_207.69.234.12
_207.69.234.13
_207.69.234.14
_207.69.234.15
_207.69.234.16
_207.69.234.17
_207.69.234.18
_207.69.234.19
_207.69.234.20
_207.69.234.21
_207.69.234.22
_207.69.234.23
_207.69.234.24
_207.69.234.25
_207.69.234.26
_207.69.234.27
_207.69.234.28
_207.69.234.29
_207.69.234.30
_207.69.234.31

403 Forbidden

http://207.69.234.10/

Forbidden

You don't have permission to access / on this server.

su.edu/jevbratt/c5/onetoone/2/inter

Subway Imperium

Menu
Info
Webmail
Webcam
Links
A.I.
Pictures
S.D.C.

Attempted microsoft virus attacks so far:
Code red: 1386
Nimda: 1515

//194.109.243.136/images/linux_p.jpg

⚠ Netscape's network connection was refused by the server 128.210.182.11.
The server may not be accepting connections or may be busy.
Try connecting again later.

OK

1999.194.10...

Not searched.

[close windows]

←   ?

...ess of the computer ...sing this site from.
...ess of the computer ...sing this site from.
...addrress of the computer ...accessing this site from.

←

cadre.sjsu.edu/jevbratt/c5/onetoone/2/

141.232.225.191
... is contacted, please wait.

[:1] [141.232.225.191]
http://141.232.225.191/

ЧПТОВАЯ МАСНАЯ
Торговля
АБиКа

āuē Ē āñÓÎ¨Ä è□Ó‰oÛÍÚ˝ - éÔÚÓ,˝fī
Íó□„Ó,Îñ

Meat & Meat Products - Wholesale

134.85.134.1

http://cadre.sjsu.edu/

134.85.134.1

... did not respond to your request.

The 'Every' interface shows the web as a range of differently coloured pixels, where the colours define top-level domains such as '.com', '.gov', '.mil' and '.edu'. In 'Migration', differently coloured blobs depict the changes between the 1999 and 2001 databases. In 'Hierarchical', you can browse the web by zooming in on the numbers. One thing Jevbratt unequivocally establishes is that the web is not such an open space as we are inclined to think – IP addresses that immediately give access to a site turn out to be quite rare. The 'Random' interface, which randomly generates IP numbers and matches them to their nearest live IP address, is a case in point. There is small chance of it actually hitting an accessible site, but the interface keeps you clicking on; it is as addictive as a one-armed bandit. If you want an exhaustive supply of 'no-go', 'log-in' and '404 – file not found' messages, use 1:1!

As with Rhizome's alternative interfaces (see pp. 52–53), the point is not so much to give easy access to discreet information as it is to find insightful ways of visualizing the coherence and connections between the assorted sites of information: a topography of the web's real estate. Such visualizations sharpen the mind when imagining a picture of the web as a whole, and Jevbratt's interfaces indicate visual approaches for charting and zooming in on such highly complex aggregations of information topoi as the World Wide Web.

55

2 . T y p o g r a p h y

2 . T y p o g r a p h y

2 . T y p o g r a p h y

2 . T y p o g r a p h y

2 . T y p o g r a p h y

2 . T y p o g r a p h y

2 . T y p o g r a p h y

2 . T y p o g r a p h y

2 . T y p o g r a p h y

Technology and the ways in which we are used to dealing with content are quite often at odds, not least because of the dismal typographic quality still prevalent on the web, which still channels vast amounts of pure reading material, texts. However, even in the field of on-screen typography serious improvements have been made.

58

1_Several systems have been developed for embedding specific fonts into web documents. Although these greatly extend the range of typographic possibilities for a designer, they are still considered as inherently vulnerable to copyright infringement. For an in-depth discussion about embedding and copyright issues, see Eric van Blokland, 'Font Embedding', www.typotheque.com/stuff/articles/embedding_longer.html or www.typeright.org

2_'It is ephemeral. The experience is fleeting. Nothing is left when it is over, except an impression.' J.Bellantoni, M.Woolman. *Moving Type* (Amsterdam, the Netherlands: RotoVision, 2000): 6.

New technology and greater bandwidth are making a significant difference when it comes to typography on the web. The coarse resolution of computer screens and the fact that material on the web can be easily copied have long put off typographers and font providers from taking much interest in the medium. New applications, however, make formatting text and using specific typefaces much easier and less risky for the fonts' copyright holders[1]. In many of these applications, letters literally have become images that can be manipulated and set into motion at will. To an extent, typography on the web has become motion typography: the inherent rhythm of words and sentences is acted out, and sound and motion become typographic.

Animating letters may at first seem rather odd in a craft that is based in the tradition of carved and printed words. However, as the legacy of cinematic titles by such designers as Saul Bass or Robert Brownjohn has shown, movement can be used effectively to accentuate the important words in a sentence (or those that the author or designer wants to draw to our attention), and to enhance the message's associative field. Brownjohn's famous opening titles for the 1963 James Bond movie *From Russia With Love* (Terence Young), for instance, set the tone for the erotic innuendo – the zip of 007's public appeal – by streaming type over the contours of a woman's body. Such use of kinetic typography may be 'ephemeral'[2] when applied as linear time-based sequences, but on the web it can become quite functional as an interactive device. Clicks or mouseovers change the size or accentuation of words; make words shift into other, related words; cause explanatory texts or further options to pop up; and set in motion small animations, which guide the visitor to the next level of a site. All these examples of animated typography take the notion of readability to the fourth dimension. Time-based typography, as we may now term it, is developing into a new brand of

Motion typography in the cinema is a prime source of inspiration and expertize for web design information design that uses type and motion (or action-dependent sequencing) to structure content in multilinear ways and to guide the reader through it.

Motion typography in the cinema is a prime source of inspiration and expertize for web design, especially when it comes to balancing and integrating text, image and sound. Web designers can learn much from the ways film directors like Jean-Luc Godard or Jacques Tati employed text and sound, not as a mere illustrative accessory to the image, but as a parallel level of communicating and emphasizing the contents of their films. Tati, for instance, frequently used sound to focus the viewer's attention on a specific spot in a visually dense scene, or to add his own ironic commentary to otherwise perfectly normal actions – the audio equivalents of such typographic accentuations as underlining or italicization[3].

Beyond the often misused employment of a background beat in a lot of cool websites, sound can be applied in typographic ways, becoming the audible equivalent of punctuation marks. Small sounds can confirm users' actions, alert them to options and alternatives, enhance hierarchies within the content (bold, regular or light sounds, to use the terminology of typographic styles), or add a spoken layer to the visual information. Converging media combined with interaction and feedback provoke new interpretations of moving type and new functions for animated typography and typographic sound on the web. The typography of interaction that is implied here is only in its infancy, but the fusion of type, image, sound and interface in a time-based environment opens exciting possibilities for designers and users.

Meanwhile, the advent of freely distributed fonts specifically designed for on-screen legibility, like Matthew Carter's seminal 1996 Verdana and Georgia, has greatly improved the readability of websites. With such fonts and with the

3_See also Michel Chion, *Le Son au cinéma* (Paris: Cahiers du Cinéma, 1985) and Michel Chion, *Audio Visions* (New York: Columbia University Press, 1999).

59

On the one hand, tried and tested typographic routines can be more easily applied to online media

4_Designers who want to be sure that their typography is both readable and reliable in HTML have a choice of four fonts they can trust as being among the defaults installed in any application on any platform: Verdana, Georgia, Courier and Arial. Times New Roman, the fifth universally installed font, is unfit for on-screen readability in small sizes.

5_Peter Bilak's wordplay on 'Flash movies', used here to imply 'fleshy', i.e. 'fat'. A pornographic association is made at the reader's own risk, but is in line with Bilak's pejorative intentions of using 'flesh' instead of 'Flash'.

technology to use and manipulate a limitless range of fonts in applications like Flash, typography has reasserted itself as a craft and as a means of structuring and enhancing the message. On the one hand, tried and tested typographic routines can be more easily applied to online media; with the Flash plug-in installed, for instance, any layout will be shown in its correct form on any browser – quite an improvement over standard HTML, which is contingent on the recipient's <u>installed defaults and fonts</u>[4]. On the other hand, developments in scripting for screen resolution and layout improve the placing, pacing and behaviour of type. Since the screen is not a fixed surface determined by the designer (as in print), designers are faced with the basic choice of either selecting a window size and risking that it will not fit the recipient's screen, or accepting they can specify a page's proportions but not its exact format and detailing. The web's technological and interactive characteristics incite designers to choose the latter: to control and detail the structure, proportion and behaviour of text in ways that are not fundamentally affected by the recipient's window size, resolution, installed fonts or colours.

More modern technologies aside, good old HTML still has much to offer when used properly. A number of young designers are beginning to feel slightly nauseated by bandwidth-devouring <u>'flesh movies'</u>[5] and are reverting to simple HTML in text-based interfaces, using the core means of type, colour and placement to compose the page. Here, typographic balance meets the demands of usability advocates, and formal rigidity is counterbalanced by an understanding of the aesthetic heart of the typographic trade. The essence of typography is balance, not form. To arrive at a pleasant read, spacing, kerning, leading and the definition of column width in relation to the page's proportion, font and type size are the

On the web, these have had to be adapted – remediated – to a fundamentally mutable display environment

traditional typographer's concerns. On the web, these have had to be adapted – remediated – to a fundamentally mutable display environment; the best web typographers, therefore, are those who combine knowledge of the old craft with a proficiency in scripting code for type behaviour in a volatile medium.

Robin Kinross is internationally recognized as a scholar and guardian of typographic taste and quality in printing

www.hyphenpress.co.uk

Hyphen Press

client_Hyphen Press, London, UK
design_Eric Kindel (concept and initial design, 1998), Jonathan Pagel (programming, 1998), Matt Patterson (programming and design, 2000)
on line_1998
relaunched_2000

Typographer, writer and publisher, Robin Kinross is internationally recognized as a scholar and guardian of typographic taste and quality in printing. Clearly, he cannot afford to have a sloppy website. In fact, the website of Hyphen Press, Kinross's publishing house, is exemplary in typographic clarity and legibility, and in the simple functionality of its interface – a few carefully prepared style sheets are all that are needed to make texts look good on screen. The light yellow-on-black type – with subtle colour accents for titles, running heads and links and enhanced by a few well-placed Java effects – produces a harmonic screen composition, which while testifying to its roots in print design performs well amidst the bustle on the web's screens.

Citrus Studio's design for a resource on the famous Russian typographic innovator El Lissitzky carefully follows a print aesthetic

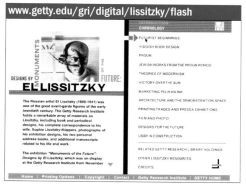

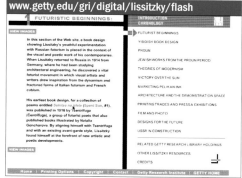

www.getty.edu/gri/digital/lissitzky/flash

El Lissitzky

client_The Getty Research Institute,
Los Angeles, CA, US
design_Citrus Studio, Los Angeles,
CA, US
on line_2000

Citrus Studio's design for a resource on the famous Russian typographic innovator El Lissitzky (1890–1941) carefully follows a print aesthetic that in almost any other context today would be considered anti-web. In this case, choosing an open-book metaphor makes sense, not only because of the subject but also because Citrus uses it in a subtle combination of stylistic quotations and screen functionality. Using red type and frames for links and red arrows for navigation connects seamlessly with 1920's avant-garde aesthetics, bridging the gap between that period and the modern day and establishing a continuity by finding a new function for the old typographer's tool box. The chronology is a case in point: on mouseover, dates light up and show the accompanying entry in the right column – an old typographic convention is used here in ways that are impossible on paper. Building the site completely in Flash has the advantage of controlling the typography, resulting in several uncommonly legible and harmonic pages on the web.

63

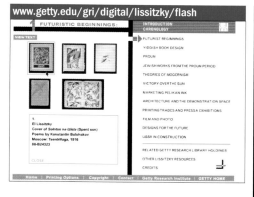

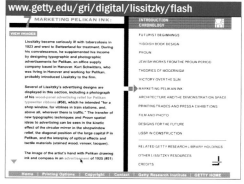

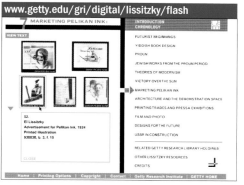

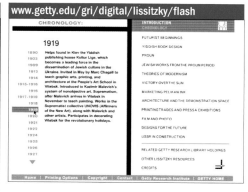

Peter Bilak is a typographer, graphic designer, performer and writer who favours clarity of form over visual exuberance

www.peterb.sk

Peter Bilak

content, design_Peter Bilak, Graphic &
Interactive Design, The Hague, NL
on line_1997

Peter Bilak is a typographer,
graphic designer, performer and
writer who favours clarity of form
over visual exuberance. Although
he can have fun with type too, any
hint of frivolity on his website is
relegated to the contents. The
interface and overall layout are
of a strict typographic austerity,
both in the choice of typeface
(Courier) and of coding (simple
HTML). Bilak has an outspoken
aversion against 'those annoying
flesh intros that you have to skip',
but manages nonetheless to use
his limited means to an end that
is visually quite appealing. The
hierarchical construction of his
screen layouts, the sparse but precise use of colour and underlining
and the transparent editorial structure make his site one of the few
that would please both usability
fetishists and design aficionados.

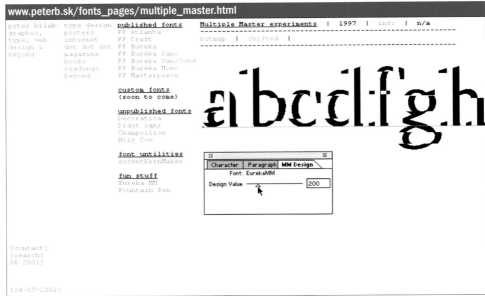

www.dot-dot-dot.org

dot-dot-dot

design_Peter Bilak, The Hague, NL
on line_2001

A similar lack of frills is evident in
the typographic style for the site
for *Dot Dot Dot*, a graphic-design
magazine produced by Bilak and
friends. In the merging boxes of
the menu, the defaults of plain
HTML quite coincidentally result in
an aesthetic of their own. The
magazine supports a no-nonsense
attitude toward graphic design and
typography that is reflected on
the webpages. However, visitors
might hope to see more attention
devoted to web-specific issues
that cannot be addressed in print.

Johanna Balusikova is Peter Bilak's partner and colleague in their fontshop, Typotheque

www.xs4all.nl/~johannab/homepage2.html

www.xs4all.nl/~johannab/homepage3.html

www.xs4all.nl/~johannab/homepage2.html

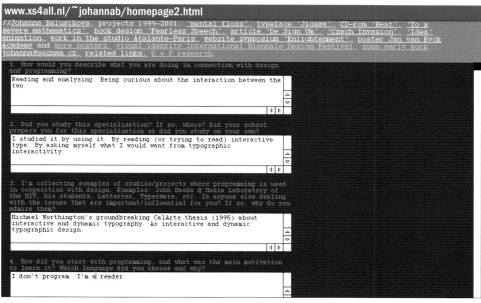

www.xs4all.nl/~johannab

Johanna Balusikova

content, design_Johanna Balusikova,
The Hague, NL
on line_2001

Johanna Balusikova is Peter Bilak's partner and colleague in their fontshop, Typotheque. Balusikova's own site is a good example of what could be described as the ASCII/HTML approach, which uses monospace lettering and the defaults of HTML as guiding principles for the site's structure, look and feel. Balusikova uses more imagery and interactivity than Bilak – a series of images that load behind a single page, short animated GIFs – but overall they share a taste for the medium's uncompromised essence, and the ensuing aesthetic.

www.typotheque.com

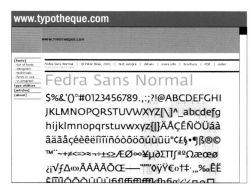

www.typotheque.com

www.typotheque.com

Typotheque

client, design_Peter Bilak, The Hague, NL
content_Digital Type Foundry
on line_2001

The 'Typotheque' site looks less austere than Bilak's and Balusikova's individual sites, but is basically composed in the same way. Bold lines structure the content on the screen in an almost nostalgic modernist style that works quite well for the matter-of-fact resource the site is obviously intended to be. These websites show that, if used well and with a feeling for typographic balance, plain HTML can be quite effective and look good.

The most uncomplicated use of the medium can be rewarding both in communicative and aesthetic ways

www.customr.nl

Customr

design_Customr, Feels Like Friday,
Amsterdam, NL

on line_2002

A further example of how the most uncomplicated use of the medium can be rewarding, both in communicative and aesthetic ways, is the small product site for Dutch design group Customr and its 'Greenlight' line – just pictures and words in the right balance. Once you have the photography and general idea for a site such as this, its actual creation can be carried out in an hour and a half. In this case, the end result is a few screens that, with an utter economy of means, tell visitors everything they need to know about the products (except the prices). A series of clickable images offers a view of each lamp's general form, construction and suggested usage, while a single information page notes the product details. Designers Willem van der Sluis and Hugo Timmermans fuse their product-design approach of a culturally intelligent visual irony and straightforward formal translation with their web design: simplicity of interaction (no interface needed!), combined with seemingly nonchalant photography and highly sophisticated computer graphics.

www.customr.nl

biodomestic lily-eau airco flat   contact   info

www.customr.nl/greenlight/flat2.html

www.customr.nl/greenlight/biodomestic2.html

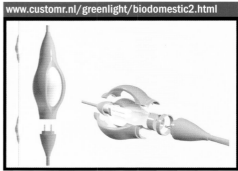

www.customr.nl/greenlight/flat3.html

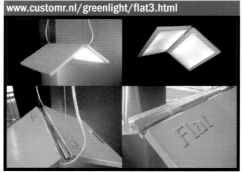

www.customr.nl/greenlight/productinfo.html

'The words of the future dance to the rhythm of a thousand heart beats'

www.zuper.com/portfolio/zx5/shockwave/...

The music of the future is visual,

Computers are not books. Computers are not televisions. A clickable book is a book without suspense.A clickable film is a boring film. There is no point in translating. Hypertext is dead. Hypertext, a poor excuse for mistaken nostalgia or just a toy for nerds. Who reads on a computer screen? If one fights excess with soberness, every simple act seems improbably grotesque. We need to re-invent

www.zuper.com/portfolio/zx5/shockwave/...

He or she will not be satisfied with mere information.

Computers are not books. Computers are not televisions. A clickable book is a book without suspense.A clickable film is a boring film. There is no point in translating. Hypertext is dead. Hypertext, a poor excuse for mistaken nostalgia or just a toy for nerds. Who reads on a computer screen? If one fights excess with soberness, every simple act seems improbably grotesque. We need to re-invent everything over and over again. No one will know us. There is no defence against the baroque. The

www.zuper.com/portfolio/zx5/shockwave/...

Information wants to be forgotten.

Computers are not books. Computers are not televisions. A clickable book is a book without suspense.A clickable film is a boring film. There is no point in translating. Hypertext is dead. Hypertext, a poor excuse for mistaken nostalgia or just a toy for nerds. Who reads on a computer screen? If one fights excess with soberness, every simple act seems improbably grotesque. We need to re-invent everything over and over again. No one will know us. There is no defence against the baroque. The human of the future is a playing one. He or she will not be satisfied with bad toys. He or she will not be satisfied with mere information. Information is not a goal, it is a means. Information overload is not a

www.zuper.com/portfolio/zx5/shockwave/...

(Life's so short. Don't bore us to death.)

Computers are not books. Computers are not televisions. A clickable book is a book without suspense.A clickable film is a boring film. There is no point in translating. Hypertext is dead. Hypertext, a poor excuse for mistaken nostalgia or just a toy for nerds. Who reads on a computer screen? If one fights excess with soberness, every simple act seems improbably grotesque. We need to re-invent everything over and over again. No one will know us. There is no defence against the baroque. The human of the future is a playing one. He or she will not be satisfied with bad toys. He or she will not be satisfied with mere information. Information is not a goal, it is a means. Information overload is not a problem, it is a consequence. Information does not want to be free. Information wants to be forgotten. The human of the future wants to be entertained. (Life's so short. Don't bore us to death.) Navigation through hyperspace should be as natural as navigation through real space. Only better. Faster. Our senses bloom in hyperspace. Not to exist. Not to exist. The human of the future will travel through data. The faster you travel the more you see. The faster you see the more you travel. The individual is dead. Reality is fiction. Simulation is real. The vehicle of the future is the networked computer. Not

www.zuper.com/portfolio/zx5/shockwave/...

If one fights excess with soberness, every simple act seems improbably grotesque.

Computers are not books. Computers are not televisions. A clickable book is a book without suspense.A clickable film is a boring film. There is no point in translating. Hypertext is dead. Hypertext, a poor excuse for mistaken nostalgia or just a toy for nerds. Who reads on a computer screen? If one fights excess with soberness, every simple act seems improbably grotesque. We need to re-invent everything over and over again. No one will know us. There is no defence against the baroque. The human of the future is a playing one. He or she will not be satisfied with bad toys. He or she will not be satisfied with mere information. Information is not a goal, it is a means. Information overload is not a problem, it is a consequence. Information does not want to be free. Information wants to be forgotten. The human of the future wants to be entertained. (Life's so short. Don't bore us to death.) Navigation through hyperspace should be as natural as navigation through real space. Only better. Faster. Our senses bloom in hyperspace. Not to exist. Not to exist. The human of the future will travel through data. Reality is fiction. Simulation is real. The vehicle of the future is the networked computer. Not hypertext but hyperspace. The metaphor wants to be free. Information will not be read or seen but experienced in simulated environments. The book is not dead. The book just is not a computer. The past is not dead. It is doubled, and doubled again. There are no doors. (Only windows.) The body is a container. The individual is a network. Space is in the mind. A heart breaks and turns into a thousand hearts. Seperation. Classification. Fragmentation. Fluidity. There is no universal center. The music of the future is visual, the pictures of the future tangible. The words of the future dance to the rhythm of

www.zuper.com/portfolio/zx5/shockwave/...

Computers are not books. Computers are not televisions. A clickable book is a book without suspense.A clickable film is a boring film. There is no point in translating. Hypertext is dead. Hypertext, a poor excuse for mistaken nostalgia or just a toy for nerds. Who reads on a computer screen? If one fights excess with soberness, every simple act seems improbably grotesque. We need to re-invent everything over and over again. No one will know us. There is no defence against the baroque. The human of the future is a playing one. He or she will not be satisfied with bad toys. He or she will not be satisfied with mere information. Information is not a goal, it is a means. Information overload is not a problem, it is a consequence. Information wants to be forgotten. The human of the future wants to be entertained. (Life's so short. Don't bore us to death.) Navigation through hyperspace should be as natural as navigation through real space. Only better. Faster. Our senses bloom in hyperspace. Not to exist. Not to exist. The human of the future will travel through data. The faster you travel the more you see. The faster you see the more you travel. The individual is dead. Reality is fiction. Simulation is real. The vehicle of the future is the networked computer. Not hypertext but hyperspace. The metaphor wants to be free. Information will not be read or seen but experienced in simulated environments. The book is not dead. The book just is not a computer. The past is not dead. It is doubled, and doubled again. There are no doors. (Only windows.) The body is a container. The individual is a network. Space is in the mind. A heart breaks and turns into a thousand hearts. Seperation. Classification. Fragmentation. Fluidity. There is no universal center. The music of the future is visual, the pictures of the future tangible. The words of the future dance to the rhythm of a thousand heart beats.

www.zuper.com/portfolio/zx5/shockwave/future_movie.html

Words of the Future
client_'Object versus Pixels' congress, Amsterdam, NL
design_Michael Samyn/Zuper!, Antwerp, BE
on line_1996

'The words of the future dance to the rhythm of a thousand heart beats.' Thus ends the text that has slowly scrolled up the screen until it has filled it, while in big bright-red type quotes from the same text are snapped on and off like slogans, faster and faster. In the background, a male and a female voice recite the text over a hard-hitting music sample. An image of the writer and maker of the page, artist and web designer Michael Samyn, appears for a split second with his eyes closed, as if murmuring, 'you better believe, brother!'. The animated text was made for the 1996 congress in Amsterdam on art and new media, 'Object versus Pixels', and contrasts this new medium with the older ones of radio, film, books, or should I say, after Friedrich Kittler, 'gramophone, film, typewriter' (see p. 185)? The text and its presentation conjure up a vision of totally converged media in which 'music of the future is visual' and 'pictures are tangible', and everything hovers in a networked space in which 'our senses bloom'. Legibility is not a prime concern here, but the combination of type, animation and sound is used effectively for remediating the content into the experience of it.

67

Artistic, critical, intelligent and fun, Young-hae Chang's site is also basic, consisting of just type, movement and music

www.yhchang.com

Young-hae Chang Heavy Industries

client_Young-hae Chang Heavy Industries, Seoul, KR

design_Young-hae Chang

on line_1999

Artistic, critical, intelligent and fun, Young-hae Chang's site is also basic, consisting of just type, movement and music – elementary Flash. Although Chang, an artist and translator living in Seoul, is as she fears the only web artist in South Korea, she received the prestigious Webby Award in the art category in 2001. Her site is a collection of web-based text pieces, little stories that are raunchy, ironic and absurdly sexy. Dancing, it seems, on the steaming rhythm of 1950's jazz licks, words and sentences hit the screen, black on white, and carry you along relentlessly in a stream of thoughts that heats up with the music. The quality lies not as so often in virtuoso software manipulation (although the pacing is pretty stunning) or in visual exuberance (quite the contrary), but in a rather old-fashioned category: literature, and quite witty as well! At the same time, it is the kind of writing that uses every aspect of the medium in which it is published to its best advantage. It has been a while since I have seen a combination of text, typography, movement and music that is so well balanced in terms of content and form. However, that does make the stories very hard to reproduce in any other medium – you will have to experience them on line.

68

www.yhchang.com

```
YOUNG-HAE CHANG HEAVY INDUSTRIES PRESENTS

DAKOTA
SAUL
RAIN ON THE SEA

RAIN ON THE SEA (KOREAN VERSION)
LOTUS BLOSSOM
HALF BREED APACHE
THE STRUGGLE CONTINUES MAC PC
THE STRUGGLE CONTINUES (KOREAN VERSION)
LA LUTTE CONTINUE MAC PC
ARTIST'S STATEMENT NO. 45,730,944: THE PERFECT ARTISTIC WEB SITE
ARTIST'S STATEMENT NO. 45,730,944: THE PERFECT ARTISTIC WEB SITE (KOREAN VERSION) MAC PC
DECLARATION D'ARTISTE NUMÉRO 45.730.944: LE PARFAIT WEB SITE ARTISTIQUE
BUST DOWN THE DOORS!
TRETE DIE TUR EIN!
THE END
THE END (KOREAN VERSION)
THE SAMSUNG PROJECT:
SAMSUNG
SAMSUNG (KOREAN VERSION)
SAMSUNG (VERSION FRANCAISE)
SAMSUNG MEANS TO COME
SAMSUNG VEUT DIRE JOUIR
SAMSUNG MEANS TO COME (KOREAN VERSION)

CREDITS
FLASH PLUG-IN DOWNLOAD
E-MAIL
```

www.yhchang.com/NEW_CREDITS.html

www.yhchang.com/LOTUS_BLOSSOM_KO.html

www.yhchang.com/LOTUS_BLOSSOM_KO.html

www.yhchang.com/LOTUS_BLOSSOM.html

www.yhchang.com/ORIENT_JAPANESE.html

www.yhchang.com/DAKOTA.html

www.yhchang.com/THE_INLAND_SEA.html

SØN ØF
A BITCH

www.yhchang.com/DAKOTA_ESPANOL.html

VAMØS

www.yhchang.com/DAKOTA.html

PUT BEER
CASES IN
HER TRUNK,

www.yhchang.com/DAKOTA.html

_ _ _ _ _

www.yhchang.com/LOTUS_BLOSSOM.html

RHYTHM!

www.yhchang.com/LOTUS_BLOSSOM.html

ISN'T
THAT
DELEUZES?"

WELCØME
TØ
SEØUL
LAND!

www.yhchang.com/DAKOTA.html

www.yhchang.com/DAKOTA.html

JØB

www.yhchang.com/DAKOTA.html

GASSY

www.yhchang.com/DAKOTA.html

?"
?

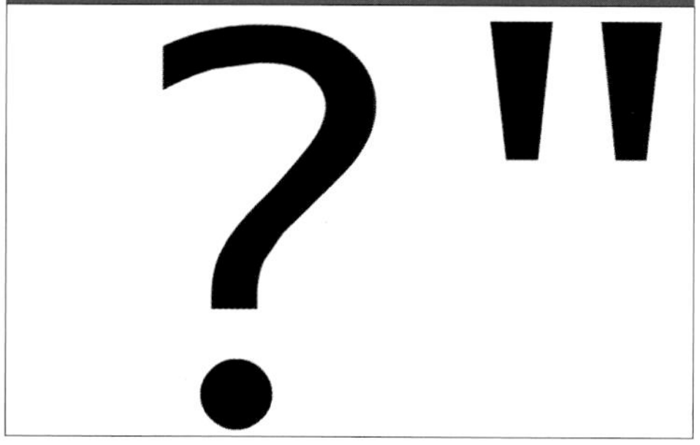

Since 1997, *Born Magazine* has fostered experimentation and collaboration between writers, artists and designers on the web

www.bornmagazine.org

Born Magazine
on line_1997

www.bornmagazine.org/projects/
storyproblem/sproblem.html

Story Problem
design_Erik Loyer, US
on line_2002

www.bornmagazine.org/projects/
blue_madonna

Blue Madonna
design_Molly Sokolow, US
on line_2001

www.bornmagazine.org/projects/walking

**Walking Together What
Remains**
design_Erik Natzke, New York, US
on line_2001

Since 1997, *Born Magazine* has fostered experimentation and collaboration between writers, artists and designers on the web by 'marrying literary arts and inter- active media'. Founded by Gabe Kean, art director of Second Story Interactive Studios, Portland, US, the site has grown into a source- book of interactive storytelling and dynamic poetry. Erik Natzke (see p. 28), for instance, collaborated with writer Chris Green to create a piece called 'Walking Together What Remains', which is composed of the images and words on dis- carded food wrappings and packag- ing picked up during a short walk. It is a nice annotated storybook that could also have been rendered in print were it not for the dynamic transitions between the 'pages'.

  Making more use of the web's resources (Flash 5 in this case), though not interactive, is Molly Sokolow's version of 'Blue Madonna', a poem written by Vandana Khanna. Juxtaposing religious concepts of holy women from her native India (young wid- ows, throwing themselves on their husbands' funeral pyres) with the christian Madonna, she revisits the

www.bornmagazine.org/mother.html

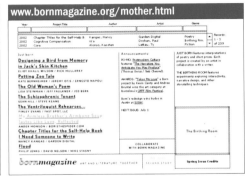

www.bornmagazine.org/mother.html

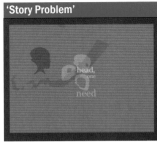

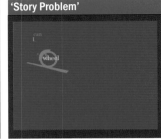

70

The piece starts in black and white with sentences erased by white lines as the text progresses down and then up the screen

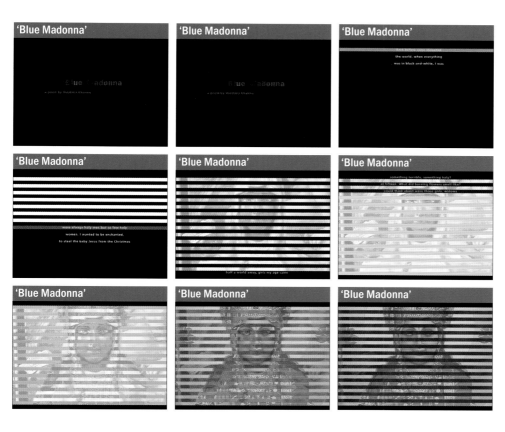

bewilderment of a child torn between two cultures. The piece starts in black and white – a child's perspective on the world – with sentences erased by white lines as the text progresses down and then up the screen. These lines then change into coloured lines over a picture of the famous Black Madonna, and, at the end of the poem, the image slowly merges with the lines to form a picture of the Indian goddess Lakshmi, who like Mary symbolizes virtue, compassion and prosperity. The dynamics of typography and image effectively communicate the confusion at the heart of the poem.

For the makers of *Born*, 'The lines between reader and artist, sound and word, motion and image are ours to play with.' Luckily, they are generous enough to allow the reader to play along, sometimes in the essential role of the 'text performer'. Such is the case in a delightfully interactive adaptation of a poem by Terri Ford, 'Story Problem', interpreted or, should I say, directed by digital media artist Erik Loyer. The poem unfolds over a three-note left-hand piano chord, freely modulating from scale to scale. Moving the mouse over the small Shockwave window draws out the words and also governs the right-hand movement on the piano. The mouse's speed, direction and location controls elements of rhythm, volume, colour, size and motion. Gradually, users begin to 'feel' the interactive possibilities, which raise such questions of performance as 'shall I play this line as a fast, mellow riff, or would it be more appropriate to interpret it as a line of staccato syllables?' It is possible to do both, save the 'results' and play them back to see and hear which one you prefer. A superb example of engaging the reader or player with the making and performance of the artwork!

71

www.3st.com

Thirst

client, design_Thirst, Barrington, IL, US
on line_1999, redesign: 2001

Thirst have developed a new look now, but their website still offers the option to enter the old site, testifying to the designers' respect for history. It is a rare sign of confidence for a design firm at the forefront of innovation not to erase their footsteps within weeks. The old site is as explorative as Thirst's current investigations into typography and (typographic) design. The main, and best, part of the content is text: musings on such grand topics as beauty or handwriting, anecdotes from the work floor, snippets of conversation between founder Rick Valicenti and his colleagues and friends. In line with the congenial tone of the site's content, its look and feel is both informal and smart in an unobtrusive way. Such details as using the standard form for writing HTML tags (as in '<recategorize> love letters </recategorize>' for 'in other words'), the use of the Courier typeface throughout, the modelling of lines or paragraphs of text in boldly coloured boxes all point to a keen and mildly ironic awareness of the web's history and core characteristics. Thirst uses the medium to its best advantage aesthetically and functionally; for instance, in their nifty 'Thirstyper' application visitors can try out a font's behaviour on line.

72

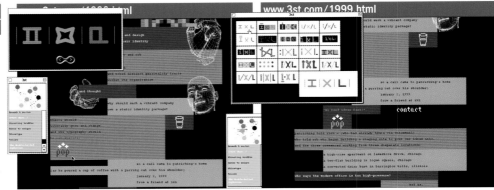

www.3st.com/1999.html

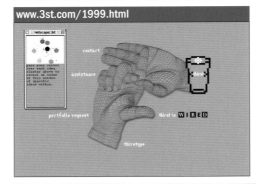

www.3st.com/1999.html

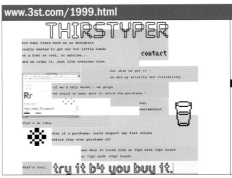

www.3st.com/1999.html

The studio's new site is equally as confident, but sports a more contemporary look and added functionality

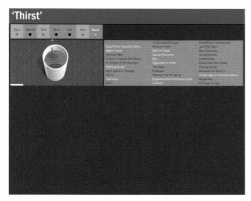

'Thirst'

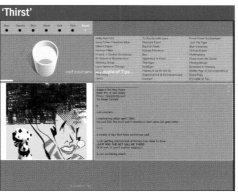

'Thirst'

The studio's new site is equally as confident, but sports a more contemporary look (in Flash) and added functionality (although I pray that one day they will incorporate a button to switch off the horrid sound loop). The new site is more businesslike, which may be an indication of the group's success, and less basic – the hands-on play with HTML has given way to a smoother interface, which, for instance, loads samples from the portfolio in grey boxes that emerge like liquid metal onto the screen. Pointless, maybe, but it looks cool and hurts no-one. One playful element allows visitors to mix the ingredients of the firm (the people) by dropping their names into a cup, at which point the things they created together are highlighted in the right-hand portfolio overview. An interesting experiment in making a human alphabet – a typographer's fascination ever since the invention of print – is Rick Valicenti's font, 'performed' by an Ukrainian webcam girl. Following a tradition of the combination of eroticism and typography that began in sixteenth-century engraving and peaked with Anthon Beeke's 1970 photographic female alphabet, Valicenti has introduced a new medium and a new form of interaction. 'Enticement, illusion – graphic design, the oldest profession.'[1]

www.thirstype.com/font_punch.html

'Thirst'

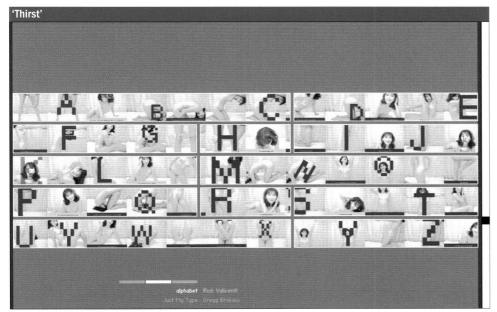

'Thirst'

73

www.thirstype.com/bydesigner.html

www.thirstype.com/playground_uic1.html

1_See also, Max Bruinsma, 'The Erotics of Type', Steve Heller, ed. *Sex Appeal* (New York, NY Allworth Press, 2000) www.xs4all.nl/~maxb/erotype.html

The online portfolio of New York studio 2x4 opens with a screen of white text on an orange background

www.twoxfour.net

2x4

design_2x4, New York, US
on line_2000

The online portfolio of New York studio 2x4, founded by Michael Rock and Susan Sellers, opens with a screen of white text on an orange background. One of the most pleasant examples of a pure-ly text-based interface I have seen, it shows that careful copywriting and hypertext are sometimes all that are needed to make a website perfectly navigable. Each link in the introduction opens a small new window with more options to look at 2x4's work. Generally, it is not always wise to do this as the screen can become a deluge of open and half-forgotten windows, but on this site it is done thought-fully and with the knowledge that the site is not so deep as to risk loosing your way among the frames. Moreover, windows that are forced to the background auto-matically close when a new link is followed from the main interface. Despite having around five-hundred lines of Javascript on the main page, the site would benefit from more sophistication in scripting type and window size for different browsers and platforms, which is, admittedly, an art in itself. Still, 2x4's site is a good example of how text can be used effectively both as an interface and as a dis-tinguishing formal element in screen design. Furthermore, in their typography for the site of New York's 2econd Stage Theatre, the designers refer back to a forerun-ner of this kind of lettering on the web: the billboard.

www.twoxfour.net

This is the 2x4 web site in which you will find an introduction to the personnel; samples of our projects (including branding and identity systems, advertising and web sites, posters, collateral materials, books, brochures and catalogues, magazines, film and video, environmental graphics and exhibition graphics); a list of the artists, musicians, galleries, museums, architects, and all-around smart people who are our clients and collaborators; various essays and articles; information about the Museum of the Ordinary; an empathy exam; a curious collection of evidentiary material of questionable origins; a messy area dedicated to work in progress, unfinished projects, rejected ideas, unresolved concepts and other things that don't quite seem to fit anywhere else; links to other people we like; pictures of our studio; and some basic information on how to find us, how to see more work, how to hire us, and what to do if you are looking for a job.

www.twoxfour.net

This is the 2x4 web site in which you will find an introduction to the personnel; samples of our projects (including branding and identity systems, advertising and web sites, posters, collateral materials, books, brochures and catalogues, magazines, film and video, environmental graphics and exhibition graphics); a list of the artists, musicians, galleries...

www.twoxfour.net

This is the 2x4 web site in which you will find an introduction to the personnel; samples of our projects (including branding and identity systems, advertising and web sites, posters, collateral materials, books, brochures and catalogues, magazines, film and video, environmental g...

web sites: (1) Princeton School of Architecture; (2) Wolf-Gordon; (3) Canadian Center for Architecture; (4) Yale University; (5) Linework by Laurinda Spear for Wolf Gordon; (6) National Design Awards; (7) Second Stage Theatre; and (8) Avi Adler.

www.twoxfour.net

This is the 2x4 web site in which you will find an introduction to the personnel; samples of our projects (including branding and identity systems, advertising and web sites, posters, collateral materials, books, br...

www.twoxfour.net

This is the 2x4 web site in which you will find an introduction to the personnel; samples of our projects (including branding and identity systems, advertising and web sites, posters, collateral materials, books, broch...

www.twoxfour.net

Graphic Authorship

By Michael Rock

www.secondstagetheatre.com

WHAT'S PLAYING?
I NEED TICKETS!
I'M A SUBSCRIBER.
WHAT'S 2ST?
I WANT TO HELP.
MORE INFO PLEASE.

www.secondstagetheatre.com

METAMORPHOSES
WRITTEN AND DIRECTED BY MARY ZIMMERMAN
Based on the Myths of Ovid

SORROWS AND REJOICINGS

RICKY JAY — ON THE STEM

MARIE AND BRUCE

www.secondstagetheatre.com

METAMORPHOSES
WRITTEN AND DIRECTED BY MARY ZIMMERMAN
Based on the Myths of Ovid

Dutch graphic-design firm Thonik derives its name from the two principals, Thomas Widdershoven and Nikki Gonnissen

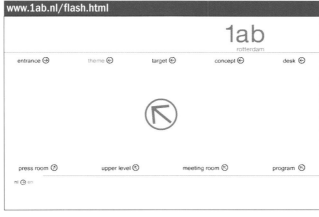

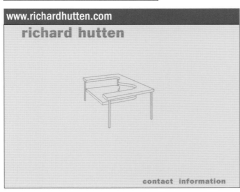

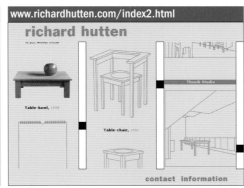

www.thonik.nl

Thonik
design_Thonik and Tijs Bonekamp,
Amsterdam, NL
on line_2001

Dutch graphic-design firm Thonik derives its name from the two principals, Thomas Widdershoven and Nikki Gonnissen, who judged their last names not very communicable outside the Netherlands. A similarly practical approach characterizes their work and their website. Known for their sometimes irreverent play with and obstruction of visual languages, they nonetheless never seem pretentious. Thonik's attitude is akin to that of the famed Dutch product-design brand Droog Design, for whom Thonik have made a catalogue.

For another client, Thonik made fifty books because they could not fit the client's multifarious output into one volume; on the webpage devoted to this project fifty covers race past the viewer. A site created for an exhibition on mobility in architecture combines timeless railway-station typography in Helvetica with an arrow that points to the position of the mouse point on the screen. Such little jokes and a more functional feature that scales the site's content seamlessly to the size of the visitor's browser window, are proof of the designers' ironic but functional regard for the web. Scaling type relative to the user's screen resolution is a very friendly gesture to on-screen readers and one that should be made more often.

75

A small portfolio site on first impression, but on closer inspection one that incorporates an aesthetic refinement, which is rare

www.quiresiste.com

Qui? Résiste

design_Pierre di Sciullo, Paris, FR
on line_2000

A small portfolio site on first impression, but on closer inspection one that incorporates an aesthetic refinement, which is rare on the web. Pierre di Sciullo, a distinguished French experimental typographer, presents his typefaces and 'occasional publication' 'Qui? Résiste' in a layout that is clearly grounded in book design yet perfectly adjusted to the screen. The main interface shows the portfolio and information sections and how they are linked. On mouseover captions pop up, and on clicking the colour of the sections change and their structure is revealed. Different sections open in separate windows – the designer controls the format. Although all levels are created on the same well-balanced grid, there is a lot of variety on the screen; Di Sciullo modulates his layouts according to the content at hand. The combination of persuasive typographic balance and a highly developed sense of colour – so important in this medium – makes visitors almost forget that Di Sciullo rarely uses the web's capacity for motion and change. Only in 'Experimental Family' in the typographic section does he use QuickTime movies to show 'Karaoké', a video experiment in which people read out loud texts in Di Sciullo's experimental typefaces. Since the majority of Di Sciullo's letters come in different variants (not just different weights), I would have liked to see more dynamics on the site. As it is, Di Sciullo's site is an important example of typographic competence and *esprit* on the web.

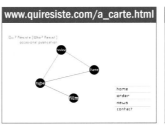

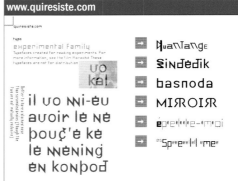

'Karaoké'

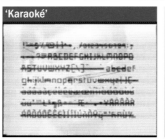

'Karaoké'

'Karaoké'

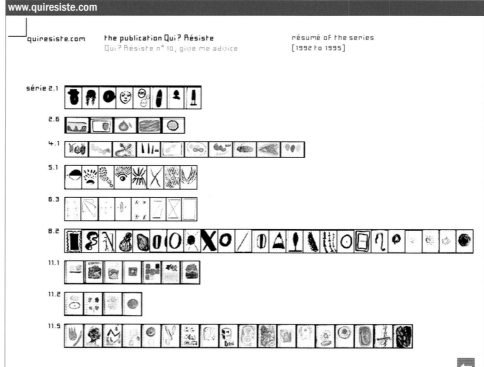

Made for a cultural festival in French Quebec, Di Sciullo's site for the Ministries of Culture and Foreign Affairs is also interesting

www.afaa.asso.fr/_externes/monbeaupays/...

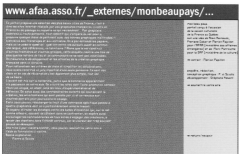

www.afaa.asso.fr/_externes/monbeaupays/...

www.afaa.asso.fr/_externes/monbeaupays/porte.html

www.afaa.asso.fr/_externes/monbeaupays/porte.html

www.afaa.asso.fr/_externes/
monbeaupays/

Mon Beau Pays
client_Ministries of Cultural and Foreign
Affairs, FR
design_Pierre di Sciullo, Paris, FR
on line_2001

Made for a cultural festival in
French Quebec, Di Sciullo's site for
the Ministries of Culture and
Foreign Affairs is also interesting.
It is intended as a portal to 'les
plus beaux sites de France' and
has links to a wealth of websites
'made by French designers, or
designers staying in France, or
passing, or departed, or coming
back'. The site is a gem of subtle
simplicity that gives access to
roughly one-hundred sites on a
single screen in Flash with a para-
graph of information on each of
them. A second page that lists the
same information in text only is
actually redundant. Grouping the
sites by genre or alphabetically in
a pop-up menu, this page proves
that a single well-organized and
well-designed window can show the
contents of a twenty-page brochure
(which is what the information in
the window would amount to on
paper), with the additional benefit
of direct access. And, laid out in Di
Sciullo's own typography, it looks
very handsome, too.

77

A group of typographers, designers and interactive artists from the northwest of England, Beaufonts provides more than letters

www.beaufonts.com

Beaufonts

design_Beaufonts, UK
on line_2000

A group of typographers, designers and interactive artists from the northwest of England, Beaufonts provides more than letters. The site shows a series of experiments and exercises that could be regarded as formal and algorithmic research for their brand of typefaces. Rectangular and chunky or smooth and rounded, the fonts betray their origin in the play between controlled procedures and random outcome that characterizes such features as 'Untiled 1' or 'Shorthand Lite'. The first is 'an exploration of graphic randomness', an engine that produces random forms within a five-by-five pixel grid; the second, a nifty Shockwave machine that lists the complete alphabet plus numerals in a thirteen-point star-shaped grid within which it 'makes symbols out of words and words out of symbols'.

'Binary Interface Structure' is an exercise in structuring a graphic interface to sixty-four units 'by binary decision-making': each click on a rectangle in the six-layer block divides it in two. Such explorations into the world of computation, 'if-then' procedures and modular construction culminate in Beaufonts's 'Chinese Whispers' project, which offers sets of modular shapes for the user to assemble into a sample letterform – a lowercase 'a' – on a ten-by-twelve grid. The resultant form is then computed to make a full alphabet and eventually a new font set. Contributions have been made by, among others, Erik van Blokland (see p. 83). Beaufonts shares its research into type, code and interactivity in the medium that is made for just such things.

www.beaufonts.com/beaufonts.html#

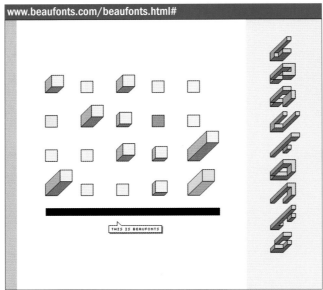

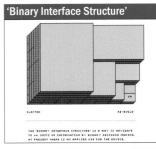

'Binary Interface Structure'

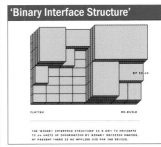

'Binary Interface Structure'

'Letterformer: Original Shapes'

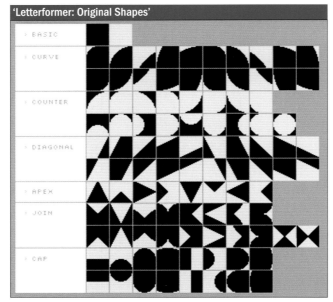

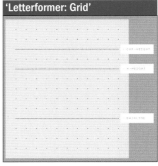

'Letterformer: Grid'

'Chinese Whispers'

'Shorthand Lite'

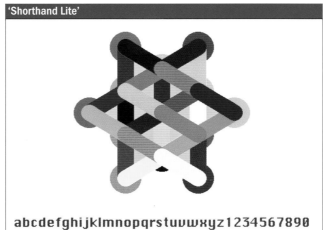

'Shorthand Lite'

'Shorthand Lite'

London-based design consultancy Fibre made this almost purely type-based site for The Fish Can Sing

The Fish Can Sing

client_The Fish Can Sing International, Amsterdam, NL and London, UK
design_Fibre, London, UK
on line_2002

London-based design consultancy Fibre (see pp. 117–19) made this almost purely type-based site for The Fish Can Sing, a 'Creative PR and Guerrilla Marketing' bureau in Amsterdam. Text only (apart from a few images deep in the portfolio section), the whole site focuses on the conceptual approach of The Fish Can Sing. One solid block of letters lists information about the company's mission, services, philosophy, clients, press and contacts. Within this block, words are highlighted on mouseover, thereby becoming the interface to the site. Strengthening the idea that every aspect of the site's content is closely connected, the screen seems to scroll back through all the pages when users click back to the index from a page deep in the site. The entire site gives the impression of being one long horizontal scroll, which technically it is not. The Javascript performing this apparently simple effect amounts to about the same number of words as those in the site's readable content; one text directs the other.

79

For a number of years now, Jonathan Barnbrook has been regarded as the angry young man of British typography

www.virusfonts.com

Virus Fonts

design_Jonathan Barnbrook, London, UK
on line_1998
redesign_2002

For a number of years now, Jonathan Barnbrook has been regarded as the angry young man of British typography. Considering Barnbrook has a deep knowledge of the history and methods of typographic and type design and a highly critical outlook on life in general and globalized Western culture in particular, you might expect a disconsolate character and ditto work. *Quod non*. What saves Barnbrook from becoming gloomy is his wit and acute sense of humour. His typefaces are visual essays in cultural awareness and, for those who might not realize it, the message is driven home in exquisitely malicious – and funny – presentation sheets. Barnbrook's most recent site presents an environment that verbally mocks the web's use as a platform for wannabe prophets and peddlers of riches and redemption. Posing as one of them, Barnbrook lures visitors into viewing his fonts, buying them, donating money, offering prayers and generally believing in him. Clearly, Barnbrook himself is a non-believer as is amply demonstrated in his juxtaposition of images from the promised land (the environment, nature, people of good will) with signs of destruction and selfish consumerism (capitalism, greed, the bomb) that appear on mouseover.

80

www.virusfonts.com

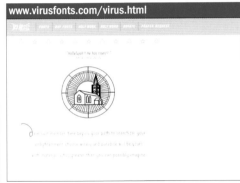

www.virusfonts.com/virus.html

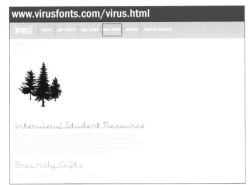

www.virusfonts.com/virus.html

www.virusfonts.com/virus.html

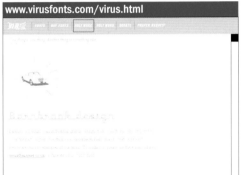

www.virusfonts.com/virus.html

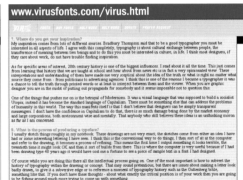

www.virusfonts.com/virus.html

www.virusfonts.com/virus.html

www.virusfonts.com/virus.html

From Drone to Melancholia, Barnbrook's fonts suggest a cultured craftsman of type

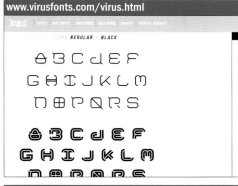

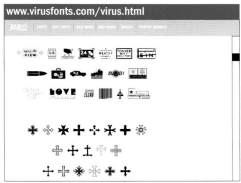

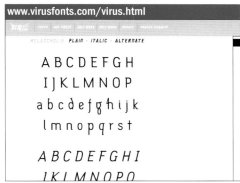

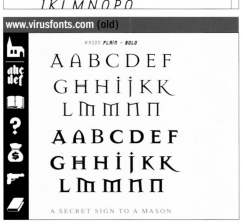

From Drone ('text without content') to Melancholia ('show how sensitive you are'), Barnbrook's fonts suggest a cultured craftsman of type who finds obvious pleasure in combining intellectual sharpness with typographic and calligraphic sophistication. Such talents and wit are also evident in his typographic designs for Adbusters, Rick Poynor's books on typography and in the book *I want to spend the rest of my life everywhere, with everyone, one to one, always, forever, now* (London: Booth-Clibborn Editions, 1997) that Barnbrook coauthored with Damien Hirst. In addition, Barnbrook has made quite a few clips with moving type, for example, for Radio Scotland, but too few of these can be seen on his website. On a few pages, Barnbrook uses movement to switch between different versions of typefaces, but it could have been used more and in more content-directed ways.

It is interesting to compare and contrast Barnbrook's old and new site; although the content has not changed greatly, the overall look and feel is quite different. The older site shares the heavy aesthetics popular in the late 1990s with bold image buttons and strong contrasts; while the newer one caters to the current taste for simple line-based imagery, lots of white space and sparse typography in a text-based interface. One of the most influential type designers around, Barnbrook is a man of his time.

81

Apart from finding some samples, visitors look in vain for content from the rich database of *Emigre* magazine on this website

www.emigre.com

Emigre

design_Emigre Inc, Sacramento, CA, US
on line_1995

Apart from finding some samples, visitors look in vain for content from the rich database of *Emigre* magazine on this website. The site is not an archive for the magazine, but a sales tool: 'This electronic version of the Emigre product catalog includes full-color images of all *Emigre* magazine back issues and posters, as well as specimens of all Emigre Fonts.' That, considering the foundry's stock list, is a lot. The main design problem, as Emigre's Rudy VanderLans once explained, is not how it looks but how it works. Bearing in mind that there are over a hundred links on the index page alone, the site looks remarkably calm. It also works effortlessly: there must be a dozen ways to arrive at the font or designer of your choice. This is a tool for people who have a reason to visit the site, which does all that it can to anticipate their queries. Of course, the typographic visual presentation is fitting for a type foundry, but it is remarkable that Emigre does not promote its own typefaces – apart from the logo, the site loads in the visitor's defaults. The most notable default Emigre has changed is the colour of the links: red instead of the ubiquitous blue, which on their site is reserved for followed links. Fonts come into view when users look up a specific designer, font, family or package. And then there is 'Typetease', an applet that allows a preview of a chosen font shown against a finely gridded yellow background – Emigre is not giving fonts away, mind you.

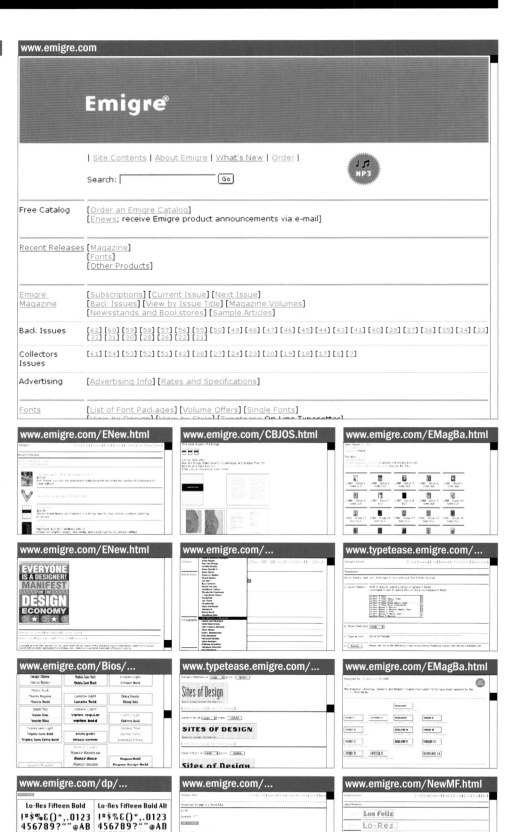

What is the language of digital media?

LettError

design_LettError (Just van Rossum and Erik van Blokland), The Hague, NL

on line_1995

What is the language of digital media? 'It's scripted!' would be LettError's answer because any pixel on the screen can be told to follow directions. This insight into the nature of computer-based media is at the root of LettError's experimental type designs. The studio has invented fonts not just with character but with attitude and behaviour, from fonts that randomly change between three different versions for each letter to engines that design myriad variations of a font on the fly. Playful, irreverent *and* steeped in the distinguished tradition of Dutch typographic design, LettError focuses on the rules of the game: the code and scripts that determine how letterforms will behave on the screen. The website is replete with substantiations of the designers' beliefs – knowledgeable texts, pranks on standard practice, self-developed code and applications, and of course their fonts. Every font has its own presentation style and in-depth explanation of its special characteristics and cultural provenance. LettError's site may not be the most sophisticated in terms of interactivity or interface design – I would love to see their dynamic letters applied more extensively on line – but it does give an insight into the designers' spirit and their innovative approach to creating digital type.

83

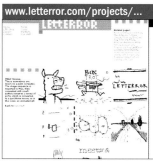

Using typograms and information graphics in an interactive way can be very persuasive

www.norm.to

NORM

design_Dimitri Bruni and Manuel Krebs,
Zürich, CH
on line_1999

Using typograms and information graphics in an interactive way can be very persuasive, especially when combined with animation and sound, as in the case of the online design lecture by the two young Swiss typographers Dimitri Bruni and Manuel Krebs who form Norm. An interactive and animated version of their printed book, the piece exposes the fundamental aspects of 2-D and 3-D design as Norm sees them. In a series of plans, the designers' argument is laid out in a stern and precise design that suggests incontestable logic. Despite its look of Swiss precision, however, this visual logic is a prime example of postmodern 'rhizomatic' thinking, where the act of establishing links between the pictograms and animated diagrams is more enlightening than the information that is actually depicted. Visitors are not passive students following the lecture – they are active participants venturing into complex media theory. This highly entertaining and playful lecture takes visitors by the hand and leads them through the four basic categories of the Norm philosophy, among which are 'things that refer to themselves' and 'things that we do not yet know'. The style of the design suggests a criticism of Robert Horn's books *Visual Language* (Bainbridge Island, WA: MacroVU, Inc., 1998) and *Mapping Hypertext* (Arlington, VA: Lexington Institute Press, 1990), offering him a lesson in taste and design sense. Norm dare to deal with complex content in a seemingly simplistic way. In doing so, they show that providing accessibility through typo-graphic clarity is now perhaps the highest artform in web design.

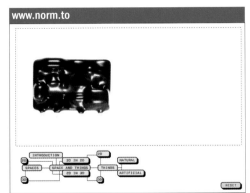

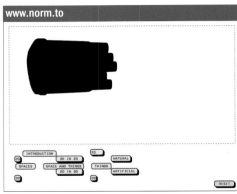

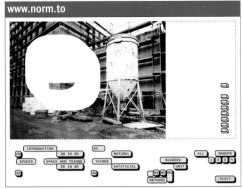

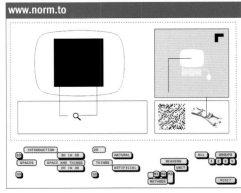

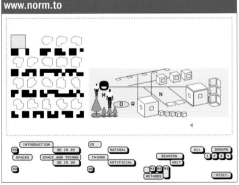

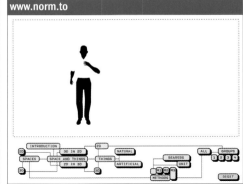

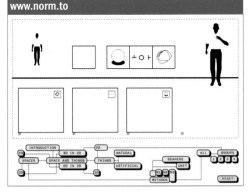

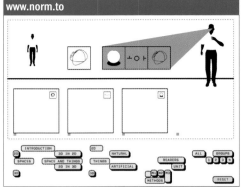

In the early 1990s, Swiss graphic and type designer Cornel Windlin was at the forefront of innovation in type design

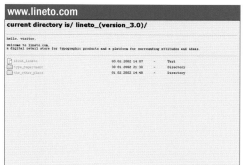

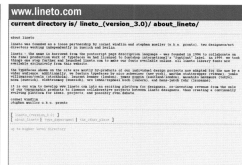

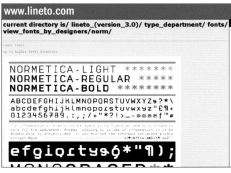

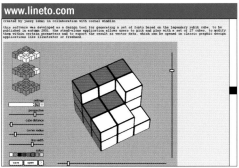

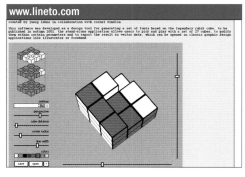

www.lineto.com

Lineto

client_Lineto, Zürich, CH and Berlin, DE
design_Cornel Windlin, Stephan Müller
on line_1999

In the early 1990s, Swiss graphic and type designer Cornel Windlin was at the forefront of innovation in type design with such fonts as Moonbase Alpha (1991) and Dot Matrix (1991–95). The former was, in his own words 'a reinterpretation of a bitmapped print-out of a 6-pt sample of akzidenz grotesk', testifying to Windlin's irreverent discourse with Swiss typographic icons. The second was an evaluation of the kind of letters that up until then had been judged as only functional for cash registers; Windlin was among the fontographers who made such lowly letters hip. In 1999, he and his Berlin colleague, Stephan Müller, launched www.lineto.com to make their fonts available on line. The site rigidly poses as being 'undesigned', its homepage copying the default directory layout you get if a site does not have an official 'index.html' start page. This approach results in an impeccable structure, reaffirmed in the headline-cum-interface at the top of every page. Each font is presented on a card, showing the letters' appearance in sometimes quite funny copy. A line accompanying Moonbase Alpha, for instance, reads, 'this font is beyond its sell-by date'. Lineto also offers a few applications or toys for tinkering with type. 'Lego Creator' lets users assemble letterforms and words from Lego blocks, while 'Rubik Maker' generates fonts based on the legendary Rubik's cube. With such experiments, Lineto fulfils its promise to evolve into a platform for exploration, collaboration and debate on all things digital and typographic.

85

There is good reason for using an almost purely text-based interface and visual design

www.fondsbkvb.nl

Fonds BKVB

client_Fonds voor Beeldende Kunsten, Vormgeving en Bouwkunst, Amsterdam, NL
design_Mieke Gerritzen, NL.Design, Amsterdam, NL
on line_1999–2001

Although the Dutch State Fund who commissioned this website supports the visual arts, there is good reason for using an almost purely text-based interface and visual design: the Fund's main means of communication is through documents. The paper machinery of application forms, memos, records, reports and statutes constitute the bureaucratic bedrock of a generous patronage for young artists and designers in the Netherlands; and Gerritzen (see pp. 26–27, 34–35, 37, 107) used this condition as the literal background for her design. On top of this, she built a straightforward and informative structure that effectively communicates the core business of the institution without giving in to the temptation of prefiguring what art is or should be about. Still, in all its modesty, the site's style does portray a visual intelligence that reflects the same qualities the fund seeks to support.

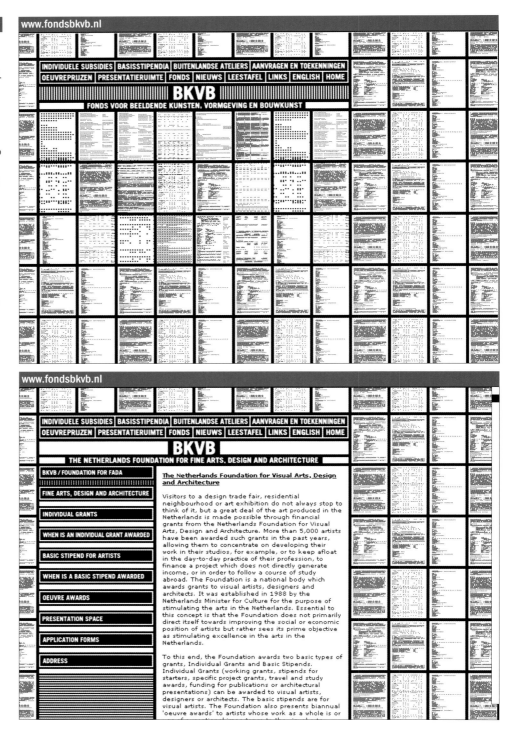

An interesting little application on the web, though not completely developed, is Niels van der Sluis's online HTML letterproof

www.werkplaatstypografie.org/bib/typefaces.html

www.werkplaatstypografie.org/bib/typefaces.html

www.werkplaatstypografie.org/bib/typefaces.html

HTML Letterproof

design_Niels van der Sluis, Arnhem, NL
on line_2001

An interesting little application on the web, though not completely developed, is Niels van der Sluis's online HTML letterproof. His final project on the *Werkplaats Typografie* (Typography Workshop) master's course in Arnhem, the Netherlands, the application enables you to test installed fonts on Mac or PC platforms. Limited to the standard HTML sizes of one to seven, it gives an apt representation of the on-screen readability of specific typefaces in particular sizes and styles. The interface might function better if the selected font and size were highlighted, if the font list and options on the left were placed in a separate frame so they did not scroll up with the text and if users could import their own text. However, the fact that a broad range of fonts in four styles and seven sizes is accessible within a single interface and after a few mouse clicks makes this a handy tool for those who design website texts.

87

The Designers Republic was one of the forces behind the typographic revolution in the 1990s

www.thedesignersrepublic.com

www.thepeoplesbureau.com

The Designers Republic

design_The Designers Republic,
Sheffield, UK

on line_2000

The Designers Republic was one of
the forces behind the typographic
revolution in the 1990s, notably for
the designers' habit of turning
everything they touched into a logo
or brand name and layering them
onto tangled heaps of decorative
data. Their typographic play with
the paraphernalia of commercialism, dubbed 'Brand-Aided Design',
has been extended to the web
albeit in a more organized fashion.
In fact TDR's site is a model
of clarity and a sophisticated
example of a purely typographic
interface. With all its apparent
simplicity, the site has a visually
interesting design, dominated by
over-proportioned and tightly
spaced titles. The studio's
characteristic play with readers'
expectations and with interface
conventions shows in the details;
on mouseover the titles change,
for example, from 'talk' to 'to' and,
on clicking, to 'you', or from 'join'
to 'exploit me'. TDR uses sound in
ways that might be called typographic. Little noises do not just
audibly affirm an action, but add a
layer of interpretation: small
'plops' for mouseover, short
'pumps' for clicks and a kind of
interference noise during the time
it takes for the requested information to load. When it is ready, it
audibly 'locks' into position.

88

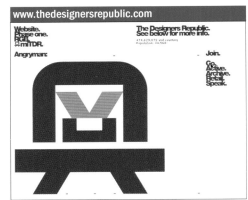

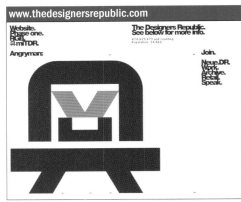

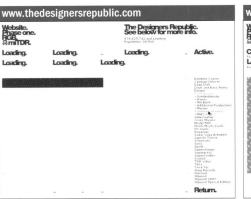

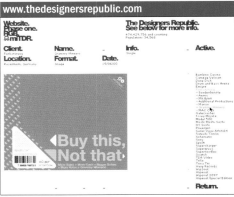

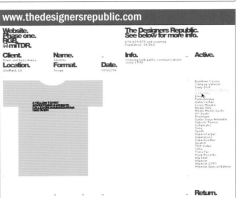

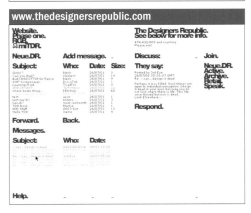

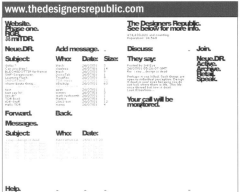

An extensive archive of TDR's work, the site also functions as a forum for discussion about their work and design in general

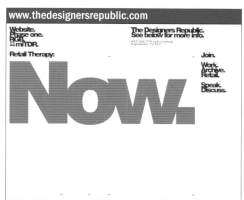

An extensive archive of TDR's work, the site also functions as a forum for discussion about their work and design in general. The site's database has been designed as a controlled visual overstatement, producing the studio's characteristic look and feel that reflects and refines the aesthetic standards of its constituency.

A parallel site, 'The People's Bureau for Consumer Information', is a blandly self-promoting shop window for The Designers Republic. Here, also, the 'right to uncensored greed' is celebrated typographically and verbally in a carefully orchestrated overstatement. As their investment charts show, these republicans will not get rich quickly, but they sure look like they are having a good time.

Animation

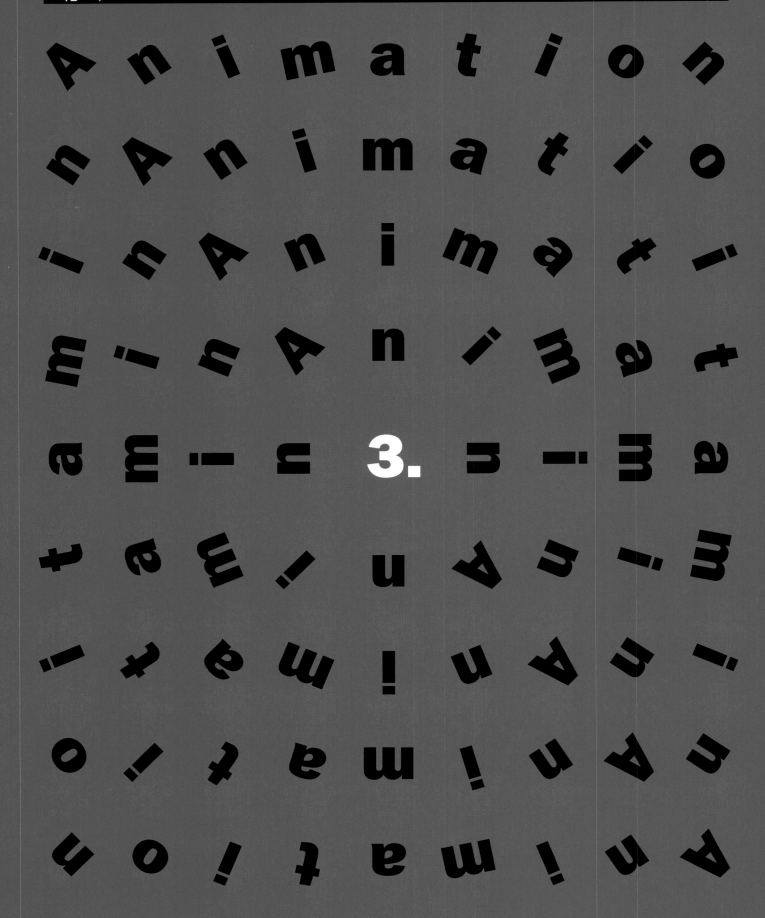

3.

The least one can expect these days is an 'intro', an opening page with moving type, animated figures, sounds and shifting colours.

Many of the most influential software innovations for the web share a propensity for motion however material the medium's 'still-mode' remains. Although movement can be highly irritating when used for soliciting attention – flickering banners and swirling buttons that want you to 'click here' – it *can* be a great enhancement of the experience. Elegant introductions that work like the opening titles of a film or the introductory pages of a book, subtle shifts in focus that guide visitors to another level of the site, funny animations, streaming video and texts, online games, all these animations can help to enliven a site's content. On a more fundamental level, they show that the web is maturing as the time-based medium it essentially is.

A growing amount of digital video makes the web incorporate more and more core aspects of television even if, for the time being, bandwidth is a problem. Increasingly, sites offer archives of digital films or schedule live webcasts of events, sometimes in combination with an online chat facility that enables viewers to respond on the spot to the proceedings. Thus, the web becomes a medium that fuses the broadcasting characteristics of television with the 'narrowcasting' quality of a personal video screening – access can be open and widely advertised or limited to a few select people. Anyone can distribute their digital video reports, video diaries, short movies or animated cartoons on the web, or simply install a webcam that shows the actual state of an office's coffee can. In fact, such uses of online digital video (or photo sequences) suggest a hybrid form of 'streaming media', an amalgamation of television formats, video art, video conferencing, surveillance cameras and home movies with more verbal and aural ways of communicating – watching, listening and reading merge.

Apart from traditional uses of time-based media in primarily linear narratives, animation can be used in quite different ways on the web, not least because of its interactive character. Even when interactivity is not the main issue,

The rubrics of interaction in this field are familiar from the play-pause mode in video

the fact that viewers can influence the pace of an online multimedia feature makes it a more personal – and interactive – experience. The rubrics of interaction in this field are familiar from the play-pause mode in video[1]. From scrolling frame-by-frame in the VCR's pause mode, through such scrolling and zoom functions in computer applications as text editors or picture viewers, to the complex combinations of static and animated information on CD-ROMs and the web, animation has developed into an important feature of hypermedia. To extend the cinematic metaphor, individual frames can function as the basic elements of a sequenced form of information, which only acquire a full meaning when animated, when 'played'. Such dynamic environments become interactive when the viewer can choose to watch either the sequence or to use single frames to focus on another level or to instigate an action. The 'up, over, down, hit' routine that defines the visual behaviour and actions of a button, for instance, can be seen as adding up to a four-frame film, with each of the four frames able to provide specific information or to trigger a different action.

The fundamental concept of animation – bringing to life – attains new meaning on the web where things take on a life of their own through 'material' characteristics, inbred behaviour and peculiar idiosyncrasies. Inanimate digital objects become active organisms thriving on user feedback. The examples of Tamaguchi, the Japanese digital pet that literally feeds on users' input, or 'Eliza', the program that uses Rogerian psychology to generate 'personal' responses to users' questions[2], show that simple feedback mechanisms can simulate the kind of complex behaviour we interpret as artificial life or artificial intelligence. When things on the screen seem alive we feel more engaged with them; animation induces empathy. And, when the screen starts reacting to our mouse movements, we start to 'feel' the screen.

1_In experimental videos, you sometimes notice a 'blip' in the continuum of the movie that, on closer inspection using the pause mode, may prove to consist of one or more frames with text. Some video makers have begun to use this 'still mode' to add another layer of information to the movie; see, for example, Michelle Martin and OS2's video *Centre of Gravity*, 1999.

2_'Eliza' was a mock psychotherapist programmed by Joseph Weizenbaum at MIT's Artificial Intelligence Lab in 1966 as one of the first exercises in making software react to and respond in 'natural language'. See, Joseph Weizenbaum's *Computer Power and Human Reason* (New York, NY: W. H. Freeman, 1972). For an online version of 'Eliza', see www.manifestation.com/neuro-toys/eliza.php3

93

The first digital environments that attempted to imbue objects on the screen with material properties were gamelike applications

94

The first digital environments that attempted to imbue objects on the screen with material properties to resemble real life were gamelike applications: balls that bounced off the frames in windows, elastic frames that gave to the pressure of the mouse point and other items that mimicked physical characteristics. By making things physically react to their environment and to external manipulation, web designers allow users to interact with objects on the screen at a far more fundamental level and encourage them to handle these items as real objects. Visual or haptic realism is not the key issue here, although it helps. More important is the idea that interacting with things on screen becomes more natural and intuitive to the user when the objects' physical properties offer a richer feedback than the standard repertoire of 'point, click, drag and drop'. The gamelike aspects of such feedback become apparent in interfaces that need to be explored and played with before users find out how they work. From a usability point of view this may seem rather counterproductive, but when an interface is well designed such challenges are seductive; once intrigued, users turn into players and want to master the game or solve the problem. A number of commercial websites have incorporated this playful aspect into their interfaces: after capturing the users' attention, the site's 'directors' can point users to whatever information they want to make prominent.

Animation enhances the experience of information. Cultural critics may lament that we do not have the patience to read anymore and that we have to be entertained into taking in information, but why should we not improve the experience when it facilitates getting the message across? More interesting than bemoaning the decline of old models of communication is to analyze how older routines are transformed and assimilated into new methods. Animated text, for instance, could be

Furthermore, animation can add a layer of information to texts or images that would be hard to achieve by other means

regarded as a blend of print-based and oral traditions – the text is read by and being read to the recipient at the same time.

Furthermore, animation can add a layer of information or interpretation to texts or images that would be hard to achieve by other means. Common words can display their hidden meaning on mouseover, a simple street map can come to life. Beyond providing information in an enhanced way, animation can entice the visitor to not just 'read' but 'act' the information; viewers become part of the drama of the content and their enactment of it enables them to intu-itively carve out their own narrative within the site's story space[3]. In this way, interacting with animated content becomes a design tool for guiding a participant along pre-structured paths between sites of information. The main task of the designer and editor, here, is to balance con-straints within the interface with room for improvisation on the part of the visitor. The designer, then, becomes a dramaturgist of the site's content.

3_See also, Brenda Laurel's *Computers as Theater* (Boston, MA: Addison-Wesley, 1991).

One of the most theatrical splash pages ever, the introduction to 'Threecolor.com' is a seventy-second Flash animation

www.threecolor.com/grad/grad.swf

Gradientors

client, design_Threecolor
on line_2001

One of the most theatrical splash pages ever, the introduction to 'Threecolor.com' is a seventy-second Flash animation. A blue ninja opposes an orange one, wins, faces five more orange enemies, defeats them all and, finally, the blue and orange ninjas eyeball each other severely before taking a last decisive leap ... at which point the 'threecolordotcom' logo appears. We will never know who won. Everything we expect from cinematic animation is present, quite a feat in this new medium: a moving camera, different angles, zooms, pans, dramatic action and a soundtrack of surging drums. All this in less than two megabytes of plain graphic expression and fading colours so typical of Flash movies. A fascinating little scene, well worth its seventy seconds, it is also the epitome of the kind of time- and bandwidth-consuming introductions that have necessitated the invention of the small interface element 'skip intro'.

www.threecolor.com/grad/...

www.threecolor.com/grad/...

www.threecolor.com/grad/...

www.threecolor.com/grad/...

www.threecolor.com/grad/...

www.threecolor.com/grad/...

www.threecolor.com/grad/...

www.threecolor.com/grad/...

www.threecolor.com/grad/...

www.threecolor.com/grad/...
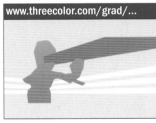

www.threecolor.com/grad/...

www.threecolor.com/grad/...

www.threecolor.com/grad/grad.swf

Amsterdam-based design group DEPT introduced an interesting link between analogue and digital media

www.bezet.nl

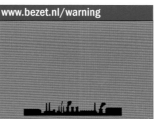

www.bezet.nl/warning

www.bezet.nl/warning

www.bezet.nl/warning

www.bezet.nl/warning

www.bezet.nl

www.bezet.nl/error

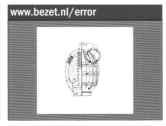

www.bezet.nl/error

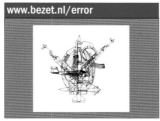

www.bezet.nl/error

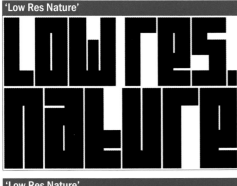

'Low Res Nature'

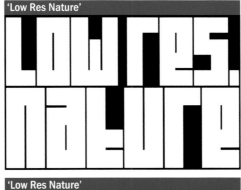

'Low Res Nature'

'Low Res Nature'

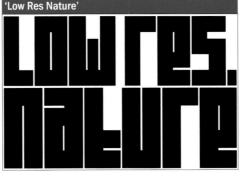

'Low Res Nature'

www.dept.nl
www.bezet.nl

DEPT
design_DEPT, Amsterdam, NL
on line_1999, 2002

Amsterdam-based design group DEPT (see pp. 32–33) introduced an interesting link between analogue and digital media when they connected a street-oriented project, consisting of monthly statements on plastic bags, to the web. The single images adorning the slogans on the bags became small animations on the site, adding movement and sound to their portable counterparts. In one, for instance, image after image of weaponry piles up into a tangled heap of deadly metal, while the accompanying sound develops into a cacophony – an apt illustration of the 'errorism' stated in the title. This is a lively elucidation of how to use simple but effective animation in the media mix of political activism.

97

Software engineer Ed Burton presented a Java toy called 'Constructor' as a job application for the design group Soda

www.sodaplay.com

Sodaplay

client_Soda, London, UK
design_Ed Burton
on line_2000

When software engineer Ed Burton presented a Java toy called 'Constructor' as a job application for the London-based design group Soda, he had no idea that it would become a classic. Working toward his Ph.D. in computer science, Burton had created the game purely as 'a toy for myself'. While thus practising his Java skills, he produced an online equivalent of artificial life: the animated geometric figures of his Java-app simulate lifelike physical characteristics in a way that turns these digital creatures into veritable online pets. It is probably this lifelike cuteness that has made the game so popular and addictive, leading *Apple Review* to call it 'a grown-up timewaster of epic proportions'. Burton obviously got the job and 'SodaConstructor', as it came to be known, counted over a million players within a month of its appearance on the web in April 2000. The application lets you play with such spiky creatures as the Hairy Caterpillar or the Dainty Walker. More importantly, it also allows you to edit them or to start from scratch – configuring lines and dots into wiry shapes, manipulating the controls for 'muscle' tension and force, mass and movement – and save your custom-made creature in the online database. Hundreds of computer-generated organisms now fill an online zoo. The game is an early and hands-on exposition of the laws of code; a hard-to-surpass example of generating interactive insight into life in the digital universe.

www.sodaplay.com/index.htm?getmodel=display+polyped

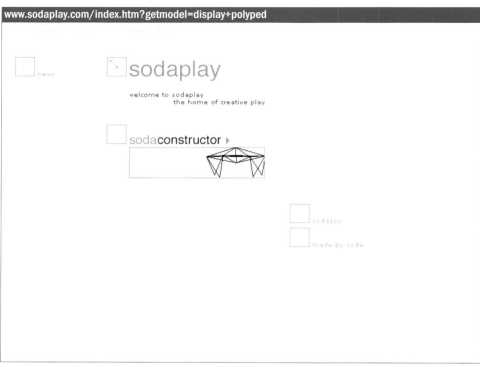

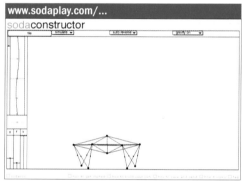

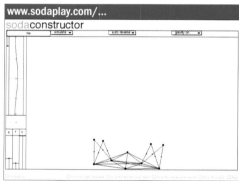

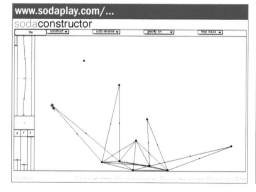

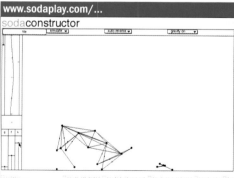

'Vector Park', designer Patrick Smith's small website, presents a few experiments in Flash

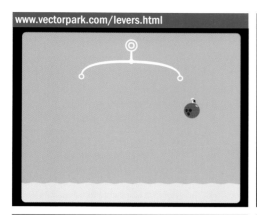

www.vectorpark.com/levers.html

www.vectorpark.com/levers.html

www.vectorpark.com/levers.html

www.vectorpark.com/levers.html

www.vectorpark.com/levers.html

www.vectorpark.com/levers.html

Levers
design_Patrick Smith, New York, US
on line_2000

'Vector Park', designer Patrick Smith's small website, presents a few experiments in Flash, created, as Smith acknowledges, because 'I just like making this stuff'. 'Levers' is a simple interactive game in which players try to balance the levers with the items that come falling out of the sky and plunge into the water. The game becomes more complex as more items appear; the players begin to ponder the relative weights of each object and are forced to conclude that although Newton's laws of gravity should not be completely discarded, a bird house *can* be heavier than a submarine. All kinds of properties, physical and behavioural, are assigned to the digital objects, turning the game into a practical discourse on materiality on screen. 'Levers' confronts – and amuses – visitors with the physicality of code, with the fact that the events on the screen are the result of the interaction of the player's manipulations not with the *objets*, but with the coding that produces them and their properties. The fun is enhanced by small surprises embedded in the objects: the bird house actually houses birds that from time to time fly out and settle on one of the levers, thereby influencing the balance; the snowman slowly melts; and the bucket can be emptied and refilled to adjust the equilibrium. Although based on interactive animation, 'Levers' is essentially a sophisticated exercise in interface design.

Maybe you have already experienced the strange way the computer translates the movement of your cursor

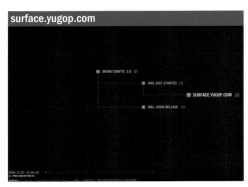

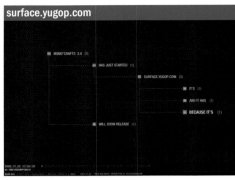

surface.yugop.com

Yugop

design_Yugo Nakamura, Tokyo, JP
on line_2000

Maybe you have already experienced the strange way the computer translates the movement of your
cursor into a graphic line or form
when you use a drawing tool?
Especially, the delaying and
deforming effect that a 9Mhz
processor has on your subtle and
gracious lines. It can provoke dis-
illusion and frustration, but should
you choose to adopt a more positive stance, it could reveal a new
way of expressing and working with
the idiosyncrasies of early computing. Yugo Nakamura, it seems, is
fascinated by the crudeness of
this method, for his site is a feast
of unusual gestural translations
into graphic and sonic environments and experiments. As a true
Shockwave virtuoso he lays down
a number of finger-tracking devices
for visitors to play with, reminding
them not only of early drawing
applications, but moreover making
them aware that they are playing in
a public arena. Some of his pieces
even invite visitors to play with others on line. Drawing will never be
the same; it has become a communal activity, something to share.
  Next to his 'Surface' experiments
is a section called 'Structure', in
which a piece shows a not entirely
non-linear interface. It is a raillery
of sorts, poking fun at the
branched hierarchies of flow
charts, while simultaneously
demonstrating quite accurately
how they work and their main
drawback (users tend to lose track
of their movement). Of course,
Nakamura provides neither 'back'
nor 'home' buttons on this page
that goes nowhere.

Animation tests the skill and ability of a designer to think in terms of action, dynamics and change

www.goingonsix.com

Goingonsix
design_Sean Donohue, New York, US
on line_2001

Animation tests the skill and ability of a designer to think in terms of action, dynamics and change. Traditional graphic-design practice very rarely deals with these phenomena. Though rooted in that tradition, the 'Goingonsix' site is an online laboratory that showcases invention, experimentation and graphic essays in animated design. The site is a learning ground, displaying attempts to broaden design vocabulary. The people responsible for this laboratory have different backgrounds and design approaches, but all share a willingness to master new techniques.

Some of the projects use limited means to achieve remarkable results, such as 'Breakout', a game by Erik Natzke (see pp. 28, 70). Unpretentious as the game is, it is still surprising that the advanced Flash programming reminds you of such video-game classics as 'Pong' and 'Tetris'. The site offers examples of a diverse array of adaptive design strategies, some of them poetic and autonomous, others incorporating intuitive navigation techniques or focusing on interactivity. Interestingly, movement is nearly always a major theme or focus, and the site offers a broad variety of sophisticated ways of thinking about movement 'out loud'.

'Breakout'

'Breakout'
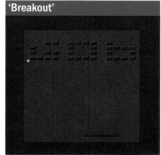

'Breakout'
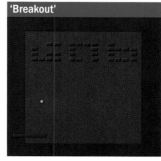

'Breakout'

'Breakout'

'Breakout'
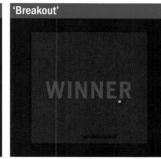

'Scrapyard'

'Scrapyard'

'Scrapyard'
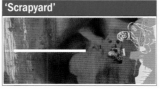

'My X_Files'

'My X_Files'

'My X_Files'

'Whispering'

'Whispering'

'Untitled.01'

If animation is a prerogative for looking innovative on the web, the Gmunk site certainly looks innovative

Gmunk

client, design_Bradley Grosh, Gmunk
studio, New York, US
on line_2001

If animation is a prerogative for looking innovative on the web, the Gmunk site certainly looks innovative. Visitors are flooded with QuickTime movies, Flash animations, Shockwave presentations and a dense amount of Gmunk's design material. Striving for better design and a mature use of the medium, the site is ideal for people whose main aim is to outdo everyone else in terms of bandwidth and reckless drainage of CPU power. Young and 'bleeding edge', Gmunk's cocktail of media is concocted with a somewhat sombre outlook on digital life. Although the site's content and redundancy of data could be criticized, its impeccable use of technology is still noteworthy. The main disturbance is the outrageous number of pop-up windows crowding the desktop. Seen from a post-everything angle, the site proves the inadequacy of traditional design criteria to describe the qualities involved. Gmunk taps into the cortex of digital exuberance, a new breed of design that will only become more visible with the growth of bandwidth and computer power. In showing that a random scribble on a paper napkin can be as viable a reason to create something digital as any clear idea on interface design, the designers at Gmunk are illustrating that computing has become second nature to them.

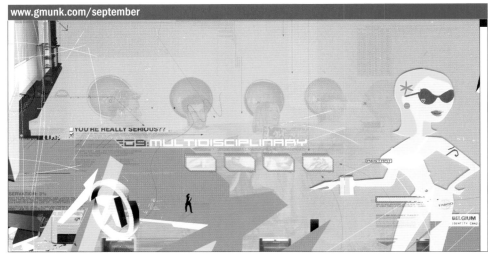

'Gmunk VS. Epyt: R1P.OFF3NSE'

'Gmunk VS. Epyt: R1P.OFF3NSE'

'Gmunk VS. Epyt: R1P.OFF3NSE'

'Gmunk VS. Epyt: R1P.OFF3NSE'

'FINN_movie'

'FINN_movie'

'FINN_movie'

'FINN_movie'

'FINN_movie'

'FINN_movie'

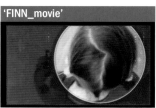
'FINN_movie'

'FINN_movie'

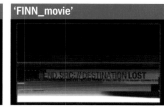
'FINN_movie'

An interesting – and working – example of converging media, 'Manhattan Timeformations' is a computer model

Manhattan Timeformations

client_The Skyscraper Museum,
New York, US
design_Brian McGrath (architect), Mark
Watkins (website design), Akiko Hattori
and Lucy Lai Wong (3-D models)
on line_2000

An interesting – and working – example of converging media, 'Manhattan Timeformations' is 'a computer model that simultaneously presents a layered, cartographic history of the lower half of Manhattan Island and an exploded timeline chronicling the real-estate development of high-rise office buildings.' The computer model correlates 370 years of urban development, facilitating comparisons between such aspects as land use, infrastructure and building sites – elements that are indiscriminately mixed on normal maps. This graphic representation of quantifiable data results in a transparent Manhattan, not in the sense of a realistic view but, in the words of Brian McGrath, with the aim of attaining a 'transparency of data'. A hybrid of cartography, information design and animation, the site provides an insight into the historic development of the city with top and side views, a layered timetable and the perspectival fly-through. Although limited in scope and depth of information, the site offers an experimental model that can be applied to more complex configurations of data.

104

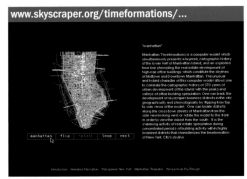
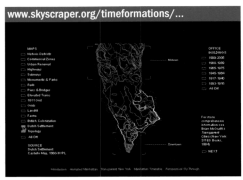
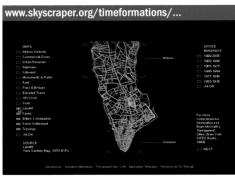
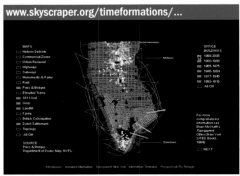
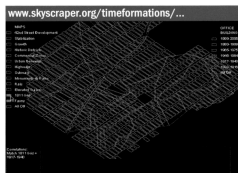
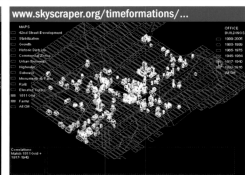
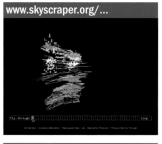
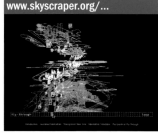

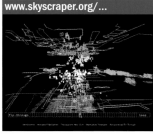

Is it a clock?

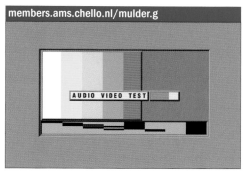

members.ams.chello.nl/mulder.g

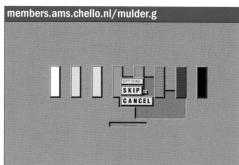

members.ams.chello.nl/mulder.g

members.ams.chello.nl/mulder.g

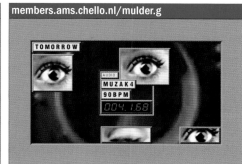

members.ams.chello.nl/mulder.g

members.ams.chello.nl/mulder.g

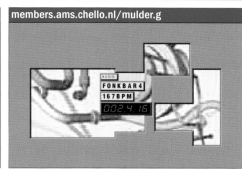

members.ams.chello.nl/mulder.g

members.ams.chello.nl/mulder.g

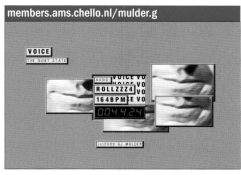

members.ams.chello.nl/mulder.g

members.ams.chello.nl/mulder.g

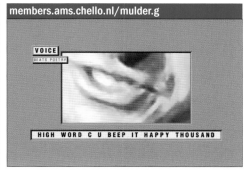

members.ams.chello.nl/mulder.g

members.ams.chello.nl/mulder.g

Today

client_Geert Jan Mulder, Amsterdam, NL
design_Geert Jan Mulder
on line_2000

Is it a clock? Is it a music channel? Is it an online application for video jockeys? It is 'Today' – all of the former and freelance audiovisual and media designer Geert Jan Mulder's private playground of randomly matching images, animation and sound. Mulder, who has an MA in computer animation from the Utrecht School of the Arts, had 'a lot of videos lying around', which he used as content for his engine. The clock, the opening image, shows the present time up to a hundredth of a second, indicating that everything you see is in real time. The combination of footage and music is generated from Mulder's database by a system that also manipulates the windows through which they are seen. Leaning very heavily on CPU resources (Mulder admits it is an 'issue of total RAM'), the site lets you follow the flow of today's sequence, or browse the log of previous days. Adjustments can be made to the speed and size of the images, choice of music tracks and the grid displaying the images. In some cases, mouse movement influences the speed of the music; in others, it simply affects the shape of the windows. At times the content becomes hypnotic and finds you raving behind the screen.

105

On completing her design masters course at The Sandberg Institute in Amsterdam, Luna Maurer left behind a new interface

Sandberg Institute

client_The Sandberg Institute,
Amsterdam, NL
design_Luna Maurer, Amsterdam, NL
on line_2001

On completing her design masters course at The Sandberg Institute in Amsterdam, Luna Maurer left behind a new interface for the institute's website that truly mirrors the school's structure and attitude: flexible, unruly and resilient. Her earlier work showed a predilection for gridded matter (as in the 'Poly' website, an experiment in branding a story space), and in the Sandberg site she uses the grid to visually structure the site's content and to give the grid a life of its own. The grid, called the matrix, is characteristic of a sturdy spider's web, elastic but unbreakable; when visitors move the mouse across the lines of the matrix in a steady movement, the lines give a little and then bounce back. This is done so convincingly that visitors can almost feel the tension and release. If the mouse is left to rest in one of the squares, the grid deforms and links are highlighted to the sides of the matrix, which when clicked on zoom out into a frame showing the relevant information. The overall effect is entertaining and functional, offering different ways to browse the matrix horizontally and vertically. It is a small site, but its characteristics sum up the web as a whole: a dynamic, elastic, changeable and rigidly structured network. It is also a rather persuasive exercise in animating, in the older sense of the word, the medium: bringing it to life.

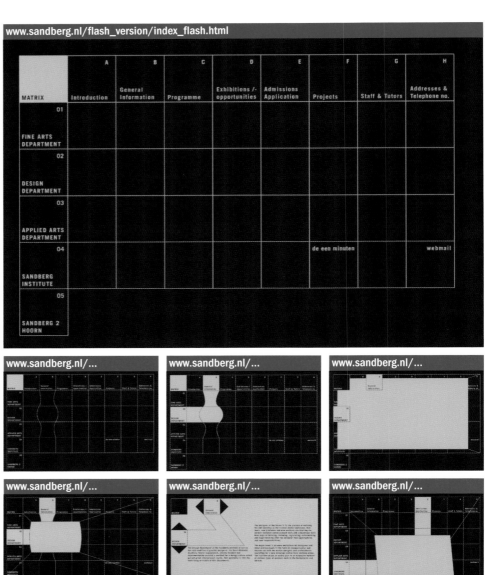

www.sandberg.nl/flash_version/index_flash.html

www.sandberg.nl/...

www.sandberg.nl/...

www.sandberg.nl/...

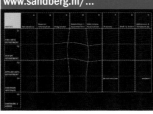

www.sandberg.nl/...

www.sandberg.nl/...

www.sandberg.nl/...

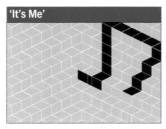

www.sandberg.nl/...

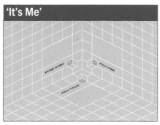

www.sandberg.nl/...

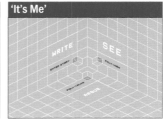

www.sandberg.nl/...

'It's Me'

'It's Me'

'It's Me'

Mieke Gerritzen connects new and unstable media to the strong Dutch tradition of bold typography, primary colours and dynamic layouts

www.nl-design.net

www.nl-design.tv

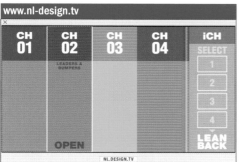

www.nl-design.tv

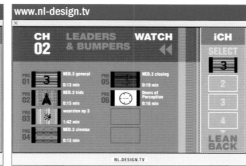

www.nl-design.tv

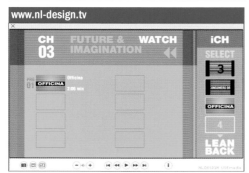

www.nl-design.tv

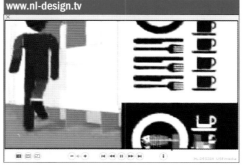

www.nl-design.tv

www.nl-design.tv

www.nl-design.net
www.nl-design.tv

NL.Design
client_NL.Design, Mieke Gerritzen
design_Mieke Gerritzen, Joes Koppers
on line_2001

A leading Dutch designer for print, television and the web, Mieke Gerritzen (see pp. 26–27, 34–35, 37, 86) connects new and unstable media to the strong Dutch tradition of bold typography, primary colours and dynamic layouts. Her own site is a case in point. It started off as a counterpart to her printed proclamation of design principles, *Catalogue of Strategies* (Amsterdam, NL: BIS Publishers, 2001), using the sloganlike chapter titles as animated banners for the screen design. 'NL.Design' is Gerritzen's loosely knit network of friends, colleagues and students (she heads the post-graduate graphic-design department at the Sandberg Institute in Amsterdam) with whom she realizes a great variety of work in a strongly consistent style. Gerritzen has an ambiguous relationship with tasteful design: few designers know how to undermine it so elegantly.

A veritable innovation is 'NL.Design.TV', the site's channel for presenting movies by Gerritzen and colleagues at the Sandberg, such as former student Luna Maurer (see opposite). Interface designer Joes Koppers (see pp. 26–27, 34–35) not only devised a completely new skin for the horrid machinelike exterior of QuickTime Player, but also added a range of functions in the process. A hybrid of browser and viewer, the channel offers a choice of options, sound and screen-size controls. It also has an extremely elegant 'casing' that gently closes when not in use, leaving a mere two-pixel-wide split in which a red dot indicates the loading status or the time played. The Bang & Olufsen of web TV!

107

On 2 October 1988, Donnie Darko received a hallucinatory message from a satanic bunny named Frank

www.donniedarko.com

Donnie Darko

client_Newmarket Film Group, IFC Films
design_Hi-Res!, London, UK
on line_2002

On 2 October 1988, Donnie Darko – euphemistically called 'a troubled teen' – received a hallucinatory message from a satanic bunny named Frank, stating that the world would end on 30 October 1988. Donnie accepted the news fairly stoically, but it marked the start of a month of destructive nightmares, which he re-created in real life. Or did he? Was anything that happened between the warning of impending apocalypse and the date of its predicted arrival real? Such is the stuff of writer and director Richard Kelly's film starring Jake Gyllenhaal, Drew Barrymore and Patrick Swayze, and reviewed as 'a daring, disturbing, visionary debut'. Equally as daring is the way the film is marketed on the web: a site that not only supplies the trailer but also a game-like environment that gives visitors more than a hunch of what the film is about. Mixing small Flash animations and movies, texts, riddles, quotes from what look like actual newspaper websites (opening in separate windows) and a sound-scape, the site is full of interactive dramatic effects that pull you into the film's atmosphere.

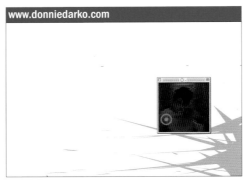

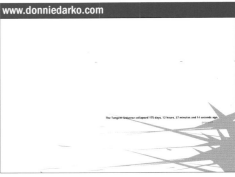

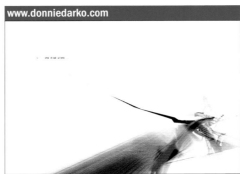

Interestingly, the film's plot hinges on different dimensions of perceiving time

'Donnie Darko Trailer'

'Donnie Darko Trailer'

'Donnie Darko Trailer'

www.donniedarko.com/the/tangent/...

www.donniedarko.com/the/tangent/...

www.donniedarko.com/the/tangent/...

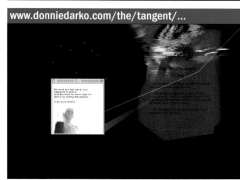

www.donniedarko.com/the/tangent/...

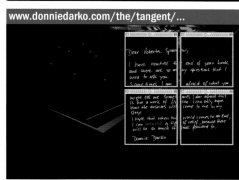

www.donniedarko.com/the/tangent/...

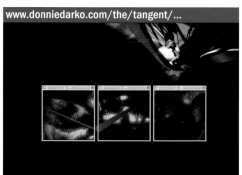

www.donniedarko.com/the/tangent/...

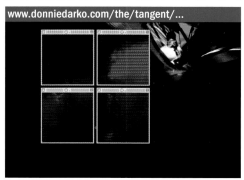

Interestingly, the film's plot hinges on different dimensions of perceiving time, and, from a media theoretical viewpoint, it could be argued that new media are better equipped to do this. Proving the point, this site breaks through standard cinematic perception and uses narrative time in a different way. With their use of hybrid imagery, media and interfacing approaches (from just reading and clicking to serious gaming challenges), the designers from Hi-Res! have done justice to this characteristic aspect of new media.

109

www.submarinechannel.com

Submarine Channel

client, design_Submarine, Amsterdam, NL
on line_2002

Submarine Channel is a network
and presentation platform
launched by Amsterdam-based
multimedia company Submarine.
Sharing a background in cinema
(International Film Festival
Rotterdam) and broadcast TV
(VPRO) and with a keen interest in
new media, founders Bruno Felix
and Femke Wolting thought the
time was ripe to fulfil the promise
of new media: the convergence of
film, TV, telecommunications and
the Internet. With a variety of
digital and interactive shorts by
Submarine and other artists, the
channel is an alternative form of
broadcasting in the new digital era.
Featuring, among other things, a
travel show to your mobile phone
('Instant Travel Service'), a very
nicely animated comic ('The Killer'
by Jacamon & Matz), commissioned stories from correspondents in Japan and the US,
Submarine Channel comes close
to showing what you could call
innovative content, a home-grown
media mix of editorial formats that
have one thing in common: they
move. Among the site's in-house
productions are 'City Tunes', 'real-
life stories, provided by you and
stylishly animated by us', and
the rather hilarious website of
'Mr. Kahoona', a would-be web
guru who gratifyingly commits
almost every violation of good
taste in web design, as illustrated
on the 'Web Page from Hell'
(see pp. 182–83).

'The Killer'

'The Killer'

'The Killer'

'The Killer'

'The Killer'

'The Killer'

'The Killer'

Syndication is important to Felix and Wolting, who work with acclaimed digital artists

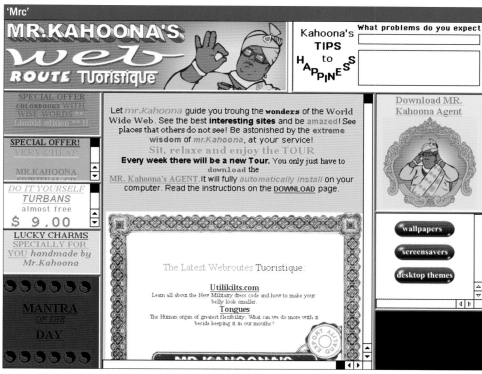

Syndication is important to Felix and Wolting, who work with such acclaimed digital artists as Rosto A.D. (known for his work on the Anouk video 'The Dark') and Douglas Gayeton to secure quality. The site's look and feel is very much like the work it shows: snappy Flash interfacing (harking back to old radio dial scales) with pop-up summaries on mouseover, a certified hip design, a nice background lounge tune and a played-down atmosphere with no marketing hysteria. Visitors may criticize the site's content for not being more ground-breaking or for being a hybrid embroidery of existing media formats and content, but maybe such criticism is due partly to the high expectations provoked by the site's format. Users want change to occur so badly in this field that the real innovations may seem to arrive slowly. If this is the case, Submarine Channel is a sign of good things to come.

111

The website for Compagnie Thor, a Belgian *troupe de dance* based in Brussels, seems to emerge from a splash animation

www.thor.be

Thor

client_Compagnie Thor, Brussels, BE
design_LAB[au], Brussels, BE
on line_2001

The website for Compagnie Thor, a Belgian *troupe de dance* based in Brussels, seems to emerge from a splash animation that brings to mind the early photographic studies of movement by Etienne-Jules Marey. In a fragmented sequence, the lines of a body in motion coincide with the lines of time. The resulting graph informs users that over eleven years Thierry Smits and his group have created ten hours and thirty-two minutes of performances. In another kind of compression, the website shows small video sequences of the various productions; by scrolling to the right, you can play around with the timing and the still images come to life at frame rates of your choosing. At the right rate of about twelve frames per second, the frames interlace to form a movie, otherwise they are seen as sequences of still images to browse through. If you move to the left, you literally go back in time, either through the sequence you just chose, or through the list of Thor's performances. Video animation and dance were made for each other; the interface allows visitors to 'time-zoom' into the movement and discover some of the intricacies of Smits's choreography. Apart from facilitating a better view of the dances themselves, this feature makes visitors aware of the fact that animation is essentially a deconstruction of movement. Thor's site grants viewers the experience of slicing time down to components of meaningful difference, which amount to the *raisons d'être* of the movement, the dance.

112

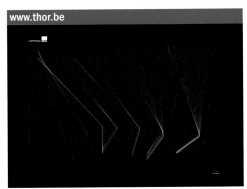

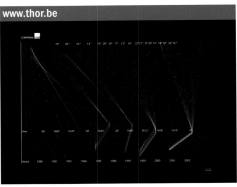

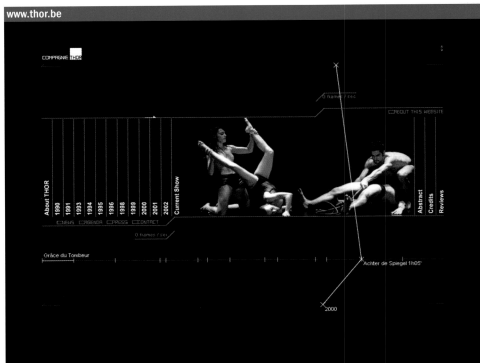

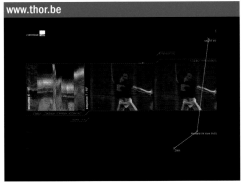

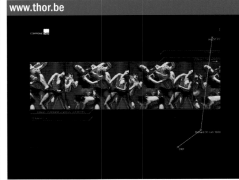

Of course, the site gives other information through the interface, connecting the performances by various timelines

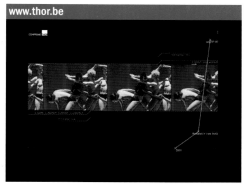

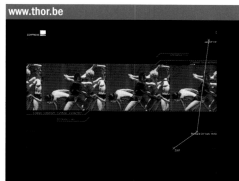

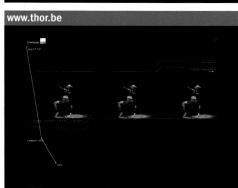

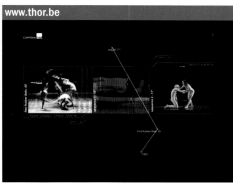

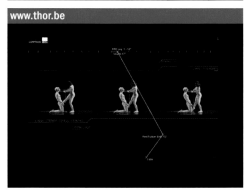

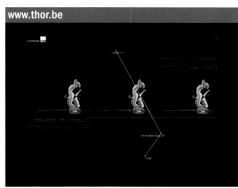

Of course, the site gives other information through the interface, connecting the performances by various timelines and providing a background for each of them. There are also press clippings, a news section and an agenda with performance dates and locations. The interface, with its constant use of visual metaphors of time, is not as transparent as users may want it to be, and the site leans heavily on the resources of the browser and CPU. However, these flaws are generously compensated for by the highly interesting and intelligent approach to communicating information about dance in a time-based manner. This superb site was made by LAB[au] (www.lab-au.com), also from Brussels, who refer to Etienne-Jules Marey in their introduction and link him to the new digital technologies of compression and navigation to arrive at 'movements in infos-pace'. A choreography of data in itself, the site testifies to the fruitful collaboration between the dance company and the information architects, 'a dance through/within information'.

113

The men's fashion site for Dior is an example of a delicate and highly suggestive use of Shockwave

www.dior.com

Dior Hommes

client_Dior, Paris, FR
on line_2001

The men's fashion site for Dior is an example of a delicate and highly suggestive use of Shockwave. Navigation is carried out by gently pressing on virtual boxes of which there are only vague outlines. The interface is obscure in a challenging way: a virtual space is suggested by patches of shimmering light, enticing visitors to investigate its workings, to play with its visual effects and to find the areas where there is a link to product information. This site is not text-book information architecture, rather it was made with one thing in mind: the Dior man. As if a result of a consultation with Rem Koolhaas, the site makes it clear that fashion is not so much about the product anymore, but mainly about experience. It is a fine illustration of the Internet as a medium for exploring the kind of virtuality that is the logical outcome of such an approach to fashion. Navigation is subtle and visitors have to find the right 'touch' – for the hasty there is little to find here. Cultivated, relaxed, smart, the site's interface epitomizes the Dior man. The Dior brand comes across as being *au courant* not only with the trends in couture, but with architecture and the visual arts as well (witness exquisite photography by Richard Avedon). Dior offers you the dream of a spectacle. The *dérive* is everywhere.

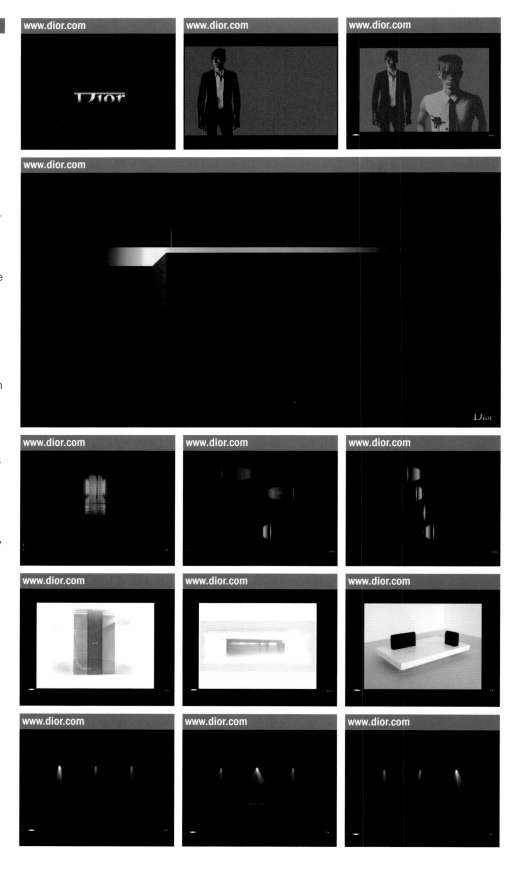

A London-based collective of artists and designers who share a decisively anarchistic view of life *and* a sense of humour

www.c6.org

www.c6.org

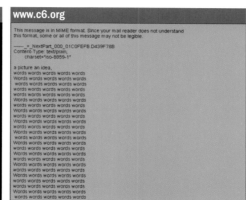

www.c6.org

C6

client_C6, London, UK
curators, design_Léon Cullinane,
Toby Lee, Sally Watkins, Asim Butt,
London, UK
on line_1998

A London-based collective of artists and designers who share a decisively anarchistic view of life *and* a sense of humour, C6 creates events from a heady mix of digital and physical performance, anarchic stenciling campaigns and fine-art propaganda. The group has opened minds in pubs, clubs and galleries, on the street and on the web. Their invocation to 'Bomb Soho' may not be meant literally – after 11 September 2001 it no longer sounds funny – but it does drive home the point that C6 is fed up with 'media whores' sipping lattes behind 'ergonomically curved desks'. As a code-slave liberation front of sorts, the designers mock the hype around new media, while showing that they do know how to deal with code at the same time. C6's shop sells T-shirts with politically incorrect imagery and slogans and demonstrates the group's work with code. Movement up and down the central frame displaying the merchandise controls the scale of the pictures and visitors can zoom in on each item as it scrolls by; movement to either side controls the speed and direction of the scroll. Elegant and effective, this is an example that should be followed more widely. The rest of the site is a strange collection of pranks, media experiments, cartoons and activity reports from C6's gallery, street shows and performances. The raw life of London's artistic scene beyond the famed Brit Pack.

115

www.c6.org/evol/com1x.gif

www.c6.org/archive/c6card.html

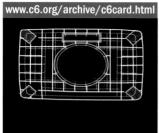

www.c6.org/archive/c6card.html

www.c6.org/archive/c6card.html

www.c6.org/c6/shop

www.c6.org/c6/shop

www.c6.org/c6/shop

If you have never been to SoHo you will probably not fully appreciate the precision with which Engine Three have made this site

www.kirnazabete.com

Kirna Zabête

client_Kirna Zabête, New York, US
design_Engine Three, New York, US
on line_2000

If you have never been to SoHo in New York City you will probably not fully appreciate the precision with which Engine Three have made this simple, elegant and functional site for Kirna Zabête's 464.5-square-metre (five-thousand-square-foot) store in Greene Street. It exudes the atmosphere of browsing the streets in the area's controlled environment of fashion, art, good taste and yuppiedom, where everything has to be just so. The website sees itself as the 'Shangri-La of shopping … a modernist materialist Mecca'. The spotless interface reflects all this, with its cosy nostalgic lounge riff – which, thankfully, you can turn off – putting visitors in the right mood of loose and laissez-faire consumerism. Small cones conceal navigation devices, which are elegantly revealed on mouseover. Small Flash animations are used humorously and effectively to lure visitors deeper into this feel-good paradise, which consists of the shop, the merchandise, the press reviews and the special events (a feature on Phil Nutley's furniture). Although the site does not deliver rich content, it does have everything you would expect; it is a case of fumbling a bit with the interface to reveal the information. Simple clicks or mouseovers result in animated responses; for example, when 'contact' is selected an animated map of downtown Manhattan zooms in on the grid, teaching visitors some essentials about the neighbourhood before pointing them in the right direction for the shop. A clean, funny and very thoughtful use of Flash animation.

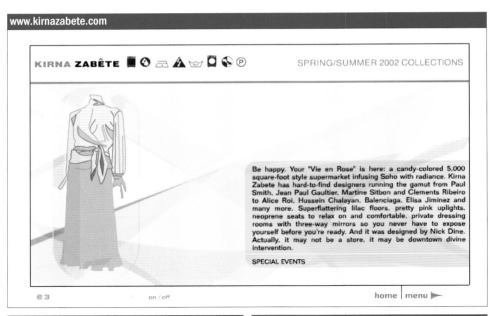

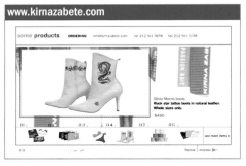

Ranking highly among design agencies in the UK, Fibre has created impeccably tasteful and sophisticated work

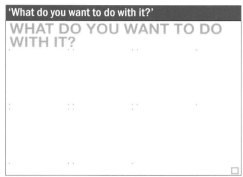

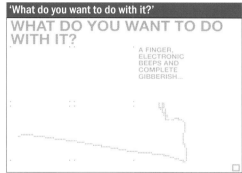

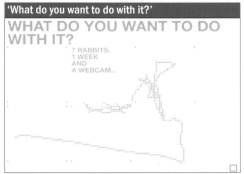

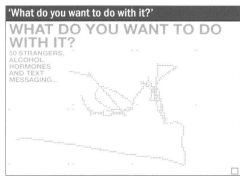

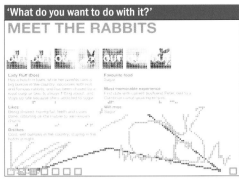

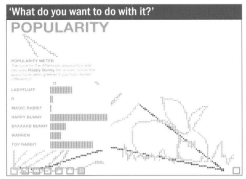

www.fibredesign.co.uk
www.whatdoyouwanttodowithit.com/index/fibre.html

What do you want to do with it?
client_ICA, London, UK
design_Fibre, London, UK
on line_2001

Ranking highly among design agencies in the UK, Fibre (see p. 79) has created such impeccably tasteful and sophisticated work as the website to accompany the ICA festival on digital arts and design, 'What do you want to do with it?', in November 2001. It not only offers information, it lets you add your own. On the site, visitors' cursor movements are traced in dotted lines across the screen. There is no avoiding this; like a child with a pencil, visitors compulsively sketch jittery lines and little drawings onto the pristine typographic surface.

The playfully digital character of the site is both in accordance and a bit at odds with the information on it; it is sometimes hard to focus on reading and not drift off to doodle. Still, for all its formal simplicity, the site is an excellent example of the kind of animated visual environment in which designers prefigure a lively experience for the visitor with very limited means. Everyone scribbles in program folders, only this one has the option to 'reset background'. As much as it is about communicating specific information, the design also amply facilitates the experience of the medium – playing around with it, 'talking back' to it in its own language. Information design *can* be fun.

117

The website for Stride Footware Collection uses animation to integrate a box-in-a-box structure with the interface of the site

Stride Online

client_Stride Footware Collection
design_Fibre, London, UK
on line_2001

The website for Stride Footware Collection, designed by Fibre, uses animation to integrate a box-in-a-box structure with the interface of the site. Although a shoe box is a rather obvious metaphor, it is used here in an amusing way, offering the site's content as surprise presents that slide out of the main boxes and reveal their content in Japanese and English on mouseover. The actual product shots are the only breach of style on the site, with dull photos of shoes sitting awkwardly in their vector-based environment. The atmospheric pictures behind the shoes are better, but they ignore the aesthetics of the rest of the site.

There are fun parts to the site, collected in a carousel, such as the soothing exercise 'Stride Meditation Online': on clicking 'reflect', a Japanese Zen garden unfolds and the mantra 'ommmm-mmm' slides past. In another example, users can search the floor for a sequence of dance steps, learning less about dancing in the process than about 'feeling' the screen for clues – animation is used in its oldest form: enticement.

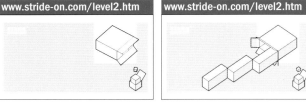
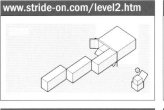
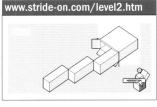
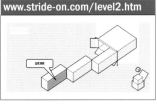
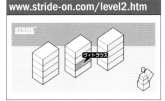
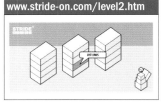
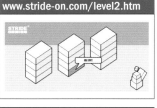
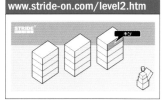
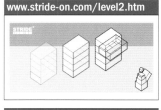

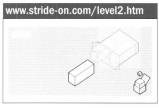
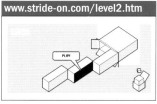
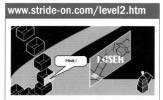
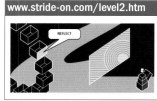
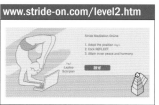
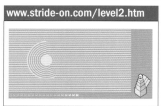

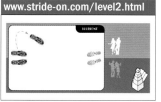
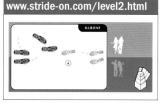
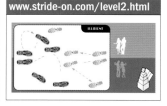

The site Fibre created for the European branch of the Japanese marketing firm Asatsu focuses on cultural differences in Europe

www.asatsu-europe.com

www.asatsu-europe.com

www.asatsu-europe.com

www.asatsu-europe.com

www.asatsu-europe.com

www.asatsu-europe.com

www.asatsu-europe.com

www.asatsu-europe.com

Asatsu Europe

client_Asatsu Europe Marketing & Communication
design_Fibre, London, UK
on line_2001

The site Fibre created for the European branch of the Japanese marketing firm Asatsu focuses on cultural differences in Europe, showing that the Japanese are fully aware of the challenges of language and perception within the European Union. The opening screen for each of the site's sections is a small animation that pokes fun at these differences; for example, the statement for Switzerland, which opens the portfolio ('work') section, reads, 'In Switzerland, you're 7 times less likely to have your car stolen than in England. But it won't always [work]', and is accompanied in the background by the sound of a car that won't start. The background photo suggests that it might be too cold. The portfolio itself is divided into bands of images and entries (video, print) that gently scroll by until visitors stop them by positioning the mouse point in the centre of the frame. Movement is used primarily to pace the information on the site and to overlay it with the client's image of smooth-operating cultural shrewdness. Using interactive movement, the designers can hide disturbing interface elements and have them slide into the frame only when they are needed or searched out.

119

Future Farmers work under the spell of a rural, Californian sense of global collectivism and collaboration

www.futurefarmers.com

Future Farmers

design_Future Farmers, San Francisco, CA, US

on line_1995

Future Farmers work under the spell of a rural, Californian sense of global collectivism and collaboration. Graphic designer and head farmer Amy Franceschini leads her fellow pioneers into cool digital pastures full of eerie flowers and fantastic animals with her own brand of Japanese kiddy design – tasteful, serene, poised and tremendously attractive. Under the surface of this fluffy dream hides a very mature design practice whose portfolio includes such big names as Nike, Adobe, Time Warner Digital, NASA, Lucasfilm and Levi's. Alongside commercial work, the farmers find the time to embark on projects that 'specialize in creative investigation and development of new work'; their 'Artist in Residence' project, for example, explores the relationship between concept and creative processes in the work of interdisciplinary artists. In the eight years of its existence, the site has become an intricate web of affiliations, cultural niches, projects and linked artists (visit, for instance, Nutrishnia.org).

www.futurefarmers.com

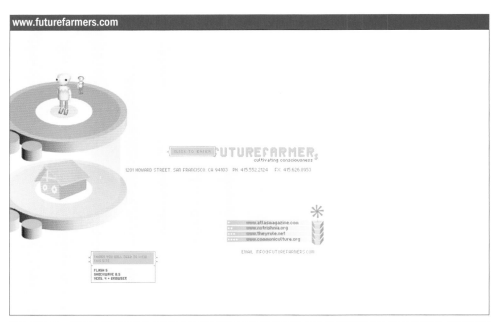

www.futurefarmers.com

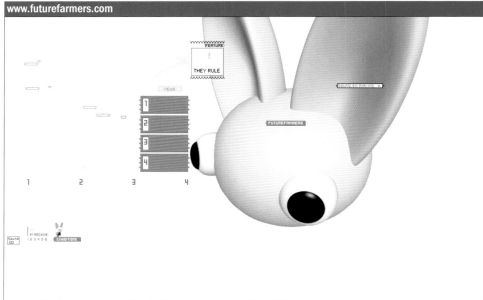

www.futurefarmers.com

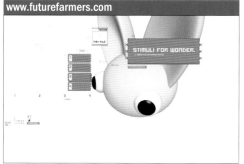

www.futurefarmers.com

For an exhibition, the farmers devised the 'Holding Patterns' installation

For an exhibition, the farmers devised the 'Holding Patterns' installation in which chandelier-like robotic birds hung from the gallery's ceiling. The Internet-based piece addressed environmental problems concerning wetlands and their migrating birds. Less 'arty' is the 'They Rule' game. Directed by farmer Josh ON, the piece provides an insight into how the US is run by big corporations and their networks. Nicely done, it shows the people in positions of control within the American economy and links to relevant sites that offer background information and sometimes stunning revelations. The list of referred sites includes 'Stop Bush 2000', 'corpwatch', 'inequality.org', 'open secrets', 'no logo' and an 'atlas of cyberspace'. So, even if you are seduced by the attractive design and the slick Shockwave interfaces, don't forget that these farmers know exactly how to reap rich visual crops whilst remaining critical and independent.

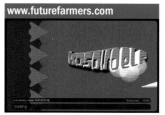

Video director and writer from Liège in Belgium, Tamara Laï converted to digital media as early as 1993

www.jimpunk.com/www/T.L.J.

T.L.J.: Javascript movie

design_Tamara Laï, Liège, BR and
Jimpunk, Paris, FR
on line_2002

Video director and writer from
Liège in Belgium, Tamara Laï converted to digital media as early as
1993. Her latest work is a new
medium in its own right, a
'Javascript movie' made in collaboration with French digital artist
Jimpunk. The short piece seems to
take over the computer for about
two minutes, causing a barrage of
windows to pop-up, slide down,
tremble and sway over the screen,
accompanied by eerie noises,
intense sighs and electronic
sounds. Staring eyes, frames
opening and drifting away, a
crouching body, faces, an empty
frame and a few snippets of text
('words which, effective like me
ablaze fire of colors and soft or
rough adjusted, functions outside
my veins'); obviously, this online
artwork is not meant to be read
like a manual. It symbolizes the
diluvial characteristics of the information society and the ensuing
desolation of a human being trying
to communicate via glass, metal
and electrons – blurred reflections
and unconnected data are your
part. Although fascinating in the
relentless way the piece usurps
the viewer's screen, it leaves you
slightly disconsolate, musing over
the demise of communication
through sensory overload or,
to quote the enigmatic French
text that closes the piece, '~~eris
et théories~~'.

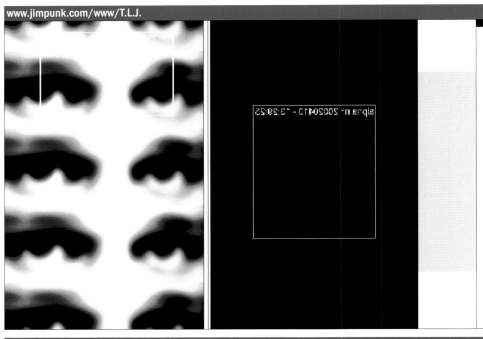

www.jimpunk.com/www/T.L.J.

www.jimpunk.com/www/T.L.J.

www.jimpunk.com/www/T.L.J.

words which,
effective like me ablaze fire of colors
and soft or rough adjusted, functions
outside my veins.

T.L.J. | T.L. | J. |

body folded its direction
with me carries more,
like matter a hypnotic fright
number you appear small number
with me,doubtful promise

sur les rôles qu'un réseau métallique maintient, ai touché, joue environ
autour de moi, ses cris m'aggravent toutefois, sans déranger mon rêve

me porte sur l'autre banquise - forêt un monde serre et effraye
quelle nature là? cherchent peut-être extrêmement, peut-être estiment,
et plaisanter qui ne présente pas à fierté moi peux que ma main gauche
sur l'eau et volent à moi

d'une étape quelqu'un va toutefois très étroitement au soleil brûlé
courses à l'herbe, bien, tristement souhaitable avant l'heure de notre mort

sous un poids de malaise non pas un son un moment soulagé sufferings
être ou ne pas pouvoir empêcher pour nous? pourquoi? cris et théories

^v^

123

Community Community Community Community
Community Community Community Community

4. **4.** **4.** **4.** **4.**

Another, and deeply cultural, consequence of the web's ability to link is that websites hardly ever stand alone – they cluster. Visitors gather not around single sites, but through portals, link lists, webrings, blogs, online clubs; in short, they form communities.

1_The French – as always – reluctant to adopt an English term, coined the word *internaute* for 'browser'.

The word 'portal' was first used to describe the kind of website that catered to the demands of a shifting population on the Internet. Where the pioneers and first users of the net were veritable *internautes*[1], exploring the web on their own or by following pointers offered by fellow travellers, the new, more consumption-oriented visitors want directions. What started as 'link lists' for like-minded people evolved into highly organized and deeply commercial collections of pointers for every taste. These portals quickly developed into a marketplace of links, banner-ridden clusters of the global brotherhood of digital doorbell ringers. The web equivalent of themed environments, portals emerged around sports, the news, cars, fashion, shopping and, of course, sex. By now the word has become derogative, indicating the commercial exploitation and expurgation of what used to be an open information space. In the 'newspeak' of international e-trade, the portal is presented as the golden gate to the promised land of customized information, but is in fact intended to monitor customers inside a controlled environment instead of facilitating unbiased access to whatever information they may want.

Still, the term portal is useful. When understood as a gateway to related (or not so related) sites, you can appreciate the portal function, although some makers would feel seriously insulted if you called their homepage a portal. Weblogs, for instance – diaries of sorts devoted to webloggers' encounters and discoveries on the web – tend to be very good portals in the gateway sense. Dedicated surfers, the 'bloggers' can be genuine trailblazers for less assiduous visitors to the web, opening up vast territories of websites on a wide range of topics sorted by personal taste – from highly specialist resources to themed communities, from an idiosyncratic look at the news to *faits divers*. Good bloggers come to be recognized as authorities on certain topics, offering a starting point for further exploration and

Independence is the key, and it shows in the design of the sites

acquiring a status that is coveted like the philosopher's stone by commercial portals. Independence is the key, and it shows in the design of the sites. Whether home-made with the help of simple applications like Netscape Composer or the more specialized Blogger (see p. 170), or fully developed professional designs, the best bloggers remain true to themselves and present a personal take on the web[2].

The web started in this way, as a space in which to exchange information among individuals with shared interests. In the era of Bulletin Boards and Usenet[3], people with an Internet connection started to group together around specific topics. The conversations and discussions that ensued were like those echoing around the central piazzas of old Mediterranean villages at the end of a work-day: a spontaneous gathering around a few opinion leaders to discuss current affairs. On Usenet, these piazzas developed into veritable communities of geographically dispersed individuals assembled around a growing range of topics, from highly specialized scientific research to self-help and lifestyle topics[4]. Crucially, the software design that made such communication possible was intended for open-source development, free distribution and peer review; it was also meant to be uncensored and self-organized. The communities themselves developed – or should I say 'designed' – rules of conduct, sets of behavioural essentials that became known as 'netiquette'[5]. It became a requirement, especially in smaller and highly focused groups, to respect the appropriate social codes lest you were 'flamed' and expelled. Participation was expected and those who just followed the course of the debates without getting involved were looked down upon as 'lurkers'.

In design terms, these text-based online environments may not look all that interesting, but they do constitute the foundation on which the web grew as a community-building medium. The newsgroup model can be recognized, for

2_'Weblog is voice. It expresses its author's everyday experience in text, illustrations, editing and design, all in one hand. Weblogs are not all encompassing critiques that pretend to stop the information invasion. On the contrary they are very precise professionally and personally guided expressions of the world its author lives in, limited to one person's experience and learning, for better or worse. Every weblog reflects the moods that come with the life lived and performed. It shows endless subtle variety, much of which will only appeal to very small audiences: circles of equally challenged people. On the other hand, thanks to the interconnectedness in its networked medium, weblogs are open for the widest imaginable perusing.' Jouke Kleerebezem's conference paper 'Daily Operations: the Weblog', 2001. www.idie.net/personalpublishing

3_For an in-depth overview of how the net has evolved as a communications and community medium see: Howard Rheingold, *The Virtual Community – Homesteading on the Electronic Frontier* (Cambridge, MA: The MIT Press 1993, revised 2000). www.rheingold.com/vc/book

4_Remarkably, the social organization that (almost automatically) shapes the workings of these online communities closely resembles social stratifications in small villages: the dignitaries and leading residents, the old nucleus of original villagers, the newcomers, the eccentric, the village idiot, the outcasts.

5_'One of the great problems with the atmosphere of free expression now tolerated on the Net is the fragility of communities and their susceptibility to disruption. The only alternative to imposing potentially dangerous restrictions on freedom of expression is to develop norms, folklore, ways of acceptable behavior that are widely modeled, taught, and valued, that can give the citizens of cyberspace clear ideas of what they can and cannot do with the medium, how they can gain leverage, and where they must beware of pitfalls inherent in the medium, if we intend to use it for community-building.' Howard Rheingold, *The Virtual Community – Homesteading on the Electronic Frontier* (Cambridge, MA: The MIT Press 1993, revised 2000). www.rheingold.com/vc/book

instance, in the 'free towns' – online digital towns – that sprung up during the mid-1990s, in which each citizen built their own home around the town square, the informational nucleus, organized according to topics, debates and functions. Communities grew to number thousands, and the free towns started to change into digital suburbia, a vast expanse of loosely connected online homesteads, which, analogous to real-life suburbs, were often grouped around the virtual shopping malls of online commerce.

Online community life is also lived to the full in the Massively Multiplayer Online Role Playing Games (MMORPGs, see pp/ 154–57). Having their origins in the same text-based environments as Usenet, the first multiplayer online games were role-playing activities in Multi-User Domains/Dungeons/Dimensions (MUDs). Players styled characters, acquired or made props and tools and collectively developed a story based on a few rules and enacted through interaction with other players, establishing further rules of conduct along the way[6]. The core design of such games mainly centred around the interface, the rubric of the interaction and the formulation of rules concerning the consistency of characters and narrative environment (it does not make sense to develop the character of a Roman soldier in a MUD on a science-fiction theme). Today's online games sport highly realistic three-dimensional environments where players can gain powers, build houses, furnish interiors, forge objects and clothe their characters at will, or with input from other players. A genuine economy has sprung up in these games, with virtual currency or tokens sometimes representing hard cash: 'real estate' in some MMORPGs has gone at auction on e-Bay for hundreds of dollars. Interesting from a design point of view, in no other format are the roles of developers, designers, writers, editors and users so entangled. If the game's interface lacks clarity or response, if it does not provide the kind of interactivity expected, or if the

6_For more information on developing social interaction skills in MUDs, see also Sherry Turkle's essay 'Constructions and Reconstructions of Self in Virtual Reality: Playing in the MUDs', *Mind, Culture and Activity: An International Journal* (vol. 1, no. 3, summer, 1994). lchc.ucsd.edu/MCA/ Journal/su94.html#constructions

If designers model characters' behaviour and the game's environment in too great a detail, players will feel like mere pawns

visual design is lacking in consistency or attractiveness, the game will not be successful. If, however, designers model characters' behaviour and the game's environment in too great a detail, players will feel like mere pawns in someone else's recreation and the game will not take off either. As Andy Cameron of the interactive design practice Antirom stated, the design must concentrate on 'potentia', providing the bare bones of the story, which the game participants will flesh out themselves[7]. How game-related communication among players evolves outside the game proper may seem marginal to its design, but, as specialists in the field confirm, it is very important: the stronger core community of players connected to the game, the more time they will invest in making it an immersive experience not only for themselves but also for the community at large[8]. Without the collective collaboration of the gamers – as co-developers , coauthors and performers of the game – the product would not exist[9].

Gaming is not the only massive concourse on the web. Ever since making a website became an easy option for everyone instead of a toilsome privilege for the digerati (web élite), the web has been a teeming agora for ad-hoc initiatives and urgent causes. The war in Bosnia, and the uprisings in Serbia are among the crises in which the web played a notable part[10]; also, without the help of the net the anti-globalization movement, organized in Independent Media Centers (IMCs), could not flourish so effectively.

Since 11 September 2001, an abundance of webpages and sites has been devoted to every conceivable aspect of the worst terrorist attack in history. Whether a simple 'thank you' posted on a number of American portals, counselling sites on how to cope with lost loved ones, personal accounts of the events or calls for action against terrorism and hatred, the communication boom spawned by '9/11' exemplifies the web's potential as a community medium (see pp. 146–51). In terms of directly reacting to current

7_'In its most fully realised form, that of the simulation, interactivity allows narrative situations to be described in potentia and then set into motion – a process whereby model building supersedes storytelling, and the what-if engine replaces narrative sequence.' Andy Cameron, www.hrc.wmin.ac.uk/hrc/theory/dissimulations.xml?id=theory.3.2

8_'It is extremely important to have this aspect both within and outside of the product. Without community, without tools of socialisation to build said community, your product will not be as successful, no matter how well you design your game.' Misty 'Beans' Matonis, community developer for 'Websites'. www.gamespy.com/mmog/stratics/june01/stratics3/index2.shtm

9_'(In multiplayer games), the aesthetic and the social are integrated parts, and this could be regarded as the greatest innovation in audience structure since the invention of the choir, thousands of years ago.' Espen Aarseth, editor-in-chief of www.gamestudies.org

10_In the early days of the Internet, Usenet played a pivotal role in disseminating essential information. 'In Usenet, every member of the audience is also potentially a publisher. Students at universities in Taiwan who had Usenet access and telephone links to relatives in China became a network of correspondents during the 1989 Tiananmen Square incident.' Howard Rheingold, *The Virtual Community – Homesteading on the Electronic Frontier* (Cambridge, MA: The MIT Press 1993, revised 2000). www.rheingold.com/vc/book

Interestingly, this publication trajectory largely bypasses the existing hierarchies of commentary in older news media

affairs, this use of the web resembles the 'letters to the editors' section in newspapers; only in this instance, letters are put on specific sites and the links to them are published through mailing lists, newsgroups, webrings and, ultimately, search engines. Interestingly, this publication trajectory largely bypasses the existing hierarchies of commentary in older news media like newspapers, magazines or television. Rather, new hierarchies, new sites of authority are constructed.

The web can be a perfect channel through which to share individual emotions and views with a community of like minds or with the world at large. Commercial portals have by now understood the potential in the persistent desire of 'netizens' to express themselves and are opening up places on the web for them to do so: such online diarylike applications as blogs, clubs or guest books offer the templates for digital suburbanites to fill in and bring to life. Design, here, is limited to creating the simplest possible interface and leaving enough room for the advertisers' banners. Ultimately, for the user, the player, the dilettante publisher, design on the web becomes a matter of tweaking the defaults.

'It can be difficult to know where to look to see the best sites', so www.linkdup.com saves users a lot of time

www.linkdup.com

linkdup

design_Preloaded, London, UK

on line_1999

Realizing that 'it can be difficult to know where to look to see the best sites', the founders of www.linkdup.com save users a lot of time and effort by collecting and archiving sites they consider to be important. At the time of writing, the categorized and cross-referenced URL database stands at over 2800 entries divided into seven categories. The 'links pool', the unfiltered database, contains another 2500 links 'awaiting validation'. Started as the link list for London-based new-media shop Preloaded, 'linkdup' has developed into a resource of quality design on the web, and its authority has been enhanced by its very clear and accommodating interface. The site's nucleus is the 'favourites' section, comprising sites catalogued and reviewed by the 'linkdup' crew. You can also browse by latest addition, the public's favourites, or search the entire database or unfiltered list; and you can 'lock' the sites you like into your own selection. Other interface elements indicate the status of a site and the technology used, offer you the opportunity to mail the URL to someone and allow a search based on technological criteria. Focusing around their own research and that of a loose neighbourhood of friends and colleagues, 'linkdup' chooses sites on fairly subjective criteria, thereby establishing a highly valued connoisseurship.

Since its inception, Sippey's 'occasional commentary on Internet technology, business and culture' has been a guiding light

www.theobvious.com/network

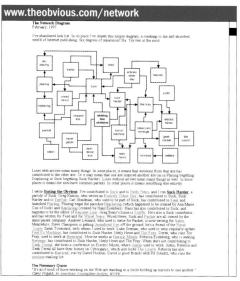

www.theobvious.com/archive.html?michael

www.theobvious.com/questions.html?000028.obv

www.theobvious.com/archive.html?michael

www.theobvious.com/archive.html

www.theobvious.com/wired

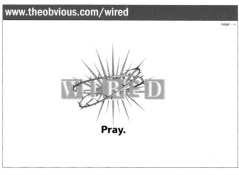

www.theobvious.com/wired/contents.html

www.theobvious.com/wired/1.html

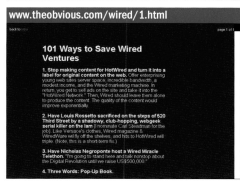

www.theobvious.com

Stating the Obvious

content, design_Michael Sippey,
Berkeley, CA, US
on line_1995

Since its inception in August 1995, Michael Sippey's 'occasional commentary on Internet technology, business and culture' has been a guiding light for those who want intelligent views on web-related issues. Apart from Sippey's witty commentary, the site has hosted a wide variety of guest authors and has confronted specialists with long-unanswered questions in the 'Just One Question' section. Sippey, an e-business developer and strategy consultant, has contributed to Suck.com (which he parodied in 'Suck Harder'), 'Time Digital', 'The Netly News' and other online publications. His site may be seen as a blog *avant la lettre*, bringing a personal view and candid observations to a dedicated community of readers, but Sippey also has a separate blog, sippey.com, in which he notes his thoughts of the day, muses on things he has found on the web – not forgetting to link to an 'obvious statement' when appropriate (which is quite often).

Aside from commentary, 'Stating the Obvious' has been involved in a hilarious pastiche of *Wired* in 1997. It also has a link to Sippey's academic background in English literature through a collection of thirty-six randomly selected fragments of text from Don DeLillo's novel *White Noise*. Each fragment has been hand-annotated with hypertext links to the web, which 'need not be followed; passing your mouse pointer over the link and reading the associated URL will usually bring forth the appropriate emotional or cultural response'. Vintage Sippey.

133

One hands-on critic of life on the web is artist, designer and entrepreneur Jouke Kleerebezem

www.lemoulindumerle.com
www.nqpaofu.com
www.idie.net

Notes, Quotes, Provocations and Other Fair Use

content, design_Jouke Kleerebezem, Nièvre, FR

on line_1998

One hands-on critic of life on the web is artist, designer and entrepreneur Jouke Kleerebezem. Based now in his own manor in rural France, Kleerebezem made a name for himself as a critical artist and curator in the Netherlands. His relatively remote location is compensated by a growing collection of websites that soundly place the house and its community in virtual space. The house and its inhabitants are described in the small informational site www.lemoulin dumerle.com; it is as 'homepage' as you can get.

The real business – the critical analysis of the Internet – takes place on a site called Notes, Quotes, Provocations and Other Fair Use[1]. With a name that almost forces you to bookmark it, it has developed into a database of Kleerebezem's own texts and a growing blog replete with web references. Summing up the cultural-political idea behind the site, Kleerebezem states, 'NQPAOFU is personal publishing, rather than a personal publication: a process, an act rather than a product. Its daily routine, its mixture of personal and "professional" information, insights, beliefs and critique, its context of other weblogs, all contribute to a connectedness, which I think is the true "belief" behind such utterances.' With a crisp and clear typography and, apart from extended internal hyperlinking, no interface to speak of, Kleerebezem shows how the web is *one* text if you are author enough to write it by combining your notes and provocations with other people's quotes and assorted 'fair use'.

www.lemoulindumerle.com

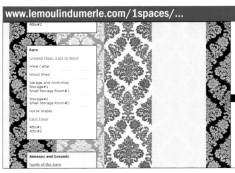

www.lemoulindumerle.com/1spaces/...

www.nqpaofu.com

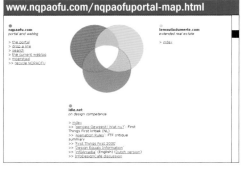

www.nqpaofu.com/nqpaofuportal-map.html

www.nqpaofu.com/nqpaofusince1998.html

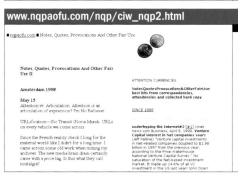

www.nqpaofu.com/nqp/ciw_nqp2.html

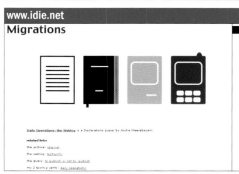

www.idie.net

134

When Kleerebezem read the 'First Things First 2000' manifesto, he got mad

When Kleerebezem read the 'First Things First 2000' manifesto, an international appeal to designers' critical faculties and social responsibility published in *Adbusters* (see pp. 140–41) and many other magazines, he got mad at what he considered to be gratuitous 'do-goodism' from a bunch of well-paid lounge idealists and decided to react against it. Kleerebezem posted a harsh critique on the Info-Design mailing list, and the next morning he registered www.idie.net 'because it is in communication networks that information empowerment emerges today'. The site, nicknamed 'I Die For Change', is intended as 'the home for launch-and-learn activism', collecting critical essays and statements by its author and linking to artists, designers, theoreticians and sites that advocate a critical-activist approach to new media, the information society and the web. Kleerebezem states, 'With idie.net, IDIE, I would want it to be more of a collaborative project. It would gain from an active participation, multiple research and development, active production and editing.' The basic simplicity of the site's design (one page, internally linked, in elementary HTML) is a programmatic statement in itself. In my view, although Kleerebezem admits that the site is 'more or less stuck in its infancy state', it is one of the best critiques 'First Things First' could have hoped for!

1_The site's initials, NQPAOFU, are the same as those of the Latin quote Jouke Kleerebezem uses as a motto: 'Nunc Qualibet Parte Alloquium Orant Fratres Urbanitatis' ('Now, the brotherhood of urbanites speak their sermons anywhere they like.').

135

Launched in March 1998 under the motto 'bastion of peace and information', this site is the weblog of British artist Paul Perry

www.alamut.com

Alamut

content, design_Paul Perry, Rotterdam, NL
on line_1998

Launched in March 1998 under the motto 'bastion of peace and information', this site is the weblog of Rotterdam-based British artist Paul Perry. In one of the first entries, he asks, 'You're wondering what's going on here?', and answers, 'I'm advertising my attention!'. In the exchange terms of the attention economy, Perry is giving more than he gets. Associative and highly idiosyncratic, the blog offers us insights into the life and mind of a dedicated reader – of books that is. The site's design echoes the love of the printed page: a crisp layout that uses differences in typeface and the occasional background colour to discern between various kinds of quotes and commentary. Be sure to leave on the 'underline links' option in your browser, since that is the only way links are accentuated; coloured text, here, is for Perry's own highlighting. This is in many respects a reader's digest, a treasure trove of ideas and pointers to sources, reviews and summaries sparked by Perry's reading of a wide variety of texts and his correspondence with other aficionados. If you were wondering what became of civilized and erudite conversation after the demise of the Paris salons, check out Paul Perry's blog. In the ongoing correspondence between such bloggers as Perry and his friend Jouke Kleerebezem (see pp. 134–35), a new salon is coming into its own.

136

www.alamut.com

ALAMUT
BASTION OF PEACE AND INFORMATION

Present
Past
Subjects
Projects
Misc

MAY 2002

WEDNESDAY, 1 MAY 2002

"What are the odds to sharing a dream? Or dreaming about something which is about to happen?' (Like your phone call? Or your comments about the sun?")

Dream Yoga by Peter Ochogrosso (online)

The Tibetan Yogas of Dream and Sleep by Tenzin Wangyal

Dream Yoga and the Practice of Natural light by Namkhai Norbu

THURSDAY, 2 MAY 2002

Drifting Identities

"I always wondered how far I can evolve without stopping being myself... It seems possible that the identity issue can be the ultimate limit to growth."

(Sasha Chislenko, Drifting Identities)

"I bade farewell to myself in the mirror."

(Jorge Borges, The Garden of Forking Paths)

Alexander 'Sasha' Chislenko (1959-2000) Extropian Last Friday and Saturday in Gent Frank Theys and I spoke about him. Frank interviewed him five years ago for his documentary Technocalyps I read Sasha's posts to the Extropian mailing list during the period I read the Extropian mailing list (1993/1994) and a couple of years ago saw fit to archive his Drifting Identities post to Alamut

"And this is just because we "define" our notion of identity as something that is preserved in the transformations we are used to seeing. When (not if) the transformations will become more drastic, this notion will be shattered. In fact, if we just look at our own lives, we go thru so many transitions that hardly preserve our identity in any reasonable definition of this word..."

(Sasha Chislenko, Drifting Identities)

Compare Spinoza, Ethics, IV, 39 scholium

But here it should be noted that I understand the body to die when its parts are so disposed that they acquire a different proportion of motion and rest to one another. For I dare not deny that "" even though the circulation of the blood is maintained, as well as other signs on account of which the body is thought to be alive "" the human body can nevertheless be changed into another nature entirely different from its own. For no reason compel me to maintain that the body does not die unless it is changed into a corpse.

And, indeed, experience seems to urge a different conclusion. Sometimes a man undergoes such changes that I should have hardly said he was the same man. I have heard stories, for example, of a Spanish poet who suffered an illness, though he recovered he was left so oblivious to his past life that he did not believe the tales and tragedies he had written were his own. He could surely have been taken for a grown-up infant if he had also forgotten his native language.

If this seems incredible, what shall we say of infants? A man of advanced years believes their nature to be so different from his own that he could not be persuaded that he ever was an infant, if he did not make this conjecture concerning himself from the example of others. But rather than providing the superstitious with material for raising new questions, I prefer to leave this discussion unfinished.

FRIDAY, 3 MAY 2002

Non-sense then, senseful now: The Garden of Forking Paths. How many times have I read this story, rehearsed this story, gone through this story before?

'... Their publication was senseless. The book is an indeterminate heap of contradictory drafts. I examined it once in the third chapter the hero dies, in the fourth he is alive...'

(Fleeing vs. advancing: A meditation on the difference between the two.)

The Garden of Forking Paths

"Absorbed in these illusory images I forgot my destiny of one pursued..."

muses the German spy Dr. Yu Tsun in his effort to communicate to his chief in Berlin the location of the English artillery. Yu Tsun flees from Captain Richard Maaden but not in the hope of escaping. For he realises that thus is ultimately hopeless, that Captain Maaden is 'implacable' in his quest No, Yu Tsun flees his adversary in order to advance, to send two messages, one to his superior, the second to his confessor, the reader: 'The author of an atrocious undertaking ought to imagine that he has already accomplished it, ought to impose upon himself a future as irrevocable as the past'. By means of a single radical gesture, always keeping to the left, Yu Tsun arrives at the center of the labyrinth, repeating/completing the radical gesture of his fore-father.

Jalal Toufic writes in Over-Sensitivity

"We may at times flee out allies, those that acknowledge our aparté, to friends, those who put it aside (friends put us aside in the room set aside, the guest room. This room set aside, where the guests replace each other, sometimes presupposes that other room, also set aside, but now locked, that of the dead. a room where all intermingle and replace the dead. They put him aside in the room set aside, the guest room so they would not have to hear what is really set aside, put in reserve, the aparté), and who are thus the in-between on a line stretching from allies to most people"

Aparte: the whispering voice, the scholium. Strange sounds from the strange apartment next door

'In every one,' I pronounced, not without a tremble to my voice, 'I am grateful to you and revere you for your re-creation of the garden of Ts'ui Pên.'

'Not in all,' he murmured with a smile. 'Time forks perpetually towards innumerable futures. In one of them I am your enemy.'

www.alamut.com/subj/subject_index.html

ALAMUT
BASTION OF PEACE AND INFORMATION

SUBJECT INDEX

Present
Past
Subjects
Projects
Misc

www.latenightpool.com/people60.html

www.latenightpool.com

www.latenightpool.com/cidade.html

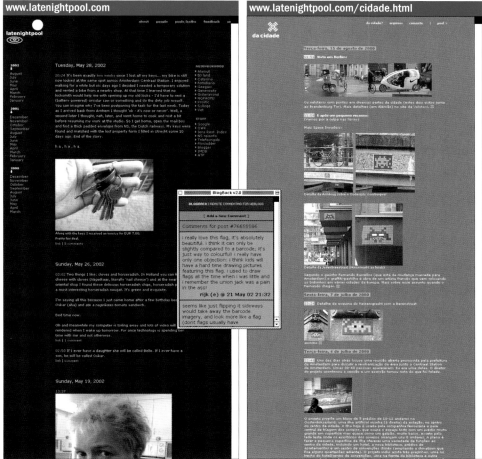

www.latenightpool.com
www.latenightpool.com/cidade.html

Late-Night Pool
content, design_Rogério Lira,
Amsterdam, NL
on line_2000

Another foreigner in the Netherlands, Brazilian graphic designer Rogério Lira maintains two blogs 'between the Centraal Station in Amsterdam and Avenida Paulista, in São Paulo', where he was born. 'Late-Night Pool' is written in English and works as a personal archive with notes on 'memories, swimming pools, dreams and transformation, and about the experience of being a foreigner in Holland and Europe'. The Portuguese-language blog ('da cidade') is about his experience of design and other means of communication in the public space in a variety of cities and is full of snapshots taken from a 'pedestrian point of view'. The two serve their author as a bridge between two continents and two cultures, and the visual focus of the Brazilian version, as Lira confesses, has to do with 'a certain distancing or estrangement' in using his native language. Made using Blogger software (see p. 170), they show both kinship and variance in their typography, treatment of links and pictures and interactivity (Lira frequently uses the information that appears on mouseover as a chance to add hidden commentary to a picture or link). Both sites testify to Blogger's flexibility and a structural part of the design of such sites must therefore be credited to the software designers. The 'neighbourhood' is another important element of blogs, which is apparent in Lira's prominent placement of his 'pool of people', a world-spanning network that meets on a daily basis via blogs and occasionally face-to-face in Amsterdam or other places.

137

www.linesandsplines.com

Lines and splines

content, design_Andy Crewdson,
Washington DC, US

on line_2000–02

Graduating in history from Berkeley University, California, Andy Crewdson became fascinated by typography and decided to share his growing awareness and knowledge with the world at large. Thus originated one of the most encompassing and concise blogs about a specific subject the web has ever known. In Crewdson's modest description, the blog was 'a way for me to loosely organize the typography-related things tumbling around in my head. Sometimes I just post observations, other times I provide links to things I've been enjoying.' The title is derived from the two main typographic forms: lines and curves. Considering the wealth of information and news on this blog, you could add that the splines represent Crewdson's steep learning curves. The type aficionado resolutely refuses to be called a designer, but of course his blog is carefully constructed, with a periodically changing masthead and layout evidence of its maker's joy in things typographic. Too bad that Crewdson decided to stop his diary in May 2002, a step that was widely mourned in typographic circles. Crewdson's new site, www.new-series.org, will collect his future articles on things typographic.

www.linesandsplines.com

Lines & Splines

Send mail

- - - -

CHART

1. Times Europa
2. IBM Selectric Classified News
3. Linotype Modern
4. Plantin Semibold
5. Eyes-down
6. *London Review* Quadraat
7. URW Grotesk

- - - -

ARCHIVES

[Select: ▼]

- - - -

$ooooh no: embedding brouhaha makes the front page of slashdot.

- - - -

Het Plantin Genootschap

- - - -

Some information from Gerard Unger about Capitolium & Vesta (both can be seen here)

- - - -

I FOUND THE FOLLOWING REVIEW HELPFUL: 'My friend is named Dan and he really likes this book. He first showed it to me outside during recess. We are both only 13 . If I had to chose over either this Ed Ruscha book or a Sega dream cast, playstation 2, alot of chocolate, a gun that looked real but wasn't, but felt real cause it was so heavy, I would choose the gun, probably because I couldn't get a gun now(I am not 21) and because none of my friends have ever seen a gun, it would be cool. But I still would like to flip through this book, but I don't know if I'd buy it, especially with my own money.'

www.linesandsplines.com

Lines & ſplines

Monday, July 23

¶ I've had good luck finding things in used books lately. A few weeks ago I got a very cheap (and in very good condition) copy of the van Krimpen *Letter to Philip Hofer* (printed letterpress at Enschedé with Spectrum on custom-made Dutch paper, designed by Sem Hartz & Bram de Does). In the back of the book was a receipt from Godine, the publishers, dated October 30, 1972 (when the book came out). The receipt is made out to Ed Foss, 'Designer — University Press of Virgina.' Ed got a special $3 discount on the book and on the receipt is a handwritten note — I'm guessing it was written by Godine himself in blue ink: 'Ed — hope you like it. Take care — keep in touch. Best.' I guess Ed didn't like it that much since it ended up at an obscure book store (or maybe he died and it was sold off, more likely).
And then today I picked up a $2.50 reprint of an article from the *Penrose Annual* (1951) about W.A. Dwiggins. It was written by Jackson Burke (forgot about Aurora), Chauncey Griffith's successor at Merganthaler, and came with a great four-page Caledonia specimen (no matter how many times I look at them,

www.linesandsplines.com

POSTONI
In 1995 Michael Keegan, Assistant Managing Editor of The Washington Post, began a redesign of the paper 'as an important improvement, not a radical change.' In commissioning a new headline type he told me: 'The Post has historically been a Bodoni newspaper and there is a desire to stay that way.' There was also a desire to keep the convention of 'up-style' headlines, in which every single word began with a capital letter. The version of Bodoni then in use at The Post, a derivative of ATF's at several removes, had very prominent capitals. The purpose of Postoni (the working nickname that eventually stuck) was to condense the face slightly and make the x-height larger so that the caps would combine more harmoniously with the lowercase. Two weights of Roman were produced, and two of Italic — The Post uses italic headlines more than most newspapers — with the overall aim of making a headline face 'a little more friendly, a little less rigid than other Bodonis.'
In the end the redesign took longer than expected. In the course of it Postoni was tested by focus groups of readers and by outside consultants. I was nervous about this, but no significant changes were called for. The redesign was launched on March 2, 1998. Michael sent me a copy with the message 'Postoni lives and breathes!'

VINCENT
In 1792 Vincent Figgins cut a roman for the body of Two-Line English (about 26-point). It came about in an odd manner. Part-way through the printing of a folio Bible in roman volume or home in 1780 completed in 1800 Joseph

www.linesandsplines.com/mercury.gif

Lucinda Williams

With its tranced-out amnesiac, oddball diners, and weird doings by sinister m with physical or sartorial peculiarities, a

www.linesandsplines.com/carter3.html

Man Who Laughs :
Dead on Revival

POSTONI BOLD
Making a Better Sell
of Treasury Securities

POSTONI ITALIC
On the Edge of

The private playing ground of web designer Robin Garms, 'Star of the East' is named after a former pub

www.staroftheeast.com/pages/galleries/...

www.staroftheeast.com/pages/galleries/...

www.staroftheeast.com/pages/numbers/helix.html

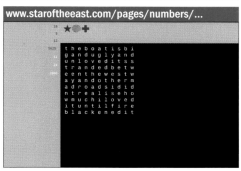

www.staroftheeast.com/pages/numbers/helix.html

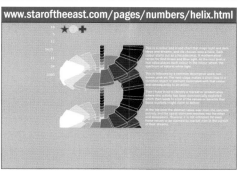

www.staroftheeast.com/pages/numbers/...

www.staroftheeast.com/pages/numbers/...

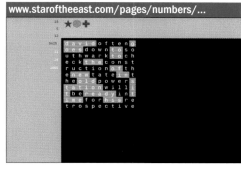

www.staroftheeast.com/pages/words/awards.htm

www.staroftheeast.com/pages/menu/...

www.staroftheeast.com

Star of the East

content, design_Robin Garms, London, UK
on line_1999

The private playing ground of web designer Robin Garms, 'Star of the East' is named after a former pub. Garms's interest in details becomes evident when he explains, 'The "shopfront" of the pub was painted gold with the name in red-oxide paint that when translated into hexadecimals, gives a deep-yellow background and dark-red type'. Precisely the basic colours of the site. However, even if every detail of the site's design has been thought through intensely, the result is 'intended to be as minimal as possible', with simple navigation devices, plain colour and a stern rectangular lay-out. The site's mystery resides in the contrast between its clear and simple design and the almost complete lack of background information regarding its content. What are these pictures about? What do the numbers mean? Who made these strange drawings? Who is this guy, and why am I visiting his site? Well, I don't recall how I got there, but I bookmarked the site because the writing is good and intelligent, the pictures are intriguing and there are a few little Flash experiments that I like very much. One such experiment is '11'; within the space of eleven-by-eleven small squares, letters shift very quickly on each of the 121 positions, freezing, when clicked and held, to form a text in which the words are divided by colour. How many texts can you write with exactly 121 letters and no spaces? 'Star of the East' screens many such small mysteries, which in the words of its maker are of 'the kind of obscurity that I have been prone to shroud my work in and that staroftheeast.com is intended to remedy in its simplicity'.

139

Based in Vancouver, Canada, Adbusters is a magazine, a website, a non-profit campaigning agency, and a way of life

Adbusters

client_Adbusters Media Foundation, Vancouver, British Columbia, CA
design_Jeff Harris, Adbusters
on line_1997

Based in Vancouver, British Columbia, Canada, Adbusters is a magazine, a website, a non-profit campaigning agency, and a way of life: 'a global network of artists, activists, writers, pranksters, students, educators and entrepreneurs who want to advance the new social activist movement of the information age'. Their strategy is called 'culture jamming', with 'jamming' referring to both obstruction and collaborative improvisation. The aim is if not to completely overthrow the whole damn cabal of consumerist propaganda called advertising then at least to jam it into a deeply uncomfortable hiccup. One way of achieving this is through 'uncommercials'; 'Obsession Fetish', for instance, takes Calvin Klein's anorexic look to its apparent pathological conclusion by showing a nude model on her knees in the bathroom throwing up into the toilet bowl.

Among the campaigns initiated or sponsored by Adbusters is the re-issue of the 'First Things First' design manifesto. Echoing the call to responsibility first expressed by British designer Ken Garland in 1964, the much debated 2000 version urges designers to dedicate their talents and resources to better causes than churning out slick packaging for gourmet dog food and the like. Adbusters' initiator

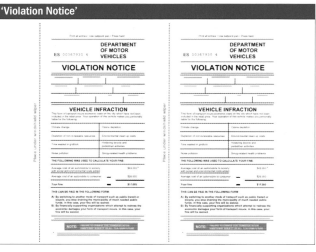

To help do just that, the site provides a 'toolbox' for each Adbusters campaign

www.adbusters.org/magazine/40/psychology/2.html

ADBUSTERS CAMPAIGNS MAGAZINE SPOOF ADS UNCOMMERCIALS ORDERS ? INFO

#40 Mar / Apr 2002

Psychology of Submission
Resistance
Intimidation
Everyday Life
Imperialism

BUY NOTHING DAY
BND Update 2001
What's in store for 2002
Debate

REDESIGN
When History Looks
Back
Psycho Design

A. Modern nation-building begins with loans, but only to plant the seeds of freedom. Privatization is the place to start. As a condition of any international loan, the debtor nation should immediately put up for sale its social services, government-owned industries and public infrastructure. This makes space for new investment. If a weak democracy is going to succeed, its government will need strong ties to successful corporations –

www.adbusters.org/magazine/437/nature/3.html

secure.adbusters.org/orders/posters/

www.adbusters.org/...

www.adbusters.org/...

www.adbusters.org/...

www.adbusters.org/...

www.adbusters.org/...

and guru Kalle Lasn reinvigorates activist instincts that are still lingering among the mass of DTP and agency workers in the design and advertising business when he incites them to 'turn the drab number cruncher you're staring at right now into the most versatile activist tool ever reckoned with'. To help do just that, the site provides a 'toolbox' for each Adbusters campaign, with downloadable posters, banners and bumperstickers. Obviously, the goal is not so much to make our visual environment less crowded with messages, but to redress the balance with critical stings. Although Adbusters has been accused of fighting its enemy by adopting the very same manipulative media approach, one thing is sure: Adbusters proves that design can make an intelligent, witty and serious difference when using the media for critical campaigning.

'The digerati meet the literati' on the Internet at 'Alt-X'

www.altx.com

Alt-X Network

client_Alt-X Digital Arts Foundation,
Boulder, CO, US
design_Mark Amerika, Joel Swanson,
among others
on line_1993

'The digerati meet the literati' on the Internet at 'Alt-X'. The site's initiator, net.artist Mark 'I link, therefore I am' Amerika, states that from its inception 'our primary mission has been to challenge the art and literary publishing establishments by supporting some of the most iconoclastic voices and visions in contemporary art and writing'. Alt-X's 'Virtual Imprints' section brings web readers classics from the recent past and anthologies of current work, available to print out, read on screen or on a Palm Pilot. There are some interesting experiments with words and images on the site, such as the funny typographic play on Ben Benjamin's 'What Would Abraham Lincoln Want To Say To Us Today?', or 'The Body', a hypertext by Shelly Jackson with an interactive drawing as the main interface, but mostly the work is rather illustrative. More experimental work is found in the 'Alt-X Audio' section, where audio-streams and downloadable MP3 files are collected into 'concept albums'. The design of the site still favours text, as may be expected from iconoclasts ;-) Browsing the site's content, it becomes clear that it has been around for quite a while; as Amerika says, 'Bits and pieces of the site are older designs. ... Which brings up a question, should we just always change the look and feel of the site to accommodate new conditions?'. Maybe not: like the collected pieces, the site's interface and the design of its contents are of their time.

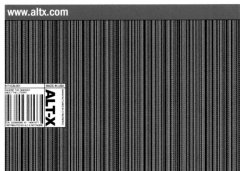

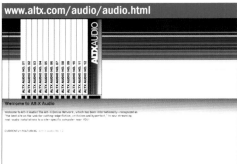

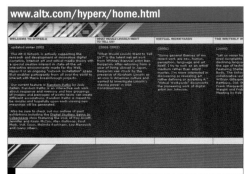

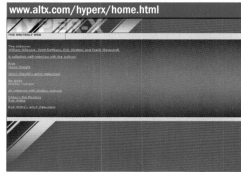

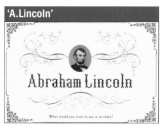

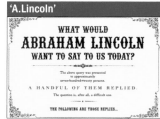

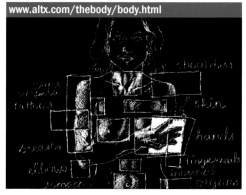

142

Associated with 'Alt-X', the 'Electronic Book Review' is an interesting web of critical debates

www.electronicbookreview.com

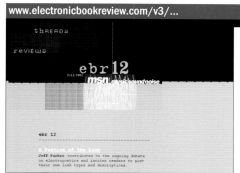

www.electronicbookreview.com/v3/...

www.electronicbookreview.com

Electronic Book Review

design_Anne Burdick, Ewan Branda,
among others
on line_1995
redesign_2001

Associated with 'Alt-X', the 'Electronic Book Review' is an interesting web of critical debates on 'electronic textuality, cyberculture, and the value of digital design literacy for scholarship and critical writing on the web'. EBR's new interface (version 3) connects the database of essays, reviews, experiments and discussions that have been added over the past couple of years. The interface has been designed as an application: it links articles once the reader has made the initial step of searching for a specific title, author, topic or thread. The 'weave' function exemplifies the idea of the database as a textile made from interlinking threads. The interface facilitates many ways of ordering and accessing the contents, like a virtual loom that weaves different patterns each time you choose a different perspective. 'Ideally I'd be designing myself out of my job as it's currently defined', comments designer Anne Burdick, pointing to the fact that, once realized, the application principally takes care of 'laying out the pages'. This is another sign that designers for the web are redefining their jobs: instead of executing the formal appearance of a communication product, they merely define the basic editorial structure of its elements. The formal expression of these 'elements' then becomes a one-off, and the designer is done once the application is in place; after that, it is up to the authors, editors and other content providers.

www.electronicbookreview.com/v3/servlet/ebr?command=view_weave

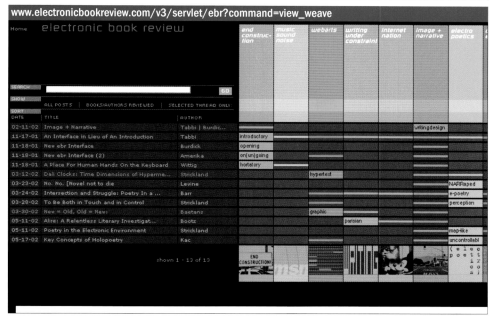

143

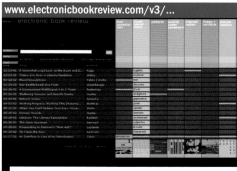

www.electronicbookreview.com/v3/...

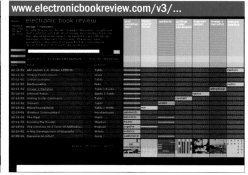

www.electronicbookreview.com/v3/...

www.electronicbookreview.com/v3/...

www.electronicbookreview.com/v3/...

Among the most successful examples of using the web as a community communication tool are the Independent Media Centers

www.indymedia.org

Independent Media Centers

design_anonymous

on line_1999

Among the most successful examples of using the web as a community communication tool are the Independent Media Centers (IMCs), the first of which sprung up in 1999 to provide 'grassroots coverage of the World Trade Organization (WTO) protests in Seattle' (seattle.indymedia.org). IMCs – there are dozens now worldwide – combine the characteristics of news agencies, multinational action centres and online discussion forums in a decidedly multimedia setting. The websites function as news media in their own right, but, at the same time, are part of a media mix that comprises a weekly print publication disseminated as PDF files (print.indymedia.org), a radio station (radio.indymedia.org) and the 'Indymedia' newsreel that can be viewed on line or via satellite television (satellite.indymedia.org). A network of collectively run media outlets, IMCs are open for anyone to publish stories and commentary, which essentially delegates the task of assessing and editing the information to the public using the sites.

The interface is geared at facilitating the triple role of the visitor as reader, editor and author of information

www.indymedia.nl

jerusalem.indymedia.org/news/

colombia.indymedia.org

italy.indymedia.org

uk.indymedia.org

sf.indymedia.org

nyc.indymedia.org

france.indymedia.org

www.tijuanaimc.org

rockymountain.indymedia.org

www.indymedia.ie

nigeria.indymedia.org

www.vaikuttava.net

www.ucimc.org

satellite.indymedia.org

radio.indymedia.org

print.indymedia.org

www.protest.net/imc-meetings

The interface is geared at facilitating the triple role of the visitor as reader, editor and author of information, with simple forms and extended tutorials to assist the ad-hoc journalist. IMCs are typically DTPed sites, and most of them in one way or another use the basic templates and interface developed on the original Seattle site. Design subtlety or formal consistency is of less importance than the smooth flow of information and ease of access. A team of dedicated volunteers makes sure the software and databases that the system runs on remain reliable. In terms of contributors, range of media, global coverage and reach, IMCs collectively resemble the large-scale news agencies they seek to check and balance. The main difference is the absence of a central organization, base or policy, making IMCs the news equivalent of such open-source projects as Linux. In both, the networked development of tools and content is challenging the older hierarchical and commercial models of development and dissemination.

Within days of the devastating terrorist attacks on 11 September 2001, this page appeared on a host of US websites

Thank You

on line_2001

Within days of the devastating terrorist attacks on the World Trade Center and the Pentagon on 11 September 2001, this page, in several versions, appeared on a host of US websites. A single page with slight variations in montage and choice of images; no credits, no source, just the simple headline, 'a heartfelt thank you'. No explanation needed, the pictures tell the story. Opening with a view of the European Union's flags at half-mast on the square before its headquarters in Brussels, over sixty photos show how the world paid its respect to the victims. A young man in black leather with a green Mohawk-style haircut brings flowers to an improvised shrine before the American embassy in Berlin, an old man kneels to do the same in Moscow, a woman cries and raises an American flag in London, two fashionable girls sob over flowers in Jerusalem, an old man in Chile holds a poster saying 'No al terrorismo', a Muslim girl lights a candle. These pages demonstrate the simplest and fastest use of the web as a community tool: no design, just content.

a heartfelt thank you

A pictorial tribute from around the World

For an exhaustive overview of web materials devoted to 9/11, visit this site

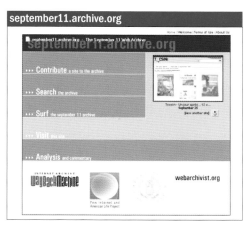

september11.archive.org

september11.archive.org

september11.archive.org/search.plx

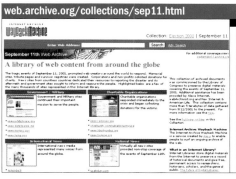

web.archive.org/collections/sep11.html

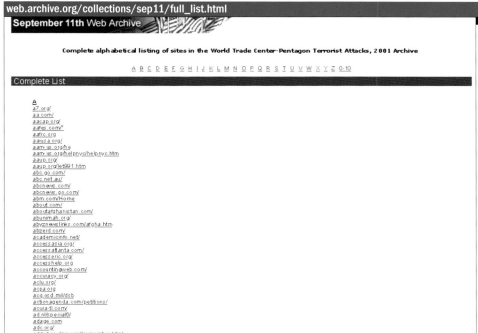

web.archive.org/collections/sep11/full_list.html

september11.archive.org

September 11 Archive

client, development_WebArchivist.org, Internet Archive, Library of Congress, Washington DC, US
on line_2001

For an exhaustive overview of web materials devoted to 9/11, visit this site. The 'September 11 Archive' is a highly laudable collaboration among the 'Internet Archive', 'WebArchivist.org' and the Library of Congress, who commissioned the archive and organized its collection and development. Only hours after the attacks the collecting activities started, with people around the world contributing URLs. The well-designed interface allows visitors to search or surf the archive containing thousands of URLs, to browse through randomly generated thumbnails of collected sites and to contribute new sites. The browse facility is especially fascinating; site after site of picture galleries, news digests, discussion forums and personal accounts from an enormous variety of sources testify that this is an illimitable subject. The web has become a fairly sophisticated means of communication – the distributed high-resolution photo resource that was in place within hours of the attacks was unthinkable only a few years ago. Maybe the most valuable consequence of the web as communication channel, however, is that its many individual threads together weave a tapestry of great informational *and* therapeutic value for those who participate in making it and for those who browse the results. We may never fully understand why 9/11 happened, but we certainly know what it meant for thousands of people around the globe who were, or felt, affected. Archiving such a body of material is an act of immeasurable cultural importance.

147

US provider Inter.net dedicated this site to 'those affected by the September 11, 2001, attack on our country'

mystory.inter.net

My Story

design_Inter.net, Veston, VA, US

on line_2001

US provider Inter.net dedicated this site to 'those affected by the September 11, 2001, attack on our country'. In a virtually un-designed but well-balanced layout, hundreds of people remember where they were and what they did when the news broke. Some are touching in their concise simplicity, and some are among the most detailed and gruesome 'live reports' I have heard, seen or read. Guy Miller from Cincinnati, Ohio meticulously, and almost obsessively avoiding any sign of stylistic enhancement, recounts what happened on the day he went to New York for a conference on the fan business. Miller records the minutest details of his ordeal – the kind of detail that makes you shiver: 'the top section of the tower seemed to be collapsing in on itself from the bottom up. There was the sound of floor hitting floor in rapid succession. It sounded like an earthquake above the ground. With each floor being a square acre, thousands of tons of concrete and steel were shedding out from the sides of the tower as it came down, falling into the streets, filling up the area at the base of the tower with debris.' With this and many other accounts, the site becomes what its initiators intended it to be, a virtual memorial that will remain up indefinitely.

mystory.inter.net

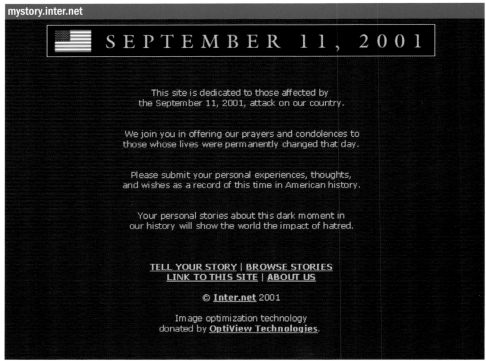

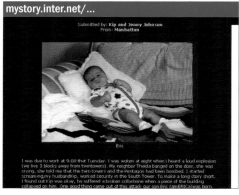

In an account on 'My Story', a New Yorker registers with alarm that her favourite Afghan restaurant has barricaded its windows

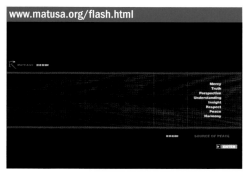

www.matusa.org/flash.html

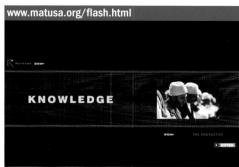

www.matusa.org/flash.html

KNOWLEDGE

www.matusa.org/flash.html

UNDERSTANDING

www.matusa.org/flash.html

ALLAH = GOD = DIOS = ALLAH

MUSLIMS AGAINST TERRORISM

www.matusa.org/home.asp

www.matusa.org/aboutus.asp

www.matusa.org/education.asp

www.matusa.org/faq.asp

www.matusa.org

Muslims Against Terrorism
client_Muslims AGAINST Terrorism (MAT)
development, design_Rayhawk Systems,
Freddy Venegas (Motion Graphics), Han
Haque (Creative Director & Producer)
on line_2001

In an account on 'My Story', a New Yorker registers with alarm that her favourite Afghan restaurant on the Lower Eastside of Manhattan has barricaded its windows and crossed out the word 'Afghan' on its display panel, obviously afraid that enraged citizens would assault the place. A more defiant but no less cautious response comes from the 'Muslims Against Terrorism' initiative, which in plain English asserts that 'Terrorism is an act against God, not for Him'. A truism, but after 9/11 nothing seems certain any more. Be that as it may, this site is a blessing for those who always wanted to know more about Islam but were afraid to ask. In a few well-laid-out pages, a choice of pointers, sources and quotes from the Qur'an go beyond soothing the minds of frightened infidels, not avoiding interpretation problems that may arise from citations like, 'and if you do respond to an attack, respond no worse than they did'. This is not a site for those who look for quick, simple answers (although even they will find some functional one liners), but a portal that serves open and mature communication between people of different creeds who agree on at least one thing: that they should not smash each others' heads in to obliterate their disputes. That this opinion is not so common in our daily existence may be deduced from the section on hate crimes, which complements the site's very balanced resource on Islam.

149

The idea to make an online memorial to the victims of 9/11 is also behind 'I Remember the Towers'

www.irememberthetowers.com

I Remember the Towers

client, design_David Gomez-Rosado,
New York, US

on line_2001

The idea to make an online memorial to the victims of 9/11 is also behind 'I Remember the Towers', a site created by David Gomez-Rosado who aims to rebuild 'the Towers out of memories'. Forming the two towers from two-thousand small cubes, each one intended to represent a memory about the structures when they were still standing, the two archetypal buildings are being built up anew in this virtual shrine. Again, some of the entries are chilling in their simplicity, such as the one in which a woman leaves the names of her two friends and the number of the floor they died on. Gomez-Rosado gives an account of the damage in the language of an information architect – behind the 'Towers' link at the bottom of the interface there are a few effective and ghastly infographics, measuring out the lost lives as 10-by-10-pixel thumbnails of faces, stacked in the rectangular form of one of the towers and in the shape of the aeroplanes. It takes a couple of seconds before you finish scrolling down the towers, about the same time it took the real ones to crumble. Although not finished, witness the links that have not been filled in (apparently intended for information on the architect of the World Trade Center and a timeline of the events), this is a very well-designed site that shows the power of good information graphics, alongside the emotional impact of personal accounts. A rare concord between statistics and stories.

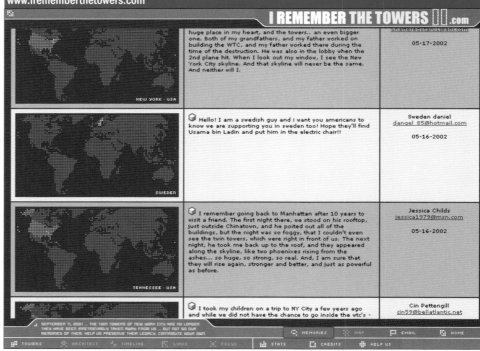

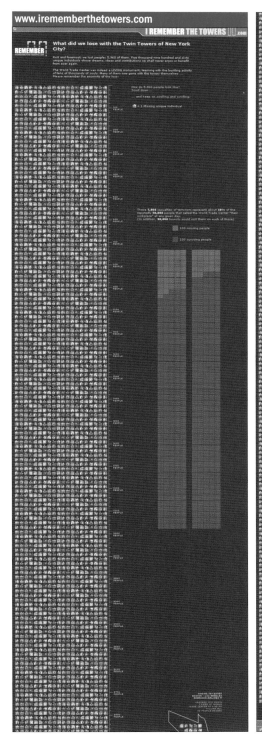

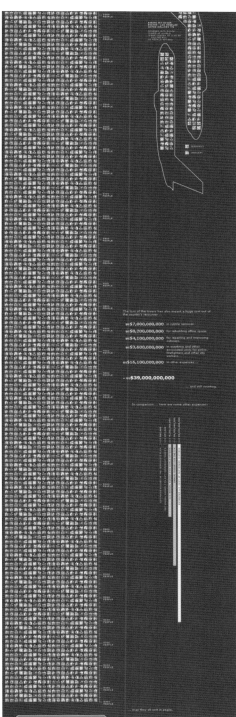

On the web, the error message '404' indicates 'File Not Found'; thus, visitors may assume that Flight 404 was lost

www.flight404.com

Flight 404

design_Robert Hodgin, Boston, MA, US
on line_2000, 2002

On the web, the error message '404' indicates 'File Not Found'; thus, visitors may assume that Flight 404 was lost. This is a narrative site about the fictional disappearance of a commercial airliner off the coast of Canada on 6 September 2001. It appeared on line after 11 September 2001, but its maker, web designer Robert Hodgin, insists that the story was conceived prior to the terrorist attacks and has nothing to do with them. In fact, the site is a radical upgrade of what started off as a portfolio for its author, who explains, 'The problem with portfolio sites is that it is too easy to make them look generic. ... What I hope to see more of in the future are <u>portfolio sites that have a sense of personality</u>'[1]. Hodgin's site certainly has personality and provides a lively form of collaborative story telling; the investigation and the database of Flight 404's passengers grow at parallel levels, illustrated or accompanied by animated images and associated Flash movies. The story is evolving with help from colleagues and contributors from around the world who have reacted to Hodgin's call for assistance in solving the enigma of Flight 404's disappearance. Akin to the *X-Files* in terms of suspense and mystification, the site features a good deal of Flash 5 experiments that demonstrate its author's skills, all contained within a very clear and balanced screen design.

1_www.netspace.net.au/lookout/archive/0009

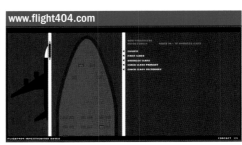
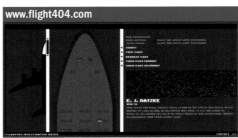

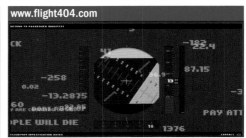

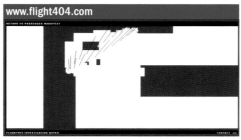

'I'd like to apologise for all this' reads the opening line keyed in by a nameless figure

www.nobodyhere.com/justme

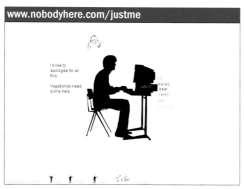

www.nobodyhere.com/justme

www.nobodyhere.com/justme/mister.php3

www.nobodyhere.com/justme/do.php3

www.nobodyhere.com/justme/...

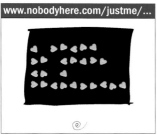

www.nobodyhere.com/justme/...

www.nobodyhere.com/justme/...

www.nobodyhere.com/justme/...

www.nobodyhere.com/justme/...

www.nobodyhere.com/justme/...

www.nobodyhere.com/justme/...

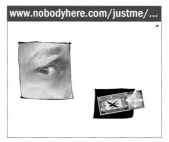

www.nobodyhere.com/justme/...

www.nobodyhere.com/justme/...

www.nobodyhere.com/justme

Just Me
content, design_anonymous
on line_2000

'I'd like to apologise for all this' reads the opening line keyed in by a nameless figure typing away at his computer. Not very confident, this guy – a latter-day version of Austrian writer Robert Musil's *Mann ohne Eigenschaften* (*The Man Without Qualities*). Running the mouse randomly across key words or clicking on hot words or pictures, you gradually gain an insight into the vexed soul of this rather old young man. If it were not for the wit and humour with which his anonymous author portrays him, he would be boring. The site is full of epigrammatic observations, funny games with small images and examples of practical *Weltanschauung* like 'Theory of Relative Happiness' – 'depress yourself and in the relief following that depression, you will experience an overwhelming sense of bliss'. Such refined logic shows a keen awareness of postmodern philosophy on the part of the author. For all its apparent simplicity of design, however, the site's pages are well coded, and visitors gradually appreciate the nifty little surprises hidden behind small images or texts; an appreciation that is shared and can be expressed in the site's commentary section, which has grown into a community of fans. With this kind of interaction and playfulness, the quality of the writing and the consistency of myriad internal links, this is one of the best hypertexts I have seen so far.

153

Since its inception, the Internet has been used as an environment for playing games

| www.unrealtournament.com |
| www.planetunreal.com |
| utbooty.unrealism.com |
| aut.unrealism.com |
| www.utonline.kolayweb.com |
| dynamic3.gamespy.com/~identitycrisis |

Unreal Tournament Online
client, design_Epic Games
on line_1999

| www.sega.com/sega/game/
pso_launch.jhtml |
| www.phantasy-star.net/pso |
| www.maidencircuit.com/home.html |
| www.geocities.com/o2pso |

Phantasy Star Online
client, design_SEGA
on line_1999

| www.counter-strike.net |

Counter Strike (MOD for Half-Life)
design_Minh 'Gooseman' Le, 'Cliffe',
among others
on line_2000

Since its inception, the Internet
has been used as an environment
for playing games, from translations of single-player 'arcade'
games to multi-user online games.
Vibrant virtual communities have
sprung up on the web not just in
the gaming environments themselves, but in ntricate networks
of sometimes hundreds of con-
current websites. With computers
and connections becoming faster,
the graphic quality of the games
has improved and so has the
gamut of actions and roles; apart
from fighting your enemies (still
the best part of player activity in
most games) in ever-growing
detail, you can team up in various
ways and construct additions to
the environment. From a visual
design viewpoint, many games are
rather bland, but this ongoing virtual carnage does result in an ever-
expanding afterlife that unfolds in
myriad sites on rules, actions,
cheats (short cuts in the game),
patches (scripts for solving software bugs in the game), maps

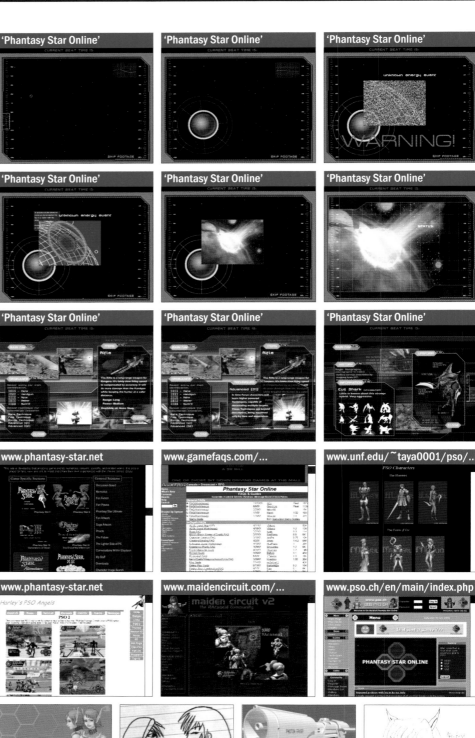

The fact that a gamer can actually make their own addition to the content, form and action of the game is telling

'Unreal Tournament'

'Unreal Tournament'

'Unreal Tournament'

'Unreal Tournament'

www.unrealtournament.com/global/gameplay.html

www.utonline.kolayweb.com/...

www.bagpipes.net/ut

www.planetunreal.com

utbooty.unrealism.com

dynamic3.gamespy.com/...

aut.unrealism.com

www.counter-strike.net

www.counter-strike.net

'Counter Strike Italy'

'Counter Strike Italy'

'Counter Strike Italy'

(3-D story environments) and sounds. The fact that a gamer can actually make their own addition to the content, form and action of the game is telling; they are not just playing, they are creating, changing and directing the game as it progresses.

In 'Unreal Tournament', players can add their own levels using the 'Unreal Engine' to model and make characters, weapons and environments. The game's scenery consists of numerous battle locations, and code-savvy gamers can add their own scenes with the help of tutorial sites (such as unreal-ized.com), which guide them – up to a point – into acting as co-developers. Another feature allows players to round up an army of co-players (or bots) and to fight collectively in games like 'Team Death Match' or 'Capture the Flag'. Such authorial and collaborative elements of online games place the players on a – virtually – equal level as the game designers. Virtually, because the ground rules have been set and the design and software standards have been defined. Within such rules a wide expanse of creativity can unfold, a large part of which is fan art; see, for example, 'Phantasy Star Net', a site devoted to SEGA's roleplaying game. A group of fan sites has sprung up around this game, too, including sites that denounce offensive players as 'thieves' and the special-interest group 'Maiden Circuit', which promotes the female 'RAcaseal' character in the game. In these and similar games, like the war game 'Counter Strike', players can leave their own tags, or organize snapshots of each other between blood baths. This is the kind of kids' role play that used to be enacted on the street, but has now moved to the net where the virtual playground spans the universe – and beyond.

155

Very few communal activities on the web are capable of attracting so many dedicated believers in the new medium as game playing

everquestonlineadventures.station.sony.com

www.eqatlas.com

www.planeteq.com

www.eqclasses.com

eq.guildmagic.com

www.loralciriclight.com

www.allakhazam.com

www.healersunited.com

www.girlsgametoo.com

Everquest Online

client, design_Sony

on line_1999

Very few communal activities on the web are capable of attracting so many dedicated believers in the new medium as game playing; nowhere does this become more clear than in Massively Multiplayer Online Roleplaying Games (MMORPGS). 'Massively' is to be taken seriously here: a game like 'EverQuest Online' has a dedicated following of about 500,000 players worldwide. It is a fantasy world with an elaborate range of characters from a variety of races and castes, each with their own specific skills and assets. With a 'focus on exciting combat, questing and character development'[1], it is immersive in the most literal sense, so much so that its addictive features have earned it the nickname 'EverCrack'. The extent of playing modules and roles, the detailing and variability of the environment and action and the many ways of collaborative and social interaction make EverQuest a 'virtual community' that intensely intersects with the 'real world'. A recent survey concluded that EQ players spend on average 22.4 hours per week playing the game[2]. And, they gather also to spend additional time 'après gaming' on message boards and forums, making game-inspired fiction and art, updating blogs, meeting in online guilds and studying reference sites and sites dedicated to discussing strategy and role-playing for specific classes of characters[3].

156

www.eqatlas.com/qeynoscatacombsmap.html

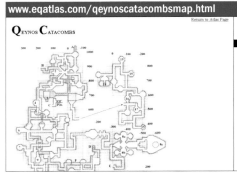

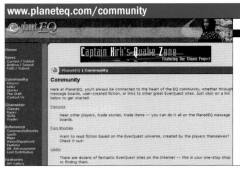

Players trade objects and services, they engage in enmity or romance, they fashion their appearance and environment

'Loral Last Inn'

'Loral Adjutant'

'Loral Charlies Healers'

'Loral Clicky'

'Loral Drak Wedding'

'Loral Raining Blood'

'Loral Thurg Bar'

'Loral Trick and Treat'

'EverQuest'

'EverQuest'

Players trade objects and services, they engage in enmity or romance, they fashion their appearance and environment; in short, they collectively create a fantasy world from the game's core design. A prime example of how the virtual world spawned by 'EverQuest' has expanded into an ongoing stream of stories, subplots and extensions, compared to which a TV soap is a one-liner, is 'Loral Ciriclight'[4]. His stories, illustrated with screen shots from the actual game, are another instance of coauthoring within the scope of the original game's gist.

The sites collected under 'girlsgametoo.com' show how close game life and real life can be – and how utterly distanced. The sites' author is called Eriste, a 'Level 20 Half Elf Rogue of Innoruuk', in 'EverQuest'; in real life, she is Julia Grimm, a 'girly-girl and nerd extraordinaire', who provides 'interior decoration' and character artwork for gamers and she keeps a log of the adventures of Eriste and Chretienne (her other 'EverQuest' character). For designers, such sites offer valuable information about the kinds of use, interactivity and social dynamics that are the yardsticks for the successful design of online communities. These characteristics cannot be underestimated at a time when the experience and scenario aspects of designing for the web are becoming increasingly essential to interface design at large. To paraphrase Voltaire, *il faut cultiver son site.*

1_Quote from the official EQO site, everquestonlineadventures.station.sony.com
2_Nicholas Yee's 'The Norrathian Scrolls' (version 2.5, 2001), a study of EverQuest at www.nickyee.com/eqt/home.html
3_See introduction to the 'Race Strategy Discussions' for the Half Elf at eqdb.allakhazam.com/strategy/races.html?race=2
4_See introduction to the Loral Ciriclight website, loralciriclight.com/about.html

Authoring

5.

Authoring
Authoring
Authoring
Authoring
Authoring

The web promises to thoroughly mix up the established hierarchies between authors (or content providers) and recipients (or users).

1_WYSIWYG is an acronym for 'What You See Is What You Get', indicating the making of a product in its preview mode when most of the code remains invisible. The functional elements of a site's structure are found in toolbars and menus where buttons and options trigger complex strings of code.

From the beginning, the web has been the ultimate in do-it-yourself. The first users were the professional software engineers that built it, but as soon as the web began to establish itself as a mass medium during the mid-1990s, computer-savvy non-professionals started to upload their own home-made pages. Now, a large part of the web's content comes from complete design amateurs. The use of the web as a popular communications medium is interesting in several ways from a design perspective. First, the fact that design dilettantes can make websites is in itself telling; how many books, magazines or movies does the average family produce and publish? Today, it is not unusual for mom, dad and the kids (and sometimes their pets) to have their own homepages or weblogs. They can do this because publishing on the web is cheap – most providers offer disc space for homepages at no charge and free (or cheap) editor programs have been developed to make websites on the basis of the installed defaults. 'WYSIWYG'[1] web editors are a case in point, but even the more code-oriented HTML text editors nowadays come in versions that work mostly from menus, templates and wizards. This enables users to build a website without typing a single line of code; all you need is a basic understanding of such structural elements of HTML as tables, frames, links, properties and tags.

With such applications, using the web resembles making its contents – navigating the toolbars structurally resembles navigating a site. Instead of giving the web designer total control over the formal end result, control of the interfaces of these authoring applications is given primarily to the web author through the tools used to format the editorial structure (i.e., to manage the cohesion between texts, images, pages and links – much like a reader would do mentally). Obviously, average users are highly dependent on the aesthetic and interactive standards that are programmed into the software by the

Still, by stressing that 'off-the-shelf' software frees users from having to forge code or master the intricacies

designer. Still, by stressing that 'off-the-shelf' software frees users from having to forge code or master the intricacies of the communication between hardware and software, I want to point to a shift in creative focus from form to content, and thus – from a user's perspective – from visual design to editorial design. To summarize, popular tools for making websites permit users to concentrate on the web as an authoring medium.

This excursion into the characteristics of popular authoring applications intends to highlight an often overlooked implication of the word 'user', the generic term for anyone accessing a website[2]: on the web, the user is not a passive recipient, but in the most essential way a maker. Users make content, not just when they are creating websites themselves, but also when they are accessing sites compiled by others. In digital communication, the combination of computer and screen is the medium for both production and presentation, so the difference between making and experiencing, between sending and receiving becomes gradual instead of absolute[3]. This notion of the recipient as active coauthor of the content brings to mind Roland Barthes's distinction between 'readerly' and 'writerly' text; the latter implies readers have an active role in establishing the meaning of a text[4]. In much the same way, visitors to a website actively construct content by choosing their own paths through a (series of) pages, or frames as I've termed it above[5]. Making a website and navigating and experiencing its content become, to a certain extent, equivalent activities. From the perspectives of both users and designers, this amounts to a shift in attention regarding content on the web: to use a cinematic analogy, users are performers of the content – they are not passively watching the movie, they are participating in it. Moreover, they are focused on improvising on, instead of merely following up, clues. In this context, designers are functioning more as dramaturgists, directors and editors of the unfolding

2_ See note 1, p. 9.

3_'The screen keeps alternating between the dimensions of representation and control.' Lev Manovich, *The Language of New Media*, (Cambridge, MA: The MIT Press, 2001): 208. On the design consequences of this assertion in the context of computer games, Manovich says, 'I think that the opposition "representation" – "control" provides a practical challenge to artists and designers of new media. ... Traditional "noninteractive" narratives (books, movies) are more concerned with representation and narrative immersion, what can be called "narrative flow". In contrast, all real-time games, from tennis to "Unreal" require the user to exercise continuous control. So the challenge and promise of combining a traditional narrative form such as a movie with a game is how to combine the two logics of narrative flow and real-time control into a new aesthetics.' (Lev Manovich interviewed by Daniel Palmer in *Real Time*, Australia, July, 2001.)

4_'L'enjeu du travail littéraire (de la littérature comme travail), c'est de faire du lecteur, non plus un consommateur, mais un producteur du texte.' ('at stake in the literary work [in literature as work], is making the reader, no longer a consumer, but a producer of the text.'). Roland Barthes, *S/Z*, (Paris: Editions du Seuil, 1970): 10.

5_ See note 1, p. 93.

161

Ultimately, in interactive environments the roles of scriptwriter, director, actor and audience essentially overlap

6_'The subject is forced to oscillate between the roles of viewer and user, shifting between perceiving and acting, between following the story and actively participating in it.' Lev Manovich, *The Language of New Media*, (Cambridge, MA: The MIT Press, 2001): 207.

7_Plutarch, *Pompeius*, 50: 'We must sail' would be the most appropriate translation from the original context, but for our purposes we may translate it literally as 'it is necessary to navigate'.

8_'This all works only if each person makes links as he or she browses, so writing, link creation and browsing must be totally integrated.' Tim Berners-Lee's online publication *Design Issues*, 1990. www.w3.org/DesignIssues/Overview.html

9_'Presumably man's spirit should be elevated if he can better review his shady past and analyse more completely and objectively his present problems. He has built a civilization so complex that he needs to mechanize his record more fully if he is to push his experiment to its logical conclusion and not merely become bogged down part way there by overtaxing his limited memory. His excursion may be more enjoyable if he can reacquire the privilege of forgetting the manifold things he does not need to have immediately at hand, with some assurance that he can find them again if they prove important.' Vannevar Bush, 'As We May Think', *Atlantic Monthly*, July 1945. www.theatlantic.com/unbound/flashbks/computer/bushf.htm

10_'The human mind ... operates by association. With one item in its grasp, it snaps instantly to the next that is suggested by the association of thoughts, in accordance with some intricate web of trails carried by the cells of the brain. ... Memory is transitory. Yet the speed of action, the intricacy of trails, the detail of mental pictures, is awe-inspiring beyond all else in nature.' Vannevar Bush, 'As We May Think', *Atlantic Monthly*, July 1945. www.theatlantic.com/unbound/flashbks/computer/bushf.htm

narrative than as authors of the story or set dressers. Ultimately, in interactive environments the roles of scriptwriter, director, actor and audience essentially overlap[6].

'Navigare necesse est'[7] – this phrase by the classical author Plutarch is echoed by Vilém Flusser, in his book *Die Schrift* (1987), when he notes 'scribere necesse est' ('we must write'). The association Flusser makes between navigating and writing is no doubt intentional and demonstrates that the essence of interacting with information is to author your own – to use the power of the pen, as Flusser says. Extending Flusser's reasoning, you might say, 'navigating is writing'. On the web, authoring, publishing and accessing (formerly, 'reading') information is carried out, to a large extent, by linking (and not by writing)[8]. The idea that making and navigating links between associated information amounts to an authorial activity is at the heart of the computer medium and the Internet. As far back as 1945, Vannevar Bush had envisioned a machine that would help people record the 'trails' they made from one item of information to another[9]. These Memex machines, as Bush called them, embody a specific way of dealing with information, modelled on the way the brain functions and compensating for its weaknesses – we may have inadequate memories, but our associative (linking) powers are awesome[10].

Since the (online) computer has become embedded in the social fabric of human communication and interaction, Bush's dream of enabling people to record and retrieve their trails through assorted sites of information is an option open to everyone. The once mysterious tool for a caste of technological wizards has become a mundane commodity. On a cultural level, this 'socialization process' entails a remediation (see p. 14) of publishing technology, or, more accurately, a re-engineering of existing publication formats and technologies. For developers and designers of these types of authoring tools, it boils down to reverse

In older media, this is not the case – being able to operate a television set in no way implies the ability to make a TV programme

engineering: they have to embed the communicative behaviour that is the intended product of the application's use into the application itself. In older media, this is not the case – being able to operate a television set in no way implies the ability to make a TV programme. The experience of navigating websites, on the other hand, qualifies as the basic training in making them.

If this is the state of the medium, what then remains of the professional designer's role? What is the difference between editorial intuition facilitated by highly specialized but easy-to-use applications that solve design issues and a developed knowledge of design as a traditional craft? Frankly, this distinction is not so easy to establish anymore. This poses a problem for designers trained in a modernist tradition, where a design for a specific commission is viewed as a model, as an imminent reality, almost as an act of faith in which everything is predestined. In modernism, a design is not a proposal; it is a prescription[11]. As we have seen, the idea of design defining the end terms of a communication product is quite antithetical to web practice. Beyond problem-solving for clients who want to use the medium unilaterally, web designers must find ways to transmute the editorial core of design into visually viable and functional solutions.

This aim is at the heart of the design profession, for designers do have an edge when it comes to understanding the relationship between particular messages, visual languages, cultural contexts and communication media. On the web, they need to translate this experience in terms of dynamic behaviour of information, and not in the usual static form of immutable data. A deeper understanding of the transformation from what used to be readers or viewers in older media to users on the web can only be gained when recipients are recognized as coauthors, codirectors and performers of the information at hand. This also implies that designers are authors in their own right[12].

11_See also, Max Bruinsma, 'An Ideal Design is not Yet'. www.xs4all.nl/~maxb/ideal-e.html

12_'Every designer is an author, a publisher who, with every intervention, adds content to the bulk of exchanges, whether commissioned or not. There is always a commissioning voice, a commissioning tradition, a commissioning way of life. Design is content, attached to other content.' Jouke Kleerebezem, 2001.

In adding content to existing messages and in mapping paths between messages, designers represent and activate the 'potentia'

13_See, Andy Cameron, note 7, p. 129.

14_'By accepting the possibility of leaving a design open-ended, by up to a point not finishing it, the designer not only leaves room for the recipient's and reader's own interpretation of the message – an emancipatory aspect, this – he also creates the space for a personal standpoint. The design now suggests that this is how things might be – it opens a dialogue about the way it itself functions in the communication process of which it is a part.' Max Bruinsma, 'An Ideal Design is not Yet'. www.xs4all.nl/~maxb/ideal-e.html

15_'It is the editorial quality of the designer that determines whether the design enables the recipient of the message to make meaningful connections with the information culture of which the message is, whether we like it or not, a part.' Max Bruinsma, 'An Ideal Design is not Yet'. www.xs4all.nl/~maxb/ideal-e.html

In adding content to existing messages, in mapping paths between messages, in associating links between data, the interface and cultural contexts, designers represent and activate the 'potentia'[13] of the information they are communicating. Beyond composing the formal aesthetic surface of a site, designers formulate the confines – and the reach – within which visitors can move through the data landscape: the design of sites becomes the structuring of sites by design.

Templates, options, structures, mappings, flow, routes – these are the terms in which the fundamental open-endedness[14] of design for the web is expressed. How can designers work with these terms that define the medium if not from the perspective of the user as fellow designer? Analogous to the growing practice of multi-disciplinarity in developing new media products, designers have had to reinvent their role as being collaborative instead of definitive; feedback becomes the touchstone of design and design becomes the art of scripting for coauthors. Shaping sites of design – places with a purpose – within oceans of disparate data is the fundamental task designers for the web share with their fellow content providers. Their contribution as the primary visualizers of content may not be as exclusive as in older media, but, instead, graphic designers for the web have become application designers, designers of the conceptual tools with which we research, deepen and expand the visual languages we all read and write on the web[15].

Of the online applications that have rooted themselves in the very structure of the web, search engines are the most fundamental

www.google.com

Google

client_Google.com, Mountain View, CA, US

design_Google International

on line_1998

ixquick.com

Ixquick

client, design_Surfboard Holding BV, Amsterdam, NL

on line_1999

Of the online applications that have rooted themselves in the very structure of the web, search engines are the most fundamental. They have become much more than 'the online version of the perfect answering machine' as one analyst described them; if linking resembles writing, as I argue, then search engines are among the most important authorial tools on the web. Metasearch engines, like Google or Ixquick, can be great aids in compiling associated samples of the hypertext the web essentially is. They facilitate the forging of paths, or 'trails' <u>as Vannevar Bush called them</u>[1], through enormous masses of linked information. Regrettably, most search engines have suc-cumbed to the temptation of mak-ing money in ways that detract from their core business of index-ing information (clotting their pages with advertising), or that are seriously at odds with it (letting the index be biased toward paying customers). The latter, particularly, corrupts the 'relevancy rates' of search results. Nevertheless, the way search engines help filter, organize and access information exemplifies a fundamental condi-tion of the web: its referentiality. Writing a site's 'meta text' becomes a key part of authoring it. When making use of the web's ref-erential potential with the help of search engines, both users and designers are participating in authoring the web.

From a visual design perspective, most search engines are interesting only because of their highly specialized way of structuring

'Netscape Composer'

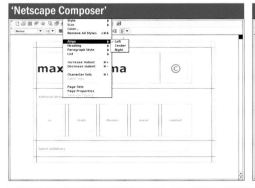

'Netscape Composer'

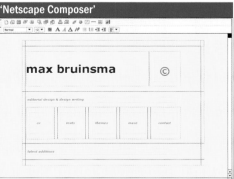

'Format'

'Format'

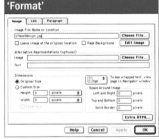

'Color Picker'

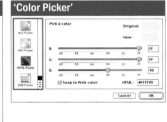

wp.netscape.com/browsers/using/...

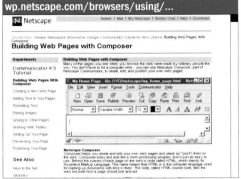

wp.netscape.com/browsers/using/...

vis-à-vis their product: is it an object or a service?

At no time in history has the sharing of ideas, opinions and expressions expanded so massively as today on the web. Literally millions of homepages publish the lives and times of 'ordinary' people around the globe; the community aspects of this publication bonanza have been explored in the previous chapter, but we should remind ourselves of the applications that have made this possible. One of the first to give complete amateurs the power to make and publish their own websites was Netscape Composer, a follow-up to the WYSIWYG editor incorporated into 'Netscape Navigator Gold 2.0' in 1995. Netscape was very early to recognize that the skill of using a browser was closely related to that of making webpages: once you can push a button on the screen to use a function, you can push a button to make it. The crux of the situation is to design the right buttons and have them perform well. In this respect, Netscape Composer is <u>a prime example of interface design</u>[1], carefully rooted in users' experience of browsers and in the layout options of widespread tools like word processors. With Composer's push-button, drag-and-drop and menu options, the dilettante web designer does not need to know a single line of HTML code to construct a functional website. In terms of rethinking, or reverse engineering, the role of designers from that of users, WYSIWYG editors are exemplary applications.

1_The pristine clarity of Composer's interface design contrasts sharply with that of Netscape's own website, which is, and has been for years despite some heroic attempts at reorganization, one of the worst examples on the web of the smothery chaos so characteristic of portals – an absurd proof that design cannot help when editorial clarity and consistency are absent.

The prodigality of home-made diaries and personal publications on the web has greatly benefited from web editors

www.blogger.com

Blogger

client_ Pyra Labs, San Francisco, CA, US
design_Derek Powazek
on line_1999

The prodigality of home-made diaries and personal publications on the web has greatly benefited from the introduction of the next generation of web editors, among which is Blogger. Practically, you could make any kind of website with this editor, but it is primarily meant for one specific genre: the weblog. Intended for daily updating the *faits et gestes* of its maker, this online application registers date and time, archives and indexes, so that the author can concentrate on providing the contents. Blogs are the apex of personal publishing and Blogger has taken care to provide a wide range of templates, each of which can be easily modified to the blogger's liking. The result is a great variety of designs, which nevertheless remain recognizable as originating from the same platform.

Blogs are interesting from a design angle because they show the level of (visual) literacy of their authors; some contain quite good writing and others may have intricate photo stories or an elaborate editorial design. In many cases, the basic structures of Blogger's templates balance even the most undesigned blogs, although some

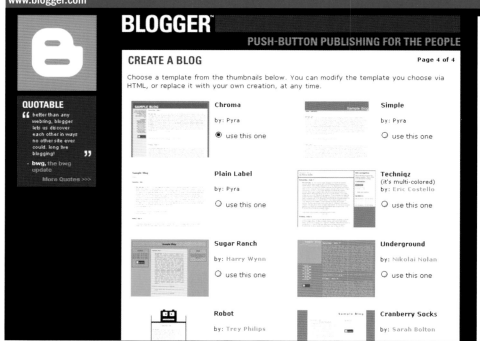

These kinds of deeper design questions could be addressed in the next generation of templates

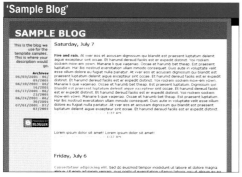

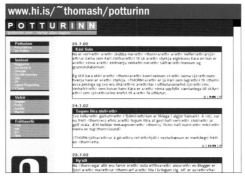

time the reader has to adjust the window or font size to make for a pleasant read. These kinds of deeper design questions could be addressed in the next generation of templates: how to maintain flexibility and the possibility of customization and still 'hardwire' into the defaults some basic parameters for page layout, typography and balance?

The way blogs are linked to each other is vital to their success; they prove that if a website does not refer to other sites it practically does not exist. Bloggers read other blogs and often provide a link list to a dozen or so colleagues. With the possibility of linking commentaries to entries in blogs, the blogger neighbourhood has evolved into a world-encompassing community – chatting, gossiping, reflecting on the guys next door, distant loves and current affairs – a globally syndicated soap opera.

Until recently, complex interactive media presentations have belonged to the realm of the professional designer

Nine

concept, design_Graham Harwood,
London, UK
on line_2002

Until recently, complex interactive media presentations have belonged to the realm of the professional designer who has mastered the intricacies of such multimedia authoring tools as Macromedia's Director (the standard in the field). 'Nine' attempts to bring the power of multimedia to the masses. The program was developed by Graham Harwood, partner in the multimedia artists collective Mongrel, who have worked extensively on media tools for local communities in London, Amsterdam, Paris and Delhi. Using as a starting point a drastically stripped down version of Director's functions, Harwood, with assistance from the Waag Society in Amsterdam, built what he calls 'a multimedia equivalent of the throwaway camera'. The program makes 'maps' of nine pictures, which form a grid on which users can upload and link photos, texts, sounds and digital video. Intuitive, fast and flexible, the application extends the range of home-used media formats, from photo albums and stamp collections to the arrangement of bric-a-brac, to the computer, making them 'modernlike and multimedia'.

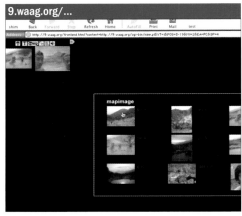

172

At the time of writing, the online application was still in its pre-beta stage

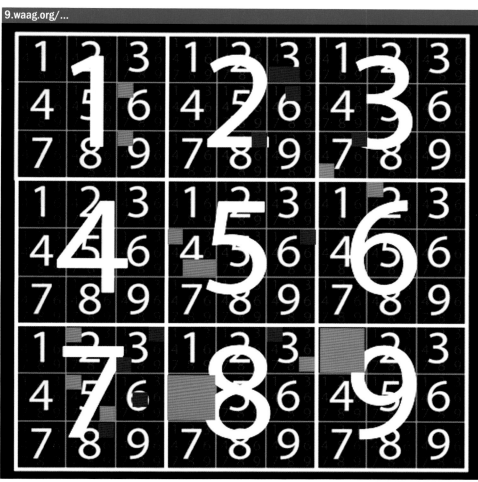

9.waag.org/...

At the time of writing, the online application was still in its pre-beta stage, but it promises to be another step in the direction of the media empowerment of 'ordinary' people. In collaboration with Imagine IC, a new Amsterdam-based centre for foreign cultures, 'Nine' will be used as an authoring tool for presenting stories about the lives and cultures of immigrants in the Netherlands, told, recorded, designed and published by themselves. The professional designers, software developers and producers will remain in the background as facilitators, not makers of the content.

9.waag.org/...

9.waag.org/...

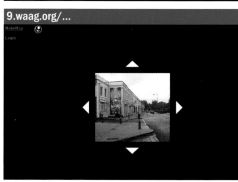

9.waag.org/...

9.waag.org/...

The most basic of online authoring tools is a small Dutch site called 'klad.nl'

www.klad.nl

Klad.nl

concept, design_Dennis Lodewijks,
Jeroen Disch, Koert van Mensvoort,
Amsterdam, NL
on line_2001

www.twofivesix.co.uk/snd

WebPlayer

concept, design_Pete Everett, UK
on line_2002

www.altx.com/ebr/ebr12/litmix

LITMIXER

concept, design_Trace Reddell, Denver,
CO, US
on line_2001

The most basic of online authoring tools is a small Dutch site called 'klad.nl'; 'klad' means draft or sketch in Dutch, and users can store short texts on the site. Nothing more, nothing less. It is as close to scribbling a note on a napkin as is possible on the web. With its marginal functions, the site fits more comfortably under the heading 'net.commentary' than 'application'. Although it might be handy to have an easily accessible place on the web for storing notes when you do not have your personal computer to hand, 'klad.nl' can also be enjoyed as a tongue-in-cheek comment on the increasing technological complexity of communication.

   Another combination of artful functionality and net.critique is 'WebPlayer' by Pete Everett. Subtitled 'Music to Watch URLs By', this little app turns HTML data into music; feed it a URL and it hums the drone embedded in the code, partly influenced by the time and date of entry. While not very elaborate in terms of musical experience, based as it is on reducing complex data to a small set of variables and procedures, the music it generates underlines the fundamental malleability of code. As for authorship, Everett remarks, 'can I really consider

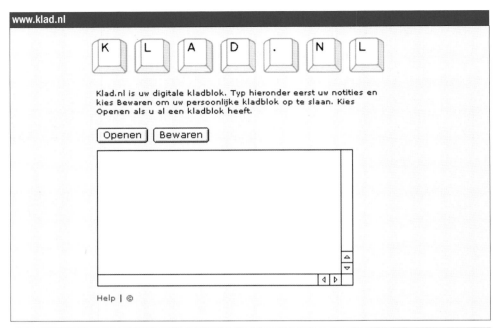

And if the output was recorded and sold, who owns the copyright?

www.twofivesix.co.uk/snd/

'WebPlayer'

'WebPlayer'

'WebPlayer'

www.altx.com/ebr/ebr12/litmix/manual_03.htm

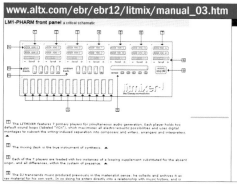

'Litmixer | LM1-Pharm'

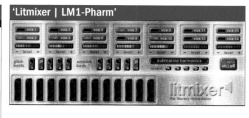

myself the composer of any output it generates? And if the output was recorded and sold, who owns the copyright? In fact, is there any copyright to be had?' In other words: what remains of authorship, which we traditionally associate with products (texts, paintings, compositions), once the structural part of a piece of art is removed from its formal end result? This is also, as I have argued earlier (see p. 143), a design issue; as Anne Burdick of the 'Electronic Book Review' observes, by designing the structure of a site so that the actual page layout generates itself, she is designing herself out of her job 'as it is currently defined'[1].

What might replace the current definition of authorship is hinted at by 'Litmixer, The Literary Remediator'. In this application (made for 'Electronic Book Review', no. 12) Trace Reddell 'applies the tools and strategies of the DJ to the performance of literary interpretation and critical speculation'. Based on passages read from Jacques Derrida's essay 'Plato's Pharmakon' ('Plato's Pharmacy'), with added effects and interactions from the piece's DJ, the 'Litmixer' is both a performance and an interpretation of the text. Whether it is 'what critical writing could look like once scholars and critics begin making use of the performative possibilities within networked environments' remains to be seen, but it does, again, question the relationship between authors, editors, designers, interpreters, performers, listeners and readers in environments where there is no possibility of hearing the 'original voice', only mazes of interpretations[2].

1_See p. 143.
2_Trace Reddell, feat. Ulf Poschardt, *DJ Culture* (London: Quartet Books, 1998), 'The remixer isn't concerned with salvaging authenticity, but with creating a new authenticity.'

Links are the essence of the web's hypertext, the raw material for using and interpreting the web

www.type01.com

Link_R.I.PPER

concept, design_type01.com,
Cape Town, SA
on line_2001

www.potatoland.org

Potatoland

concept, design_Mark Napier,
New York, US
on line_1998

netflag.guggenheim.org

net.flag

concept, design and Java
programming_Mark Napier, New York, US
editor, research_Liza Sabater
research assistant_Josep Arimany Piella
Java programming_Zach Lieberman
on line_2002

Links are the essence of the web's hypertext, the raw material for using and interpreting the web. So, why bother with all the redundant data around them? Link_R.I.PPER's response is unequivocal: lose it. Feed this small app a URL and it strips everything from the webpage leaving only the URLs that link to other pages and other sites. In all its simplicity, 'Link_R.I.PPER' is a hands-on critique of what the web is all about. Like 'Litmixer' and 'WebPlayer' (see previous pages), it is an example of an interesting mix of intellectual exploration, application design and critical writing. These 'thought toys', which are becoming more and more popular, express critical analysis *as* application design. Unlike 'Litmixer' and 'WebPlayer', 'Link_R.I.PPER' does not have an elaborate 'manual' that positions the app in the context of the critique it expresses. However, it could be 'read' as an applied illustration of Richard Rogers's book *Preferred Placement* or Manuel Castells's articles on the 'Network Economy', where both argue that the cultural effectiveness of a website (or any individual) is

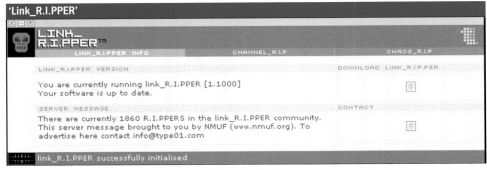

'Link_R.I.PPER'

'Link_R.I.PPER'

'Link_R.I.PPER'

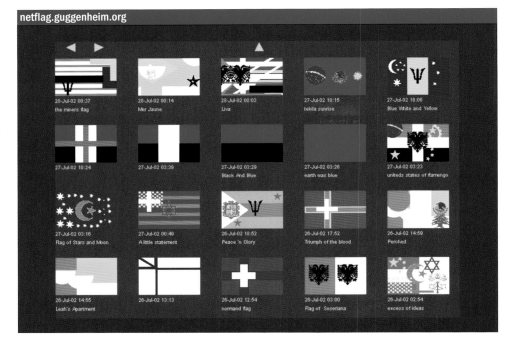

netflag.guggenheim.org

'net.flag Editor'

'net.flag Statistics'

'Flags of the Web'

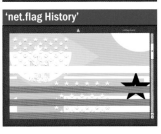

'net.flag History'

'net.flag History'

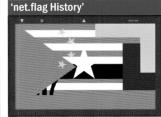

'net.flag History'

Another instance of playful destructiveness is Mark Napier's 'Potatoland'

www.potatoland.org/riot/riot.html

'Riot'

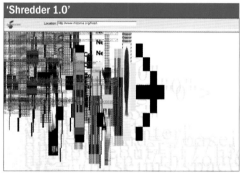

'Shredder 1.0'

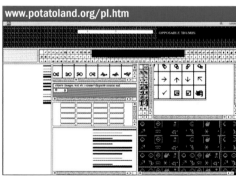

www.potatoland.org/pl.htm

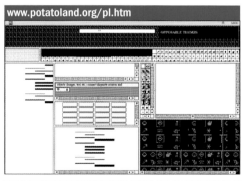

www.potatoland.org/pl.htm

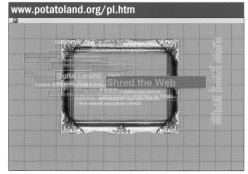

www.potatoland.org/pl.htm

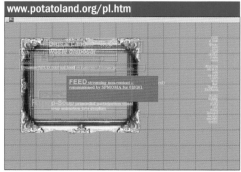

www.potatoland.org/pl.htm

a function of the way they are linked to others[1].

Another instance of playful destructiveness is Mark Napier's 'Potatoland'. This painter turned net.artist is the author of the now famous 'Shredder' (1998), an application that hauls the sites you give it through a digital mincer to produce 'a new Internet experience'. Once more, the fundamental adaptability of code and the virtuality of all web design is illustrated. To stress these points *and* to emphasize the untenability of nationalism on the web, Napier's 'net.flag' project for the Solomon R. Guggenheim Museum allows visitors to gener- ate an ever-changing interactive flag for the Internet by taking elements from existing national flags. Older projects share this anarchistic quality, such as 'Riot', an alternative web browser that builds its page by combining text, images and links from the most recent pages that any user has been to. In contrast to net.artists like Alexei Shulgin and Jodi.org (see pp. 42–43), Napier uses a more outspoken interactivity, which forces visitors into a position of critique and makes them feel more responsible for the havoc that results from using his applications.

1 See bibliography, p. 184.

Presenting visitors with 'an open-ended interplay of words and pictures', Icontext is an ASCII-tool that makes small icons

artcontext.com/icontext

Icontext

concept, design_Andy Deck, New York, US
on line_2001

Presenting visitors with 'an open-ended interplay of words and pictures', Icontext is an ASCII-tool that makes small icons with monospace characters; you can 'write' images with it. As its maker states, 'Icontext is a hybrid of telecommunication, drawing, and word processing software'. Each character is also associated with a colour and this double meaning forces users to 'negotiate the balance (or imbalance) between image and text'. The database of 'icontexts' is proof that it is hard to equally distribute text and image aspects of icons – they remain different languages. The database is open for re-use or available as a starting point for new drawing sessions, resulting in a strategy of collaboration and negotiation on the part of visitors; two concepts that are vital to any new art that is emerging not only within the realm of online media, but also in the broader framework of contemporary art. Not many icontexts will stand the test of art or net reviews (we will have use for artists for a while ;-), but 'Icontext' is a viable, and sometimes funny, experiment in making an interactive and collaborative authoring tool.

'Icontext Sitemap'

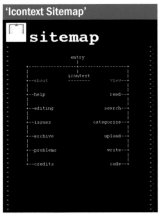

artcontext.com/icontext/...

artcontext.com/icontext/...

artcontext.com/icontext/html/index.php

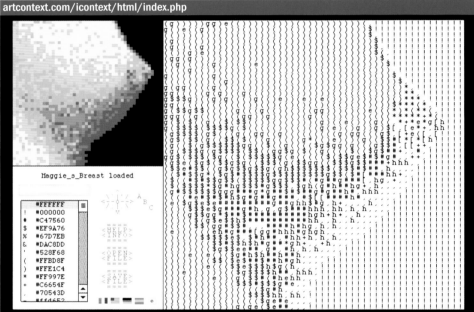

artcontext.com/icontext/html/index.php

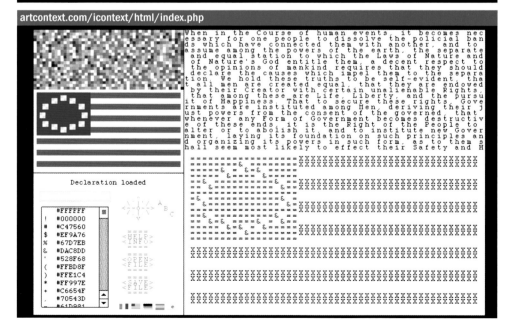

Gicheol Lee's site is a series of typographic and code experiments

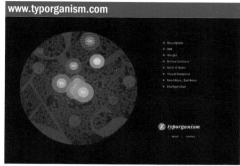

www.typorganism.com

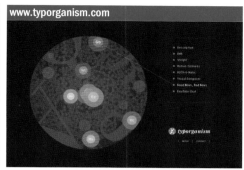

www.typorganism.com

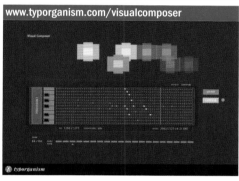

www.typorganism.com/visualcomposer

www.typorganism.com/visualcomposer

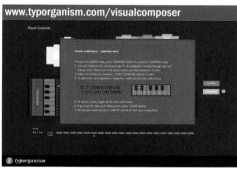

www.typorganism.com/visualcomposer

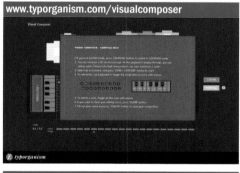

www.typorganism.com/visualcomposer

www.typorganism.com/goodbadnews

www.typorganism.com/goodbadnews

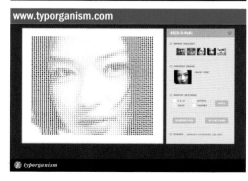

www.typorganism.com

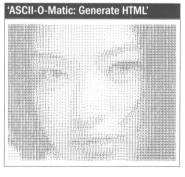

'ASCII-O-Matic: Generate HTML'

www.typorganism.com

typorganism
concept, design, programming_
Gicheol Lee, New York, US
on line_2002

Gicheol Lee's site is a series of typographic and code experiments, one of which is another ASCII-tool that lets visitors upload small images and have them translated into 'ASCII-art'. Such playfulness with the pixel character of (small) letters has been employed in graphic design for quite a while, with the most famous example being the text of Marx's *Communist Manifesto* (1848) set to form a portrait of the author. Now that computers can easily and swiftly complete the translation, ASCII renderings are becoming more and more popular with artists in various media because they symbolize the essential connection between the text of code and anything that results from it.

The 'Visual Composer' is another small experiment that points to the intimate connection between all media governed by code. Its central concern is how code interacts with a combination of sounds and visual effects. Clicking a virtual punch card produces a kind of piano roll that, when played, links pixelated light bursts to a sound. You can concentrate on writing the music, but also reverse priorities and focus on making an aesthetically pleasing visual score. In 'Good News, Bad News', Lee contrasts two different sets of cultural codes – the news as brought to you by CNN and the news you yourself would share with the world. Feeds from both sources – one automated, the other interactive – display the gap between public and personal on the web. Designers who help to bridge this gap are cultural agents in the best sense.

179

Austrian designer Lia Schitter's site is a genuine temple of intervention

www.re-move.org

Re-Move

concept, design_Lia Schitter, Vienna, AT
on line_2000

Austrian designer Lia Schitter's
site is a genuine temple of intervention. In eight Shockwave
experiences, or 'playscapes'
as she calls them, visitors can
intervene in digital, graphlike
landscapes spawned from
mathematical procedures. With
an interface that may be called
intuitive because it reveals its
workings only when used,
'Re-Move' challenges visitors
to fight or influence the pre-
programmed stream of events.
The sheer beauty of the dynamic
graphs can make it hard to concentrate on the means at your
disposal to alter the events, but
this drawback only causes a
temporary disruption. The
playscapes show the unbridled
reorganizational potential of
generic code, and the various
scenarios are abstract meditations
on the processes of interaction
and automation. Such interactive
pattern generators reveal that
complete control, even when
programmed, is attainable only
in theory. Visitors and users dis-
rupt the processes in an almost
Heisenbergian sense (where the
mere act of looking influences
the process that is being watched),
removing linearity from the course
of events.

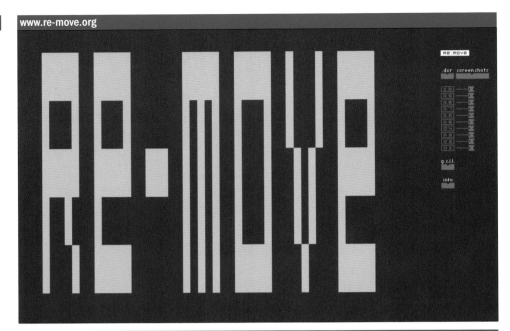

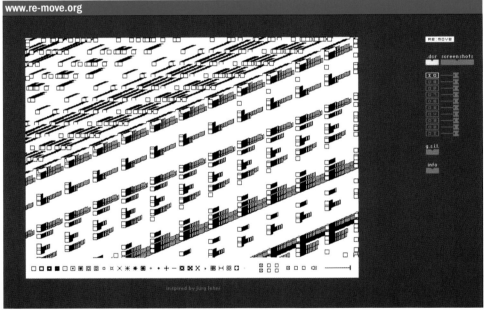

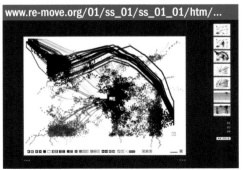

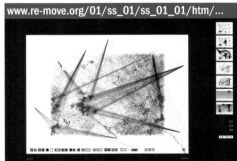

www.re-move.org/00_gsi01/18/htm/03.htm

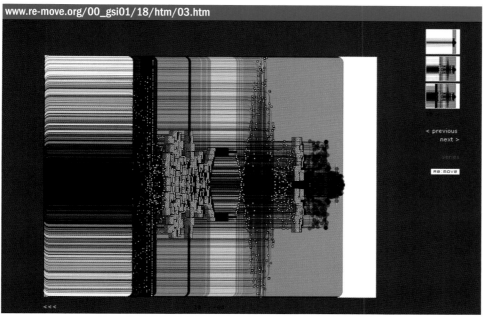

www.re-move.org/08/ss_08/ss_08_01/htm/02.htm

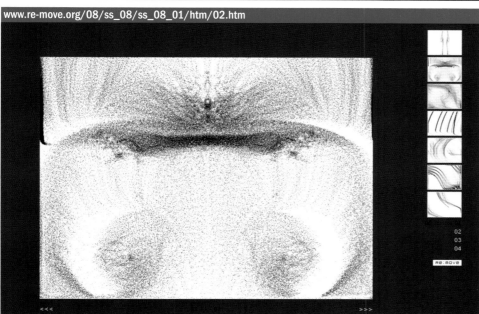

www.re-move.org/06/ss_06/ss_06_01/htm/...

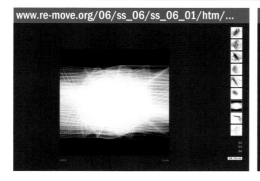

www.re-move.org/08/ss_08/ss_08_01/htm/...

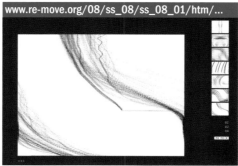

Jay Boersma knows all about HTML and such stuff as websites are made of

Web Page from Hell

design_Jay Boersma, re-vision.com,
Steger, IL, US
on line_1999

Jay Boersma knows all about HTML and such stuff as websites are made of, and to make sure you know that minding your code is not enough, his frontpage neatly sums up every bad editorial and inter-face-design decision you can make. Unfortunately, it seems to be common practice: look at any big portal site's homepage and you are bound to see a disconcerting number of similarities with Boersma's 'Web Page from Hell'. The most frequently perpetrated error is the uncontrollable urge of many webmasters to squeeze access to *every* bit of information on the entire site into the home-page instead of precisely mapping a site's structure. Plus, they make space for the banner ads that pay the bills, provide for ample redun-dancy and show the solicitations to subscribe to free updates and mailing lists. Boersma's page has all this and more. For example, the line '(CNET Yellow. Used with per-mission.)' under 'main navigation' is a gibe at CNET's information architects, who proclaimed that a site's navigation should *always* be in a frame to the left and *always* be in yellow. Of course, it is not where you put it, but how you use it. Having had what not to do drummed into your head, you can click any of the myriad links and be transported to Boersma's tutorials on how to treat HTML right. Word!

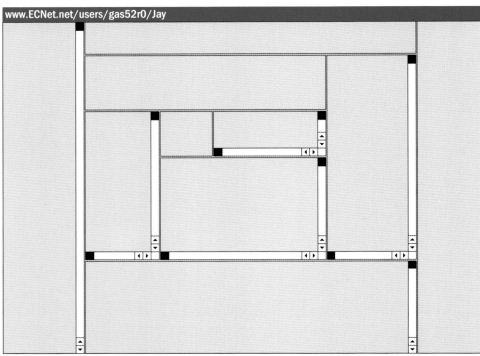

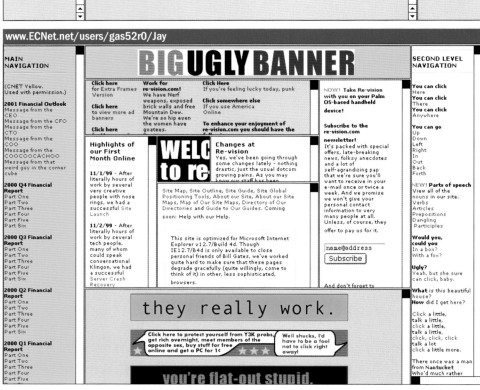

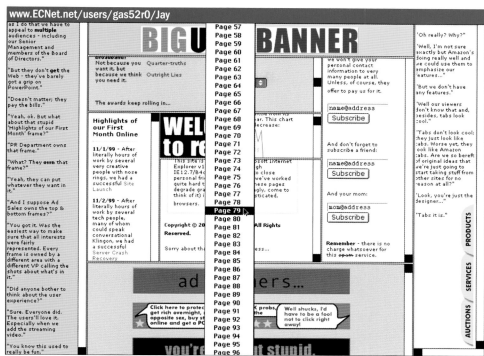

'Hell to Go'

Bibliography

Abbate, Janet
Inventing the Internet (Inside Technology)
Cambridge (MA), US: The MIT Press, 1999
Janet Abbate recounts the key players and technologies that allowed the Internet to develop. Her main focus is on the social and cultural factors that influenced the Internet's design and use. Her story unfolds as an often twisting tale of collaboration and conflict among a remarkable variety of players.

Barthes, Roland (trans. Stephen Heath)
Image, Music, Text
London, UK: Fontana Press, 1977
The French critic and semiotician Roland Barthes was one of the most important literary theorists of his century, and his work continues to influence contemporary theory and cultural studies. *Image, Music, Text* collects best writings on photography and cinema, as well as fascinating articles on the relationship between image and sound. (Of particular interest: 'Introduction to the Structural Analysis of Narrative' and 'The Death of the Author'.)

Bertol, Daniela with David Foell
Designing digital space: an architect's guide to virtual reality
Chichester, UK and New York (NY), US: Wiley, 1997
The first in-depth book on virtual reality (VR), aimed specifically at architecture and design professionals, steers you through the learning curve of this new technology. Detailed coverage of the virtual universe – data representation and information management, static and dynamic worlds, tracking and visual display systems, control devices, and more.

Bolter, Jay David
Writing Space: The Computer, Hypertext, and the History of Writing
Hillside (NJ), US: Lawrence Erlbaum Associates, 1991
Electronic version, 2000
Jay David Bolter's study of hypertext and the history of writing from cuneiform and hieroglyphics to the computer is quite simply the finest book about hypertext available. It comes both as a book and as a hypertextual electronic text.

Bolter, Jay David and Richard Grusin
Remediation: Understanding New Media
Cambridge (MA), US: The MIT Press, 1999
Taking up where Marshall McLuhan left off, Jay David Bolter and Richard Grusin offer a theory of mediation for our digital age. They argue that new visual media achieve their cultural significance precisely by paying homage to, rivalling and refashioning such earlier media as perspective painting, photography, film and television. They call this process of refashioning 'remediation'.

Bonsiepe, Gui
Interface: An Approach to Design
Maastricht, NL: Jan van Eyck Akademie, 1999
This collage of edited papers, articles and interviews presents a wide variety of topics that are, according to Bonsiepe, crucial in understanding the paradigm shifts in the concept of design due to the influence of information technology. He argues that all design has to be re-interpreted as 'interface design'.

Bukatman, Scott
Terminal Identity: The Virtual Subject in Postmodern Science Fiction
London, UK: Duke University Press, 1993
In his book, Bukatman surveys the electronic age, computer culture and cyberpunk sci-fi, which attempts to define the societies and individuals that cybernetic culture will create. Drawing on a vast array of sci-fi literature, comics, films and criticism, as well as numerous postmodern authors, Bukatman argues that the human/machine interface is fast approaching a symbiotic relationship.

Burnham, Van
Supercade: A Visual History of the Videogame Age 1971–1984
Cambridge (MA), US: The MIT Press, 2001 (www.supercade.com)
Supercade is the first book to illustrate and document the history, legacy and visual language of the video-game phenomenon. From Pong to Pac-Man, Asteroids to Zaxxon, Burnham chronicles the golden age of video games. Practically every game you can remember from that period is mentioned, and there are excellent screenshots, interesting facts, impressive photos and amazing anecdotes.

Carroll, John M.
Making Use: Scenario-Based Design of Human-Computer Interactions
Cambridge (MA), US and London, UK: The MIT Press, 2000
Very insightful book on the design process. Carroll combines humility with scarily deep knowledge about the ways we are learning to design information systems. This masterful book provides a platform for an understanding of the design process in a world of complex systems and constant change.

Cassell, Justine and Henry Jenkins, eds.
From Barbie to Mortal Kombat: Gender and Computer Games
Cambridge (MA), US and London, UK: The MIT Press, 1998
A wide-ranging collection of essays that examines the rise of the 'Girls' Game Movement' and the consequences of separating girls from boys in cyberspace and the marketplace. Both supporters and opponents of the idea have equal space to deliver their thoughts and convictions.

Castells, Manuel
The Rise of the Network Society
Cambridge (MA), US and Oxford, UK: Blackwell Publishers, 1996
This book is unrivalled in ambition: to make sense of the global social dynamics as they arise out of a myriad of changes around the world. It is a cross-cultural analysis of the major social, economic and political transformations at the end of the twentieth century. Part one of his already famous trilogy.

Coyne, Richard
Designing Information Technology in the Postmodern Age: From Method to Metaphor
Cambridge (MA), US: The MIT Press, 1995
Coyne's book puts the theoretical discussion of computer systems and information technology on a new footing. Shifting the discourse from its usual rationalistic framework, he shows how the conception, development and application of computer systems is challenged and enhanced by postmodern philosophical thought.

Crary, Jonathan
Techniques of the Observer: On Vision and Modernity in the Nineteenth Century
Cambridge (MA), US and London, UK: The MIT Press, 1990
A dramatically new perspective on the visual culture of the nineteenth century, reassessing problems of both visual modernism and social modernity. This analysis of the historical formation of the observer is a compelling account of the pre-history of 'the society of the spectacle'.

Crary, Jonathan
Suspensions of Perception: Attention, Spectacle, and Modern Culture
Cambridge (MA), US and London, UK: The MIT Press, 1999
A major historical study of human attention and its volatile role in modern Western culture. It provides a historical framework for understanding the current social crisis of attention amidst the accelerating metamorphoses of contemporary technological culture.

Deleuze, Gilles and Félix Guattari (trans. Brian Massumi)
A Thousand Plateaus: Capitalism and Schizophrenia
Minneapolis (MN), US: University of Minnesota Press, 1987
This book is viewed by many as a must-read for understanding the nature of networks and horizontal conglomerates of milieus, and thus the Internet. However, it is imperative to state that the book's original aim was to change the face and practice of philosophy. The dynamic duo envisioned a philosophy moving at infinite speeds in a mad creation of concepts. Although technology has changed greatly since 1995, you cannot say that the internet allows you to data-travel at infinite speed. ... Still, *A Thousand Plateaus* has undeniably influenced the course of media theory.

Dobrila, Peter Tomaz and Aleksandra Kostic, eds.
Eduardo Kac: Telepresence, Biotelematics, Transgenic Art
Maribor, SI: Association for Culture and Education, KIBLA, 2000
This collection of essays covers approximately the last decade of Eduardo Kac's artistic production. Arranged roughly in chronological order, the essays cover numerous telepresence works and conclude with Kac's more recent experiments in genetic manipulation. It finishes with an essay by Kac himself on his 'GFP Bunny' Alba (the fluorescent rabbit).

Dourish, Paul
Where the Action Is: The Foundations of Embodied Interaction
Cambridge (MA), US: The MIT Press, 2001
In this book, Paul Dourish addresses the philosophical bases of human-computer interaction. He looks at what he calls 'embodied interaction' – an approach to interacting with software systems that emphasizes skilled, engaged practice rather than disembodied rationality. Based on the phenomenological tradition, the publication shows how this perspective can shed light on the underpinnings of current research on embodied interaction.

Flusser, Vilém
Ins Universum der Technischen Bilder
Göttingen, DE: European Photography, 1985
Flusser belongs to the group of optimistic authors who dare to confront the new media and images with a 'ganzheitlichen' ('all-embracing') theory. Not only are the media new, but through them a new life form or societal form (trans)forms itself. Although highly critical, Flusser is a true believer in the possibilities of a telematic culture and society in which we fruitfully coexist with our technology.

Flusser, Vilém
Die Schrift: Hat Schreiben Zukunft?
Göttingen, DE: Immatrix Publications, 1987
Here, Flusser concentrates on whether or not writing has a future. In a brilliant and highly structured way he deals with such themes as the history of writing, the crisis of linearity, the phenomenology of media, the future of subjectivity, new cultural codes and, ultimately, a new anthropology, all as part of a critique of the telematic society.

Flusser, Vilém
The Shape of Things: A Philosophy of Design
London, UK: Reaktion Books, 1999
This book puts forward the view that our future depends on design and the bringing together of new ideas from science and art, economics and politics. Flusser presents a new way of looking at everyday objects and technology.

The Internet dramatically extends our scope and reach

Goldberg, Ken, ed.

The Robot in the Garden: Telerobotics and Telepistemology in the Age of the Internet

Cambridge (MA), US: The MIT Press, 2000

The Internet dramatically extends our scope and reach. Thousands of cameras and robots are now accessible on line. Goldberg brings together current writings about such issues as telerobotics, telepresence, Internet art and the status of the real in a virtual age. The contributors frequently disagree with one another, an indication of the intellectual vitality of this work.

Hertz, Noreena

The Silent Takeover: Global Capitalism and the Death of Democracy

London, UK: Heinemann, 2001

Providing a new and startling take on the way we now live and who really governs us, Noreena Hertz analyzes how corporations across the world manipulate and pressurize governments by both legal and illegal means. Hertz explains, for example, how protest, be it in the form of anti-globalization protests or the boycotting of genetically altered foods, is often becoming a more effective political weapon than the ballot box.

Johnson, Steven

Interface Culture: How New Technology Transforms the Way We Create and Communicate

San Francisco (CA), US: HarperEdge, 1997

With a distinctively accessible style, *Interface Culture* brings new intellectual depth to the vital discussion of how technology has transformed society. Many discussions focus on how interfaces help us work by adapting to our ways of thinking and our real-world metaphors, but Johnson also jumps to look at how our thinking and world view are altered by our computer interfaces.

Kahn, Paul and James M. Nyce, eds.

From Memex to Hypertext: Vannevar Bush and the Mind's Machine

Boston (MA), US and London, UK: Academic Press, 1991

Memex, a computer that was never built, was described in 1945 by pioneer computer engineer Vannevar Bush, and foreshadowed the principles and operations of today's personal computers. Bush's writings about Memex are collected here for the first time, interspersed with essays by historians and computer researchers.

Kittler, Friedrich (trans. Geoffrey Winthrop-Young and Michael Wutz)

Gramophone, Film, Typewriter

Stanford (AR), US: Stanford University Press, 1999

Kittler broadens Foucault's discourse theory on textual archives into a wider media band, incorporating phonographic and cinematic data streams and undermining the hegemony of literary writing. For Kittler, media determine our 'posthumanity' and have been doing so in technological earnest at least since the phonograph broke the information-storage monopoly held by writing.

Kittler, Friedrich

Aufschreibesysteme 1800/1900

München, DE: Fink, 1987

Kittler's prime work, *Aufschreibesysteme* (*Discourse Networks*) is an attempt to rewrite history from a media theoretical perspective. Inspired by thinkers like Nietzsche, Foucault, Derrida and Lacan, he sets out to reveal the archaeological background of writing: the connection between writing and the notation systems with which texts are mediated. This historical study takes the period 1800–1900 as the basis for a critique of contemporary coding systems.

Klein, Naomi

No Logo

London, UK: Flamingo, 2000

A very well documented analysis and critique of branded culture. Equal parts cultural analysis, political manifesto, mall-rat memoir and journalistic expose, *No Logo* is the first book that uncovers

the sins of corporations run amok *and* explores and explains the new resistance that will change consumer culture in the twenty-first century.

Landow, George P.

Hypertext 2.0: The Convergence of Contemporary Critical Theory and Technology

Baltimore (MD), US: John Hopkins University Press, 1997

Landow's widely acclaimed book was the first to bring together the worlds of literary theory and computer technology. In this second edition, Landow shifts the reader's focus from Intermedia to Microcosm, Storyspace, and the World Wide Web.

Ludlow, Peter, ed.

Crypto Anarchy, Cyberstates, and Pirate Utopias

Cambridge (MA), US and London, UK: The MIT Press, 2001

In this book, Ludlow extends the approach he used so successfully in *High Noon on the Electronic Frontier* to offer a collection of writing that reflects the eclectic nature of the online world, along with its tremendous energy and creativity. This time, the subject is the emergence of governance structures within online communities and the visions of political sovereignty shaping some of those communities.

Lunenfeld, Peter

Snap to Grid: A User's Guide to Digital Arts, Media and Cultures

Cambridge (MA), US and London, UK: The MIT Press, 2000

Peter Lunenfeld inverts the seemingly undesirable mapping of charming human imperfection onto rigid technology to produce a more appealing process of dialogue between man and machine. In a wide variety of topics ranging from the Beastie Boys to Heidegger and back again, he critically focuses on the demands put upon us by electronic culture.

Lunenfeld, Peter, ed.

The Digital Dialectic: New Essays on New Media

Cambridge (MA), US and London, UK: The MIT Press, 1999

A smart collection of mostly academic essays, which aims to identify a dialectic at the heart of the digital technologies currently reshaping the way we see and know the world. Lunenfeld's elegant running commentary does a nice job of teasing out the common concerns of the wide-ranging contributors (Errki Huhtamo, Michael Heim, N.Katherine Hayles, among others).

McLuhan, Marshall

Understanding Media: The Extensions of Man

Cambridge (MA), US: The MIT Press, 1994 (1st ed. 1964)

This classic evaluates the influence of a wide variety of media on man, his senses and his culture, giving an insight into the development of man and his technological 'extensions'. Electronic media provide instant knowledge and immediate, broad-based communications, effectively increasing man's awareness of the world about him and thereby shrinking the world to McLuhan's 'global village'. Required reading for anyone involved in contemporary culture.

McLuhan, Marshall

The Gutenberg Galaxy: The Making of Typographic Man

London, UK: Routledge & Kegan Paul, 1962

One can almost think of *The Gutenberg Galaxy* as the 'prequel' to *Understanding Media* because *Galaxy* does for print technology what *Media* does for electronic technology. Basically, McLuhan assesses how European civilization went from a 'listening' mode of receiving information to a 'reading' mode.

McLuhan, Marshall and Eric McLuhan

Laws of Media: The New Science

Toronto, CA: University of Toronto Press, 1988

McLuhan puts forward a solution to the problems that Aristotle formulated in his 'Four Causes'. McLuhan calls his response the 'Four Effects' – retrieval, enhancement, obsolescence, reversal. Reputed as brilliant.

Maeda, John

Design by Numbers

London, UK: The MIT Press, 1999

Labour in most art and technology projects is divided between the artist who comes up with the conception and the technical person who provides the know-how. John Maeda combines the two; he views the computer as an artistic medium in its own right. The book is a reader-friendly tutorial on the philosophy and nuts-and-bolts techniques of programming for artists.

Manovich, Lev

The Language of New Media

Cambridge (MA), US and London, UK: The MIT Press, 2001

Lev Manovich offers the first systematic and rigorous theory of new media. His questions are: what are the ways in which new media rely on older cultural forms and languages and what are the ways in which they break with them? His answers draw on the histories of computer science, art, design, photography, video and other electronic media, in particular the key cultural form of the twentieth century – cinema.

Negri, Antonio and Michael Hardt

Empire

Cambridge (MA), US: Harvard University Press, 2000

Hardt and Negri demonstrate the new political order of globalization in this bold work. They link this philosophical transformation to cultural and economic changes in postmodern society – new forms of racism, new conceptions of identity and difference, new networks of communication and control and new paths of migration.

Nelson, Ted

ComputerLib/Dream Machines

Microsoft Press, 1987 (1st ed. 1974)

One of the first cult books of the computer generation and embraced by hackers and other cultural entrepreneurs, *ComputerLib* is a landmark of vision and a celebration of the possibilities of modern information technology. The man who coined the word 'hypertext' makes it clear that computers are to be understood as literary machines.

Nielsen, Jakob

Usability Engineering

Boston (MA), US and London, UK: Academic Press, 1993

'Usability' is the measurement of how easy or difficult it is for a user to be productive with a piece of software. 'Usability engineering' is the formal study of usability. It grew out of research on the way people interact with their environment. The author offers more than a handful of guiding principles for creating better software.

Nielsen, Jakob

Designing Web Usability: The Practice of Simplicity

Indianapolis (IN), US: New Riders, 1999

For the 'old school' of Human Computer Interaction (HCI), this is the bible of usability. Interesting to some, boring and totalitarian to others, Nielsen certainly knows how to stir up a rather bleak arena. His conception of design would make the old Bauhaus boys and girls turn in their graves, but, apart from setting back a century the debate about what design could or should do, Nielsen's books neatly sum up most of the problems with which designers for the web are faced. That in itself makes it a must-read.

This book continues the exploration of the social construction of technology

Nye, David E.
American Technological Sublime
Cambridge (MA), US and London, UK: The MIT Press, 1994
This book continues the exploration of the social construction of technology that David Nye began in his award-winning book *Electrifying America*. Here Nye examines the continuing appeal of the 'technological sublime' (a term coined by Perry Miller) as a key to the nation's history, using as examples the natural sites, architectural forms and technological achievements that ordinary people have valued immensely.

Reeves, Byron and Clifford Nass
The Media Equation: How People Treat Computers, Television, and New Media Like Real People and Places
Cambridge, UK: Cambridge University Press, 1996
The equation referred to in the book's title is 'media equals real life'. The conclusion Reeves and Nass draw from the series of experiments they outline in the book is that people treat and respond to media in just the same way as they treat and respond to other people in everyday social interactions.

Rheingold, Howard
The Virtual Community: Homesteading on the Electronic Frontier
Cambridge (MA), US and London, UK: The MIT Press, rev. ed. 2000 (complete online version: www.rheingold.com/vc/book)
Cyberculture authority Howard Rheingold was the first to write about online communities in this style – part travelogue, part anthropological guide. This classic explores the entire virtual community, beginning with a selective but probing look at the author's original online home, 'The Well'.

Rheingold, Howard
Tools for Thought: The History and Future of Mind-Expanding Technology
Cambridge (MA), US and London, UK: The MIT Press, rev. ed. 2000 (1st ed. 1985)
An excellent slice of 'retrospective futurism' that shows how we arrived at our largely wired world and where we might find ourselves in the future. It also explores some might-have-been scenarios that seemed likely in the 1980s. *Tools for Thought* reminds us that today's wild ideas are what bring tomorrow's radical change.

Rogers, Richard (ed.)
Preferred Placement, Knowledge Politics on the Web
Maastricht, NL: Jan van Eyck Academie, 2000
Shifting the debate on web analysis to date, this book, instead of celebrating the web and its prospects for creative artistry, democracy and e-commerce, calmly goes 'backstage'. How do search engines really work? What would be an adequate map be of the internet? What is web epistemology?

Ronell, Avital
The Telephone Book: Technology, Schizophrenia, Electric Speech
Lincoln (AL), US: University of Nebraska Press, 1989
A must-read for anyone wishing to understand the strange convergences that have made up American technology, literature and culture over the last century. It is an original and philosophically important text. Bizarre, disjointed, 'jarring'. Yet, its themes and investigative technique represent important ways of examining tangled (post)modern literature and culture.

Sassen, Saskia
Globalization and Its Discontents
New York (NY), US: New Press, 1998
Sassen offers new ways of thinking about the benefits and disadvantages of globalization. Groundbreaking essays on the new global economy from an 'expert observer'. Her essays deal with such topics as the 'global city', gender and migration (reconceived as the globalization of labour), information technology and the new dynamics of inequality.

Shedroff, Nathan
Experience Design
Indianapolis (IN), US: New Riders, 2001
A book about today's intersection of such disciplines as interaction design, information design, visual design and related methodologies, which are seen as parts of a whole; the design of experiences. The book does not just address the designing of online experiences (such as websites), but approaches all design – including products, services, environments and events – as the design of experiences.

Sheff, David
Game Over: How Nintendo Zapped an American Industry, Captured Your Dollars, and Enslaved Your Children
New York (NY), US: Random House, 1993
A thorough study of Nintendo's history, its pitfalls and its successes. More than 150 years old, the company started as a card and tobacco manufacturer in the 1800s. *Game Over* shows the workings, hidden story and weird choices behind this computer-game giant.

Stefik, Mark
Internet Dreams, Archetypes, Myths and Metaphors
Cambridge (MA), US and London, UK: The MIT Press, 1996
This fascinating book claims that there is no longer any technological determinism left for the Internet because we have the ability to make the technology do whatever we want. The only constraint upon its development lies in the limits of our imaginations; so, what the Internet becomes will depend upon how we conceptualize or even 'dream' about it.

Weber, Samuel (ed. Alan Cholodenko)
Mass mediauras
Stanford (CA), US: Stanford University Press, 1996
In this collection of essays, Weber investigates what is left of Walter Benjamin's notion of the 'aura' in our mass-mediated culture. Has the auratic quality of artworks indeed been replaced by the emergence of such reproduction media as film and television, or does it live in the age of digital multiplication, in the guise of the 'massmediaura'?

Weibel, Peter and Timothy Druckrey, eds.
Net Condition: Art and Global Media
Cambridge (MA), US: The MIT Press, 2001
The second volume in Druckrey's 'Electronic Culture: History, Theory and Practice' series examines the way modern media and their global reach influence social, political and physical space. This interesting book investigates the worldwide 'net culture' in artistic, social, political and economic terms. Too bad its graphic design is horrible.

Winograd, Terry and Fernando Flores
Understanding Computers and Cognition: A New Foundation for Design
Boston (MA), US: Addison-Wesley, 1986
One of a few good examples showing that computing and critical design can coexist. The authors explore new design principles in respect to cognitive science. Although slightly outdated, it is still valuable for current discussions.

Winograd, Terry, ed.
Bringing Design to Software
Boston (MA), US: Addison-Wesley, 1996
This book is composed of chapters by different proponents of design. Many chapters are illustrated by examples of good design that are not created using software, presumably because there are so few good software-based examples to cite! Winograd has added a short profile after each chapter, which attempts to relate the general lessons from the chapter to the specifics of software design. (contributors include Gillian Crampton Smith, Mitchell Kapor, Donald Schön).

Zielinski, Siegfried
Audiovisions, Cinema and Television as Entr'actes in History
Amsterdam, NL: Amsterdam University Press, 1998
The production, distribution and perception of moving images are undergoing a radical transformation. The classic institutions for the mediation of film – cinema and television – are revealed to be no more than interludes in the broader history of audiovisual media. This book interprets these changes not simply as a cultural loss but also as a challenge: the new audio visions have to be confronted squarely to make strategic intervention possible.

Country codes

Country codes

AD	Andorra	FJ	Fiji	MG	Madagascar	SY	Syria
AE	United Arab Emirates	FK	Falkland Islands	MH	Marshall Islands	SZ	Swaziland
AF	Afghanistan		(Malvinas)	MK	Macedonia (F.Y.R.O.M.,	TC	Turks and
AG	Antigua and Barbuda	FM	Micronesia		Former Yugoslav		Caicos Islands
AI	Anguilla	FO	Faroe Islands		Republic of Macedonia)	TD	Chad
AL	Albania	FR	**France**	ML	Mali	TF	French Southern and
AM	Armenia	FX	France, Metropolitan	MM	Myanmar		Antarctic Territories
AN	Netherlands Antilles	GA	Gabon	MN	Mongolia	TG	Togo
AO	Angola	GB	Great Britain	MO	Macau	TH	Thailand
AQ	Antarctica	GD	Grenada	MP	Northern Mariana	TJ	Tadjikistan
AR	Argentina	GE	Georgia		Islands	TK	Tokelau
AS	American Samoa	GF	French Guiana	MQ	Martinique	TM	Turkmenistan
AT	**Austria**	GH	Ghana	MR	Mauritania	TN	Tunisia
AU	Australia	GI	Gibraltar	MS	Montserrat	TO	Tonga
AW	Aruba	GL	Greenland	MT	Malta	TP	East Timor
AZ	Azerbaijan	GM	Gambia	MU	Mauritius	TR	Turkey
BA	Bosnia and	GN	Guinea	MV	Maldives	TT	Trinidad and Tobago
	Herzegovina	GP	Guadeloupe	MW	Malawi	TV	Tuvalu
BB	Barbados	GQ	Equatorial Guinea	MX	Mexico	TW	Taiwan
BD	Bangladesh	GR	Greece	MY	Malaysia	TZ	Tanzania
BE	**Belgium**	GS	S. Georgia and S.	MZ	Mozambique	UA	Ukraine
BF	Burkina Faso		Sandwich Isls.	NA	Namibia	UG	Uganda
BG	Bulgaria	GT	Guatemala	NC	New Caledonia	UK	**United Kingdom**
BH	Bahrain	GU	Guam	NE	Niger	UM	US Minor Outlying
BI	Burundi	GW	Guinea Bissau	NF	Norfolk Island		Islands
BJ	Benin	GY	Guyana	NG	Nigeria	US	**United States**
BM	Bermuda	HK	Hong Kong	NI	Nicaragua	UY	Uruguay
BN	Brunei Darussalam	HM	Heard and	NL	**Netherlands**	UZ	Uzbekistan
BO	Bolivia		McDonald Islands	NO	Norway	VA	Vatican City State
BR	Brazil	HN	Honduras	NP	Nepal	VC	St Vincent and
BS	Bahamas	HR	Croatia (Hrvatska)	NR	Nauru		the Grenadines
BT	Bhutan	HT	Haiti	NU	Niue Island	VE	Venezuela
BV	Bouvet Island	HU	Hungary	NZ	New Zealand	VG	Virgin Islands (British)
BW	Botswana	ID	Indonesia	OM	Oman	VI	Virgin Islands (US)
BY	Belarus	IE	Ireland	PA	Panama	VN	Vietnam
BZ	Belize	IL	Israel	PE	Peru	VU	Vanuatu
CA	**Canada**	IN	India	PF	French Polynesia	WF	Wallis and
CC	Cocos (Keeling) Islands	IO	British Indian Ocean	PG	Papua New Guinea		Futuna Islands
CD	Congo,		Territory	PH	Philippines	WS	Samoa
	Democratic Republic	IQ	Iraq	PK	Pakistan	YE	Yemen
CF	Central African Republic	IR	Iran	PL	Poland	YT	Mayotte
CG	Congo	IS	Iceland	PM	St Pierre and Miquelon	YU	Yugoslavia
CH	**Switzerland**	IT	Italy	PN	Pitcairn Island	ZA	South Africa
CI	Côte D'Ivoire	JM	Jamaica	PR	Puerto Rico	ZM	Zambia
	(Ivory Coast)	JO	Jordan	PT	Portugal	ZR	Zaire
CK	Cook Islands	JP	Japan	PW	Palau	ZW	Zimbabwe
CL	Chile	KE	Kenya	PY	Paraguay		
CM	Cameroon	KG	Kyrgyzstan	QA	Qatar		
CN	China	KH	Cambodia	RE	Réunion		
CO	Colombia	KI	Kiribati	RO	Romania		
CR	Costa Rica	KM	Comoros	RU	**Russian Federation**		
CS	Former Czechoslovakia	KN	St Kitts and Nevis	RW	Rwanda		
CU	Cuba	KP	North Korea	SA	Saudi Arabia		
CV	Cape Verde	KR	**South Korea**	SB	Solomon Islands		
CX	Christmas Island	KW	Kuwait	SC	Seychelles		
CY	Cyprus	KY	Cayman Islands	SD	Sudan		
CZ	Czech Republic	KZ	Kazakhstan	SE	Sweden		
DE	**Germany**	LA	Laos	SG	Singapore		
DJ	Djibouti	LB	Lebanon	SH	St Helena		
DK	Denmark	LC	St Lucia	SI	Slovenia		
DM	Dominica	LI	Liechtenstein	SJ	Svalbard and		
DO	Dominican Republic	LK	Sri Lanka		Jan Mayen Islands		
DZ	Algeria	LR	Liberia	SK	Slovak Republic		
EC	Ecuador	LS	Lesotho	SL	Sierra Leone		
EE	Estonia	LT	Lithuania	SM	San Marino		
EG	Egypt	LU	Luxembourg	SN	Senegal		
EH	Western Sahara	LV	Latvia	SO	Somalia		
ER	Eritrea	LY	Libya	SR	Surinam		
ES	**Spain**	MA	Morocco	ST	São Tomé and Principe		
ET	Ethiopia	MC	Monaco	SU	Former USSR		
FI	Finland	MD	Moldavia	SV	El Salvador		

Domains

AERO	Air-Transport Industry
ARPA	Old-Style Arpanet
BIZ	Business
COM	Commercial
COOP	Cooperatives
EDU	US Educational
GOV	US Government
INFO	Informational
INT	International
MIL	US Military
MUSEUM	Museums
NAME	Individuals
NATO	Nato Field
NET	Network
ORG	Non-Profit Organization
PRO	Professional

Neighbourhood

This page associatively maps the designers of the sites reviewed in this book. Since, as I have argued, the web is a community medium, I thought it would be interesting to show my own network of direct acquaintances and distant links via the web. It is not exactly a statistically correct model, but the curves do represent a neighbourhood of designers from my personal point of view; closer or more distant in terms of personal or virtual contact. The inner curve is composed of designers who are friends or direct colleagues, while the outer curve lists designers whose work I know only through their web presence. As with any neighbourhood, the criterion in this diagram is less a matter of objective or subjective design quality and more to do with personal proximity. Any critic of the web should be aware of one fact: the 'global village' is mapped differently for each of its inhabitants.

Max Bruinsma

Mieke Gerritzen / 22-23, 34, 35, 37, 86, 107

Joes Koppers / 22, 26-27, 34-35, 107

Luna Maurer / 106, 107

DEPT / 32-33, 97

Marcel van der Drift / 153

Anne Burdick, Ewan Branda / 143

David Karam, Gigi Biederman / 40-41

Peter Bilak / 64, 65   Johanna Balusikova / 65

LettError: Just van Rossum, Erik van Blokland / 83

Emigre: Rudy VanderLans, Zuzana Licko / 82

Submarine: Bruno Felix, Femke Wolting / 110

2x4: Michael Rock, Susan Sellers / 74

Jouke Kleerebezem / 134-35

Paul Perry / 136   Rogério Lira / 137

Thonik: Thomas Widdershoven, Nikki Gonnissen; Tijs Bonekamp / 75

Dennis Lodewijks, Jeroen Disch, Koert van Mensvoort / 174

Mark Amerika, Joel Swanson / 142

Pierre di Sciullo / 76, 77

Geert Jan Mulder / 105

Robin Kinross, Eric Kindel, Jonathan Pagel, Matt Patterson / 62

Trace Reddell / 174

Aaron Betsky, Benjamin Weil, Perimetre-Flux / 46-47

The Designers Republic / 88-89

Alex Galloway and Mark Tribe / 52, 53

The Getty Research Institute, Citrus Studio / 63

Peter Luining / 44

Graham Harwood, Waag Society / 172-73

Niels van der Sluis / 87

Future Farmers: Amy Franceschini / 120-21

Zuper!: Michael Samyn / 67

Adbusters: Kalle Lasn, Jeff Harris / 140-41

jodi.org: Joan Heemskerk, Dirk Paesmans / 42-43

Léon Cullinane, Toby Lee, Sally Watkins, Asim Butt / 115

Yugo Nakamura / 100

Jef and Gael Morlan / 31

Young-hae Chang / 68-69

Cornel Windlin, Stephan Müller / 85

Dimitri Bruni and Manuel Krebs / 84

Thirst / 72-73

Customr / 66

Beaufonts / 78

preloaded / 132

Erik Natzke / 28, 70, 101

LAB[au] / 112-13

Engine Three / 116

Jayson Singe / 30

Andy Crewdson / 138

Erik Loyer / 70, 71

Robin Garms / 139

Alexei Shulgin / 45

Lisa Jevbratt / 54-55

Daniel Brown / 29   9-11 / 147

Michael Sippey / 133   Inter.net / 148

Threecolor / 96

Robert Hodgin / 152   MTV2, Digit / 50-51

Molly Sokolow / 70-71   Rui Camilo / 39

Dior Hommes / 114

Hi-Res! / 108-09

Soda: Ed Burton / 98

James Schoenecker / 49

CounterStrike / 154, 155

Andy Deck / 178   Ixquick / 166, 167

David Gomez-Rosado / 150-51

Lia Schitter / 180-81   Google International / 166, 167

Fibre / 79, 117-19   Patrick Smith / 99

Boris Müller, Sven Voelker / 48   Mark Napier / 176, 177

link_R.I.PPER / 176, 177   Gicheol Lee / 179   Klimate / 38

Brian McGrath, Mark Watkins, Akiko Hattori, Lucy Lai Wong / 104

Tamara Laï, Jimpunk / 122-23   Phantasy Star On Line / 154, 155

Jay Boersma / 182   Pete Everett / 174, 175   Netscape Composer / 168, 169

Pyra Labs / 170-71   Muslims AGAINST Terrorism, Freddy Venegas, Han Haque / 149

Bradley Grosh, Gmunk studio / 102-03   Independent Media Centers / 144-45

EverQuest Online / 156-57   Unreal Tournament Online / 154, 155   Jakob Nielsen / 36

Index

Index

First published in the United Kingdom in 2003 by Thames & Hudson Ltd, 181A High Holborn, London WC1V 7QX

www.thamesandhudson.com

ISBN 0-500-28384-2

Written by Max Bruinsma, NL
www.xs4all.nl/~maxb

Contributions by Sjoukje van der Meulen, US, NL and Willem van Weelden, NL

Designed by Annelys de Vet, NL
www.annelysdevet.nl

Cover photo by Paul Barbera, AU, NL
www.paulbarbera.com

Printed and bound in China by C & C Offset

For updates on the websites and URLs in Deep Sites, see
www.xs4all.nl/~maxb/deepsites